RIPPLES
OF BATTLE

RIPPLES OF BATTLE

How Wars of the Past

Still Determine How We Fight,

How We Live, and How We Think

Victor Davis Hanson

DOUBLEDAY

New York   London   Toronto   Sydney   Auckland

PUBLISHED BY DOUBLEDAY
A division of Random House, Inc.

DOUBLEDAY and the portrayal of an anchor with a dolphin are
trademarks of Random House, Inc.

Book design by Donna Sinisgalli
Maps by Jeffrey L. Ward after maps by M.C. Drake

Library of Congress Cataloging-in-Publication Data
Hanson, Victor Davis.
Ripples of battle : how wars of the past still determine how we fight, how we
live, and how we think / by Victor Davis Hanson.— 1st ed.
    p.   cm.
1. Military art and science. 2. Civilization, Western. 3. World War,
1939–1945—Campaigns—Japan—Okinawa Island. 4. Shiloh, Battle of, Tenn.,
1862. 5. Delium, Battle of, Greece, 424 B.C. 6. World War, 1939–1945—
Influence. 7. United States—History—Civil War, 1861–1865—Influence.
8. Greece—History—Peloponnesian War, 431–404 B.C.—Influence. I. Title.

U27.H38 2003
355.02—dc21   2003044043

ISBN 0-385-50400-4

October 2003
First Edition

1 3 5 7 9 10 8 6 4 2

To the memory of Victor Hanson

F Company, 2nd Battalion, 29th Regiment, 6th Marine Division

Killed in Action, May 18, 1945—Okinawa

Contents

List of Maps

Introduction

On my rare visits to the local cemetery, I am always struck by the unremarkable grave of Victor Hanson. The inscription is as spare as the stone itself—name, state, rank, dates of birth and death, and nothing much more except the nondescript "29 Marines / 6 Marine Div / World War II." Unlike the other impressive tombstones of relatives in the family plot, there are no inscribed res gestae, not even a "loving father" much less a "beloved grandfather." A man who dies tragically, young, and alone does so without capital, either monetary or human. When he leaves behind no progeny, it is evident in the modesty of his commemoration.

But then his mother died in childbirth, his father was blinded in the vineyard by a sulfur-machine accident. He was killed at twenty-three, without wife or children, his body eventually shipped back and reinterred in Kingsburg, California. And because Victor was an only child, when he died on Okinawa, his father Victor Hanson's thin line perished as well. Had his memory vanished as well?

Certainly there are no Hansons left of Victor's direct ancestry to appreciate the significance of his modest epitaph, whose calculus—death recorded on May 19, 1945, serving in the 29th Regiment, 2nd Battalion, Company F of the 6th Marine Division—reflected his presence at the nexus of one of the worst days of the bloodiest campaign in the Pacific theater, the final assault and capture of Sugar Loaf Hill and its environs. William Manchester, of the same regiment, wrote of the bloody assaults on Sugar Loaf:

> Infantry couldn't advance. Every weapon was tried: tanks, Long Toms, rockets, napalm, smoke, naval gunfire, aircraft. None of them worked. If anything, the enemy's hold on the heights grew stronger.

The Japanese artillery never seemed to let up, and every night Ushi-jima sent fresh troops up his side of the hill. We kept rushing them, moving like somnambulists, the weight of Sugar Loaf pressing down on us, harder and harder. And as we crawled forward, shamming death whenever a flare burst over us, we could almost feel the waves of darkness moving up behind us. In such situations a man has very little control over his destiny.

Victor was shot as his company beat back the last death-charges of sui-cidal Japanese to defend the hill, dying on Okinawa on the evening (May 18) before those who were left of his 29th Marines were finally relieved and evacuated from the battle. The official history of American operations on Okinawa reads, "A platoon of Company F also tried to advance along the ridge toward the west, but the leader was killed and the platoon withdrew under heavy mortar fire." The authors then summarize the sacrifice, "On the next day, 19 May, the 4th Marines relieved the exhausted 29th Marines. During the 10-day period up to and including the capture of Sugar Loaf the 6th Marine Division had lost 2,662 killed or wounded; there were also 1,289 cases of combat fatigue. In the 22nd and 29th Marines three battalion com-manders and eleven company commanders had been killed or wounded."

In addition, the official history of the 6th Marine Division remarked of the exposed position of Company F on Sugar Loaf on the day of Victor's death that "heavy fire continued to come from Horseshoe Hill and company F was dispatched in that direction. The assault was perfectly maneuvered; the Marines went right to the crest, where the fight developed into a grenade battle at close quarters with a terrific mortar barrage."

To read accounts of those savage uphill assaults against entrenched Japanese is to wonder not why Victor was killed on May 18, but how in God's name had he lived that long? After all, in just a few days, three thousand Marines were killed or gravely wounded in and around Sugar Loaf Hill, more Allied soldier casualties than lost on Monte Cassino and about the same number as on Tarawa. His 29th Regiment suffered 82 percent casualties on Okinawa and for all practical purposes had ceased to exist.

Yet without ostentatious stones, lasting works of fame, or any surviving immediate family, had the childless, young Victor Hanson really perished on that godforsaken hill with dozens of his friends on May 18? Surely not. Growing up, I heard his name nearly daily. My father was his first cousin, but the two were more like brothers, given their near-identical ages and lifelong companionship; for a time they lived side-by-side on adjoining farms, went to the same college, and joined the Marines. And so it was that the last half century our parents talked often about this mysterious dead man. "If only Vic had lived," the refrain went, followed by all sorts of counterfactuals concerning the subsequent sad fate of his father, his high school and college prospects, whom he might have married, children reared, partnerships entered with my father, grandparents consoled, college work that presaged future success, farms saved—rather than people saddened, sickened, and cast adrift, and homesteads soon to be sold or lost. I began as a child almost to resent this shadowy moral exemplar, who had died without making a mistake, thus leaving his namesake with the burden of emulating such character.

My mother and father both offered these what-ifs, since all three of them had left farms in central California to attend the College of the Pacific together up in Stockton. "He was a wonderful man," I would hear from her as a youth. After my mother's death, Victor's high school girlfriend, now widowed in her eighties, with great-grandchildren, often emerged from the past to keep up the refrain of praise and honor; she has now supervised the construction of a small memorial to the four fighting Hansons in the center of Kingsburg Memorial Park, once the site of their ancestral homestead. She visits still, and just a few weeks ago left me a formal handwritten note that ended:

> Cpl. Hanson, only son and child of Victor Sr. and grandson of Nels and Cecilia Hanson, was killed in action on May 19, 1945—age 23 years and 3 months, along with another 12,500 valiant young men. The *Kingsburg Recorder* said of Victor Jr.—"He reflected the gentility emanating from his grandmother Cecilia (reared by her when he became a motherless infant). Those who knew him, all apprised him as a gentle man." Victor Hanson, Jr. never returned to his home on 1965 18th Avenue, Kingsburg, California—Hanson Corner. He was awarded the Purple Heart posthumously.

From his surviving yellow letters on Marine stationery, I had already sensed just that humility, unusual even for the accepted modesty of that better age. And then recently I received a phone call from eighty-year-old Michael Senko, who occupied the foxhole where Victor died, and without warning had replied to my efforts in learning about Victor's last moments. He too emphasized his "gentleness," adding that he was a "perfect guy"—this remembrance from over a half century later. In a letter to his grandparents from basic training at Camp Lejeune, North Carolina, after briefly and nonchalantly detailing all sorts of trial amphibious landings, marathon marches, and assorted tests of endurance, Victor was far more concerned with the health and safety of his octogenarian surrogate parents back home here in the 1940s small farming town of Kingsburg. The final paragraph reads: "I'm really glad to hear that you are all fine, because I wonder all the time if you are all O.K. I'm just fine, couldn't be better and never weighed more. I guess I weigh over 200—not enough hard work I guess. Well I guess I better close for now. Hoping this letter finds you all well and fine, Love Victor."

Occasionally a few sketchy details would emerge about his demise. "A damn machine gun got him from when he wasn't looking," my Swedish grandfather offered twenty years after Victor's death, before coughing in midsentence and in anger—his own lungs had been ruined from gas in the Argonne. Other vague accounts mentioned his company being cut off and surrounded. Until this May I have often wondered how anyone knew of his last moments.

"They had no business putting those boys there on Okinawa in that way," my dad also on occasion spit out at the end of one of his angry monologues. "They played right into Jap hands. Hell, we were bombing Japan to bits anyway, and they could have just passed that damn island by. But no, that was not the Marine idea of how to get things done." What an odd thought: my generation who knew no battle had thought that we bombed too severely and unduly punished the Japanese; my father's who fought the war was convinced that the air war was too late and not enough—and thus did not prevent the Japanese from punishing fellow Americans on places like Okinawa.

Both cousins had, in fact, joined the Marines; for an altercation with his officer my father was drummed out of basic training but not formally charged—the embarrassing details were never revealed to us—on the stipulation that he join the Army Air Corps, which eventually led him to something as equally horrific as Okinawa. Still, even armed with that disclosure I never quite understood why his anger was sometimes turned inward; surely it was not from a failure to fight on Okinawa side-by-side with Vic. At his other outbursts the remorse appeared even more bizarre, as he hinted that had the murderous B-29s—he had flown on thirty-nine missions from Tinian over Japan as a central fire-control gunner—firebombed Japan earlier and harder, Okinawa would have been irrelevant. In his logic, if a three-hundred-plane B-29 aerial armada had carpeted Japan in 1944 rather than in the spring and summer of 1945, Victor would perhaps have had garrison duty only, mopping up a few stalwart resisters on the charred island of Kyushu. Given the dreadful incendiary missions he had flown—only his crew and one other of the sixteen bombers in his original squadron survived—I, the solicitous and embarrassed college student in the mid-1970s, had once tried to offer solace. "Well, Dad, it's hard to think you guys were slow; after all, you just about burned down the entire country in two months as it was."

Most of my fellow university students at the time—to the degree they even knew or thought of World War II—in lockstep condemned the bombing, both conventional and atomic, as barbaric an act as Vietnam was then. My strange father, alone in the world, I gathered, felt that the horrific firestorms had been too little and too late! Such are the lifelong wages of rage when farm boys reluctantly leave their homesteads to kill those who have killed their own.

Victor's Marine picture was—and still is—on our wall. Where his effects of a half century earlier went I don't know. Only a few were apparently given to my late father. They usually turned up only by accident when I was a child. One day in 1962 in the barn I pulled out of the rafters a massive thirty-five-ounce Louisville Slugger with "Victor Hanson" burned into the wood; we used it for five years, put in screws, tape, and resin until at last it shattered with age and overuse. It was a massive bat, fitting seventeen years earlier for a young Swede of well over six feet three inches and 200 pounds.

When I went to UC Santa Cruz in the early 1970s, I took his college briefcase, then already thirty years old, with "VH" stamped in two places. Its age and queer construction on occasion brought offers of purchase from affluent would-be renegades from Los Angeles, who found its strange canvas and leather bindings, now stuffed with Greek and Latin books, either exotic or perhaps even organic. "His grandmother bought it for him," my father explained, adding, "With his degree he was supposed to be an officer, not join the Marines at the front." Even at eighteen I had been aware of the ludicrous contrast between the two Victor Hansons leaving the farm with that same satchel—one halfheartedly entering the indolent, self-absorbed culture of UC Santa Cruz, the other eagerly departing for the inferno of the United States Marine Corps of 1944.

Despite the daily reminder of the monogrammed briefcase, I tried to forget about Victor, but he nevertheless seemed to return on the most unlikely of occasions. Four years later at graduation, the pleasant parents of a Japanese friend from Okinawa ate with us at a postbaccalaureate dinner. I spotted my father sitting nearby and grimaced at what I knew would—had to—follow; this was, remember, Santa Cruz in 1975 (nearly thirty years to the month after Victor's death). Our roommate's mother made a perfectly sensible remark about the Americans and the hardships of her childhood growing up in wartime Japan; her husband from Okinawa also mentioned the war and the American bloodletting on the island.

In the smiling, laid-back atmosphere of a June graduation on Monterey Bay, everybody became more candid amid the white wine, the polite chatting, and the table talk. Could we not all agree about what the Americans had done? Comfortable in the university climate of rising diversity, attuned to what they saw as the new American enlightenment of shame and remorse over the recent bombing in Vietnam, someone let slip the B-29s, the firebombings, the suicides on Okinawa, and all those regrettable acts of American barbarity.

It was all downhill from there. I have tuned out everything of my beet-red father's response to these gracious middle-aged Japanese except his last crude sentence: "It was not enough for what the Japanese did." In their defense, who at such a place and at such a time—the students and their folk at Santa Cruz were not of the warrior class—could anticipate Victor's ghost?

His letters to his grandparents mostly worried that he might not be good enough for the Marines, that should he fail various endurance tests, he might not make the cut for jungle fighting overseas, that through some imagined lapse of muscular strength—he was a highly sought-after scholarship college athlete who, with my father, played for Amos Alonzo Stagg at the College of the Pacific—he might not be a good enough Marine and so be replaced by someone more deserving, someone better. In one note to his grandparents, he expressed concern that the Marine-issue rifles might be insufficient for jungle warfare:

> Could you be on the lookout for a .45 cal. Automatic Pistol? The model is 1911 or 1911A1. They don't issue them to you any more but they are desirable to have besides a rifle in combat. They come in handy in case your rifle or carbine fails to fire. They look something like this [a sketch follows]—that's a rough idea. If you happen to run across one and it is a good one we'll buy it; you can use the money I sent you to put in the bank. I think you can get a new one from $45 to $60, but I don't believe you'll be able to find a new one. Let me know if you have any luck. . . . Today it is sure a beautiful day, nice and spring like. We still have cold mornings. Well I guess I better close for now. Love, Victor

I imagine that his two eighty-five-year-old immigrant grandparents immediately left their small Swedish farm to drive up to Fresno in search of a .45 pistol for their grandson so that he might kill, rather than be killed by, the Japanese. To no avail; whether they found one or not, I have no knowledge.

As I said, in the spring of 2002 I made efforts over six decades later to discover whether a single man from F Company was still alive—anyone who had either survived the hell of Okinawa or sixty years of life subsequent, or might have known Victor Hanson. For nearly sixty years, what was left of my family had known about Victor's last hours apparently only from the official Marine letter of condolences. A first lieutenant, Robert J. Sherer, had written our family of Victor's death on July 26, 1945: "Our Company had attacked and seized Crescent Ridge on the enemy held Naha-Shuri line on 18 May and we were digging in for the night when we began to receive heavy fire from an enemy machine-gun to our left. It was at this time that Corporal Hanson was wounded. He was given medical attention immediately, but lived only a short time. He was given a fitting burial. . . ."

What I soon discovered was quite startling. There *were* indeed survivors of Company F—and their recollections left me quite stunned. Richard Whitaker—a veteran of F Company, 2nd Battalion, 29th Marines who was wounded on Sugar Loaf Hill the night Victor was killed, and a prominent hero in George Feifer's moving *Tennozan: The Battle of Okinawa and the Atomic Bomb*—helped me locate a few surviving members of Fox Company. Among them was none other than Robert J. Sherer!

After last writing the Hanson family *fifty-seven years ago*, now in his eighties he once more, on February 28, 2002, kindly sent me a second letter about Victor in the same elegant and dignified prose: "Victor Hanson, Jr. had been trained and was serving as a Fire Team Leader. He was a Corporal and was recognized as an outstanding Marine and leader. . . . I can recall seeing Corporal Hanson standing to hurl a grenade and being hit by fire from the enemy machine gun. My 'Runner,' PFC Ryan in the foxhole next to me was similarly hit by machine gun fire. Both died immediately, as did PFC Madigan. Sgt. Bill Twigger was wounded in the thigh and was ordered evacuated."

Just a few days after the letter from Robert Sherer came the previously mentioned phone call from a 6th Marine Division veteran, Mike Senko, with a wealth of detail about Sugar Loaf and accounts as moving as Sherer's. And then arrived the next day an unbelievably dignified narrative from none other than once-wounded Bill Twigger, who, like Robert Sherer, six decades later shed more particulars upon Victor's death not before known to any in our family. "The news came down the line that Vic Hanson had caught an enemy machine-gun burst in his right thigh, and, before a corpsman could reach him to administer aid, he bled to death. The report was quickly confirmed that by reason of the shock of so massive a wound, Vic did not endure prolonged suffering, but died virtually instantly."

And then Bill Twigger finished with a final, heartrending anecdote— which I think I can quote without embarrassment to the parties involved: "There is a tragic sequel to this event. Upon hearing of Victor's death, young Peter Madigan lost his moorings, rose from his thus-far secure position and with loud shouting and cursing rushed into the open only to be cut down by rifle fire." In explanation and recollection, Twigger wrote of Madigan's near simultaneous death, "Trivia and vulgarity had no places in Victor's vernacular. A hulk of a guy, the heftiest of us all, he was befriended by the 'runt' of the bunch, Peter Madigan." Twigger elaborated on what a fine person Madigan had been, in moving language, like Sherer's, that today's graduate students could only hope to emulate.

But still this was not the end to this strange unfolding cycle of events. Finally, on March 31, 2002, *on the eve of the fifty-seventh anniversary of the landing on Okinawa*, I received an unexpected call from one Louis Ittmann, another veteran of Fox Company who had also learned of my inquiry. Yes, he too had known Victor Hanson quite well, and confirmed the picture of him—a massive, good-natured Swedish college graduate who bled to death from a machine gun burst on Sugar Loaf Hill. After an engaging conversation, Louis Ittmann finished by requesting something quite unexpected: would I, he asked, *like Victor's ring?*

Ring?

Was this 1945 or 2002, I thought—and was I a comfortable forty-eight-year-old professor, or the old Swedish patriarch Nels Hanson, tottering out in his vineyard at eighty-one, stricken with the news of his lost grandson? Ittmann then explained. In a premonition of his death on Sugar Loaf Hill, Victor had earlier asked his friends to, in the event of his demise, remove his treasured ring and send it home. They had tried; but in attempting to deliver it to Kingsburg, California, out of courtesy they had first called our farm. The distraught family—my uncle, grandparents, and cousins—was too upset to come to the phone. Thus the good steward, Louis Ittmann, since that awful night fifty-seven years ago, had watched over Victor's ring. On May 21, 2002, it arrived in the mail, its band cut, either from wear or the necessary efforts to remove it from the finger of Victor sometime after he was brought down from Sugar Loaf Hill. I am now holding it as I write this, and as a classicist I am mesmerized by the engraved silhouette of a Roman legionary. When did Victor buy it? And why was a Roman soldier on a ring of a farm boy in central California of the late 1930s and 1940s?

Since my parents are dead and the rest of most other Hansons as well, those and other questions I suppose will remain unanswered. But I do know that I have never communicated with more gracious men than those 6th Marine Division veterans of that awful night on May 18 on Okinawa—Whitaker, Sherer, Senko, Twigger, Ittmann, and a few others—who kindly and freely shared their remembrances with me by letter and phone some fifty-seven years later. There was no bitterness evident in their prose and in their voices against the questionable strategy of sending them all head-on against the entrenched and veteran crack troops just weeks before the war's end; nor any lasting hatred mentioned of the Japanese; nor apologies for their tough combat; nor anything but moving appreciation expressed for this present country, especially in this current trial of our own.

When I asked whether there could have been another way to win Okinawa, one sighed and said, "Maybe—but Okinawa was an island of thousands of enemy soldiers in our way to Japan, and we couldn't just leave that many of them behind us. We were at war." When I pressed further whether the tactics of head-on charges against entrenched troops made sense, the general consensus was, "Who knows? But that was the Marine way and we accepted it. It was our job to take the island, and we did it." Despite the horror of what they went through, there seemed a Virgilian sense of pride in their sacrifice: *Forsan et haec olim meminisse iuvabit* [Perhaps there shall come a day when it will be sweet to remember even these things].

Given the large number of American dead on Okinawa, I do not believe that the good and experienced men who planned the storming of Okinawa—Operation Iceberg—in the luxury suites of the San Francisco St. Francis Hotel were all that wise in the manner of their war making. Neither do I give all that much credence to the United States Army's official narrative of the campaign, which concluded with the confident excuse, "The military value of Okinawa exceeded all hope." I acknowledge that both traditional and revisionist historians have only scorn for those like me who question the need for or the logic of Iceberg—and I can offer no alternative to the strategy of taking the island that might have ensured fewer dead on either side. Surely I do not know how the Americans could have gone ahead with plans to invade Japan with the knowledge that they either could not or would not eliminate first a veteran army of 110,000 Japanese on Okinawa at their rear. And I also know that others more illustrious died on Okinawa—Ernie Pyle, Gen.

Simon Bolivar Buckner himself, and several Medal of Honor winners. And I grant that the death of a twenty-three-year-old farm boy I never met from Kingsburg, California, pales besides two hundred thousand combined Japanese soldiers and Okinawan civilians incinerated, blown apart, and slowly starved to death that summer. Yes, I accept all that, but I also know of the wide ripples of one man's death, and as I look at his ring they have not ended—at least not quite yet.

"Great battles," Winston Churchill remarked, "change the entire course of events, create new standards of values, new moods, in armies and in nations." They do, and we Americans, individually and collectively alike, have not yet seen all the "new moods and values" created "in nations" by September 11, 2001. The longer-term ripples of that attack are still washing up— long after the first tidal waves of horror that swept over us in the days following the crashing of airliners into the symbols of American economic and military power.

We know that there are three thousand dead. A trillion dollars in capital has been lost; $100 billion in property damage was incurred; and millions of Americans were put out of work. The government itself was transformed— citizens worldwide were delayed and disrupted by increased security measures. Access to public facilities is now restricted. Private nagging fear and doubt about future attacks remain. We will not grasp for years the full interplay of events set in motion by the sudden vaporization of thousands in the late summer of 2001. The orphans and children of orphans not yet born will not—cannot—forget September 11 because they are now part of it forever.

The victims of the World Trade Center, the Pentagon, and the crashing airliners did not fall in pitched battle. They were not even armed. None were expecting their fate. Yet they were nonetheless combat casualties of self-described warriors—indeed, the first terrible fatalities of what may prove to be a long war. And because battle by its very nature radically changes history in ways that even other seminal events—elections, revolutions, inventions, assassinations, and plagues—cannot, it will require decades before historians can chart all the aftershocks that followed September 11.

Churchill's "great battles" often dispel the easy assumptions of peacetime, as democracies, once attacked, are aroused from their somnolence to deadly and unpredictable fury. Before the carnage at Shiloh, Ulysses S. Grant forecast that the Civil War would be ended by "one great battle." Afterward—with more casualties on April 6–8, 1862, than in all of America's wars up to that time—generals realized that in a novel fight with rifled muskets and canister shot, a great number of young men on both sides would have to die before the South would accept Union primacy. A previously labeled "crazy" Sherman would use his sudden Shiloh fame and the new realities of total war to think the once unthinkable—and in a few months lead thousands on the March to the Sea.

Just as Grant and his generals woke up from Shiloh on April 8 to a new world, so did Americans on September 12. In a blink the old idea of easy retaliation by using cruise missiles or saber-rattling press conferences seems to have vanished. With the end of that mirage, the two-decade fear of losing a single life to protect freedom and innocent civilians also disappeared. Past ideas of restraint, once thought to be mature and sober, were now in an instant revealed more to be reckless in their naïveté and derelict by their disastrous consequences. In the years to come we may well see far more nightmarish things in our military arsenal than bunker-busters and daisy-cutters. Americans once feared to retaliate against random bombings; terrorists now wonder when we will stop—as the logic of September 11 methodically advances to its ultimate conclusion. Aroused democracies reply murderously to enemy assaults in a manner absolutely inconceivable to their naïve attackers.

At peace and in affluence, many Americans look back in revulsion at Hiroshima, but hardly any of these moral censors were mature enough in 1945 to remember Okinawa. They can hardly appreciate what suicidal fanaticism in April, May, and June of that year had taught past generations: over 12,000 American dead, 35,000 more wounded, and over 300 ships damaged. In fact, 35 percent of all American combatants who fought in and around Okinawa were casualties. The Japanese lost 100,000 killed and another 100,000 civilian casualties—much of it in hand-to-hand fighting on this large island, but an island minuscule in comparison with the far better defended and as yet unconquered Japanese mainland.

Far more often than a suicidal attack on people at work, battle consists of a few hours of reciprocal and organized killing in which thousands of soldiers collide to decide the fate of thousands more to the rear. In the melee, heroism, bravery, or even superior technology cannot guarantee survival. Combatants often perish due to accident and simple bad luck, with consequences that become apparent often only decades later. Battle also is not merely a logical continuance of politics, but an abnormal event in which thousands of warriors—most often in the past, young male adults—are freed to kill each other for a few hours, a dramatic and strange experience bound to change their lives and the fate of their families and friends for centuries thereafter.

Battles are deliberate and entirely human-inspired. Not being accidental occurrences, they can be even more calamitous to the human psyche than the occasional greater carnage caused by natural disasters or human catastrophes—such as mine explosions or raging fires and floods that fall as acts of God upon the entire civilian population. It is said that divorce can be worse for children than the demise of a parent; so too the battle dead are harder to take for their surviving kin than fatalities from the highway or plague. You see men, not gods, are deliberately responsible for the dead of battle, in the conscious effort to slay other humans and not through mere carelessness or errors in judgment. In time we can come to accept the deaths of loved ones if they fall into chasms or die of infection—less so when we know that their youthful bodies were torn apart by angry humans without help from nature.

People forgive the ravages of water and flame, but less so Japanese, American, or German slayers. Battle—again so unlike nature—brings with it bothersome and nagging ideas of preventability, culpability, causation, and responsibility married to the lingering notions of what-if?, whose fault?, and he, *not* it, did this. Anger, passion, and revenge always erupt from battle. "Remember the Alamo," ". . . the *Maine*," or ". . . Pearl Harbor" inflames nations in a way that the far greater losses from polio, Hurricane Carla, or the Anchorage earthquake cannot. We do not bury even heroic lifeguards or smoke jumpers in Arlington National Cemetery or put them atop bronze horses. Hundreds of firemen perish each decade, but rarely instantaneously and in great number trying to rescue thousands of their kin while under attack by a foreign enemy.

The social sparks that fly from battle ignite entire societies and soon become the flames of history. Herodotus reminds us that in war, fathers bury sons rather than sons fathers. Euripides insists that wives and mothers, like those of his *Trojan Women* who grieve and suffer over their lost ones, have it worse than soldiers themselves. Historians remind us that our own Civil War was a "rich man's war, and a poor man's fight." The forces of opposition to American segregation that had remained dormant in peace were awakened by World War II—as the nonwhite fought well for a country they loved but that did not accord them full political equality.

Battles, then, rip open the scabs of wounds of generational rivalry, the age-old competition between the sexes, class struggle, and racial strife. Already Americans ask, "How could aliens so easily enter the United States and under what auspices?"—as the government in response moves radically to reassess the Immigration and Naturalization Service. Meanwhile, the once reactionary idea of profiling suspects by age, gender, religion, and ethnicity should have disappeared—but apparently not altogether when the 19 murderers of 3,000 innocents were uniformly young, male, Islamic, from the Arab world, and living stealthily in the United States.

Battle is the raucous transformer of history because it also accelerates in a matter of minutes the usually longer play of chance, skill, and fate. Mistakes become fatal in seconds rather than remaining irrelevant lapses of day-to-day existence. Deaths are not the singular and often anticipated events among families, but occur en masse, wholly unexpected, and often horrifically. Education, training, and aristocratic pretension may become meaningless in combat. Many of those with the top-dog views at the World Trade Center were doomed; janitors and clerks on the bottom floor lobbies had a better chance of flight. A destitute homeless person found safety on the sidewalk five blocks away by his very failure and subsequent distance from society's sophisticated and visible machinery, while a Harvard MBA, distinguished record of hard work and rare discipline, ensured that a stockbroker was in the line of fire as an easy target who had the grand views of Floor 93.

So battle is a great leveler of human aspiration when it most surely should not be. Stray bullets kill brave men and miss cowards. They tear open great doctors-to-be and yet merely nick soldiers who have a criminal past, pulverizing flesh when there is nothing to be gained and passing harmlessly by when the fate of whole nations is at stake. And that confusion, inexplicability, and deadliness have a tendency to rob us of the talented, inflate the mediocre, and ruin or improve the survivors—but always at least making young men who survive *not* forget what they have been through.

Usually, military historians examine decisive battle in either a strategic or tactical context—the role of Lepanto or Hastings in deciding the larger pulse of wars, which end, renew, or are unaffected by a single day's butchery. Just as commonly, scholars see battle more as the science of how to destroy thousands through maneuver and technology. Books abound on Hannibal's encirclement at Cannae, the stealth of Arminius, Rommel's use of Panzers, or LeMay's devilish brew over Tokyo. But rarely do we appreciate battles as human phenomena or the cumulative effects—the ripples—that change communities for years, or centuries even, well after the day's killing is over. And to do that we must reexamine some well-known battles of the past in different ways, and measure others that heretofore have not warranted much attention on the grounds of their tactical irrelevance, bad timing, or absence of suitable witnesses and recorders.

Great men are cut down in battle who could have saved thousands of other lives; families ruined for centuries due to a single bullet. And by the same token, the supposedly mediocre emerge from battle, with the acclaim and opportunity to match their innate (and previously unknown and untapped) talent. Plays, poems, and novels are written because of a day's fighting, art commissioned, philosophy born. Whole schools of thought are created or deemed flawed by a battle.

In this regard I plead guilty to the classical notion—more or less continuous from Herodotus and Thucydides to the close of the nineteenth century—*of the primacy of military history.* In theory, of course, all events have equal historical importance—the creation of a women's school in nineteenth-century America, the introduction of the stirrup, the domestication of the chicken, or the introduction of the necktie. And such social or cultural developments, whether they are dramatic or piecemeal, do on occasion change the lives of millions.

Yet in reality, all actions are still not so equal. We perhaps need to recall the more traditional definitions of the craft of history—a formal record of past events that are *notable* or *worthy of remembrance.* Whereas *I Love Lucy* might have transformed the way thousands of Americans in the 1950s and 1960s saw suburban life, women's roles, or Cubans, it still did not alter the United States in the manner of a Yorktown, Gettysburg, or Tet—in creating, preserving, or almost losing an entire society. It was an event of the past, but not necessarily either notable or worthy of remembrance or commemoration.

Nor are all battles themselves equal. Ostensibly, the greater the number of participants, the more critical the tactical, strategic, and political stakes at play—and the more blood on the butcher's bill, the more likely is the engagement to make history. From what we know more than a century after the fact, Gettysburg—whether we look at Lee's climactic failure to topple the North, the heroism on Little Roundtop, the sheer number of dead and wounded, or Lincoln's address—was more momentous than Pea Ridge fought in March 1862 to ensure that Missouri would remain in the Northern camp. All remember Salamis, where Western civilization was saved in its eleventh hour from Xerxes; few recall Artemisium weeks earlier, where storms and Greek courage helped hold off for a time the invading Persian fleet.

Scholars argue over the so-called "great battles" as historians and compilers continue to publish such lists—in no clear agreement whether Antietam or Vicksburg, Normandy Beach or the Bulge, Stalingrad or Kursk were the real seminal events. Yet my purpose here is not to enter that fray other than to discuss its existence in the epilogue. Rather, I wish to show that while all battles are not equivalent in their effects upon civilization, they do share at least this common truth: there will be *some* fundamental and important consequences beyond other more normal occurrences, given the unnatural idea of men trying to kill each other in a few hours in a relatively confined space. Battles really are the wildfires of history, out of which the survivors float like embers and then land to burn far beyond the original conflagration. To teach us those important lessons we must go back through the past to see precisely how such calamities affected now lost worlds—and yet still influence us today.

In that regard, I have selected across time and space three less well-known battles of spears, black powder, and modern guns to show how our lives even today have been changed in ways we do not readily appreciate—and by a few hours long ago that few recall. Most of us know something of

Marathon, but almost nothing of the obscure battle of Delium in 424 B.C. Gettysburg is part of the American heritage, less so Shiloh a year earlier. Books and films herald Normandy Beach; almost none commemorate the far greater losses on Okinawa—a savage event less well known than Iwo Jima, where far fewer were killed.

These battles in themselves are tragic—not always inherently evil, yet much less very often good. Instead, moral appraisals of battle rest with the nature of the combatants, the causes for which men kill and die, and the manner in which they conduct themselves on the battlefield. Yet battles at least alter history for centuries in a way other events cannot. And we should remember that lesson both when we go to war and try to make sense of the peace that follows.

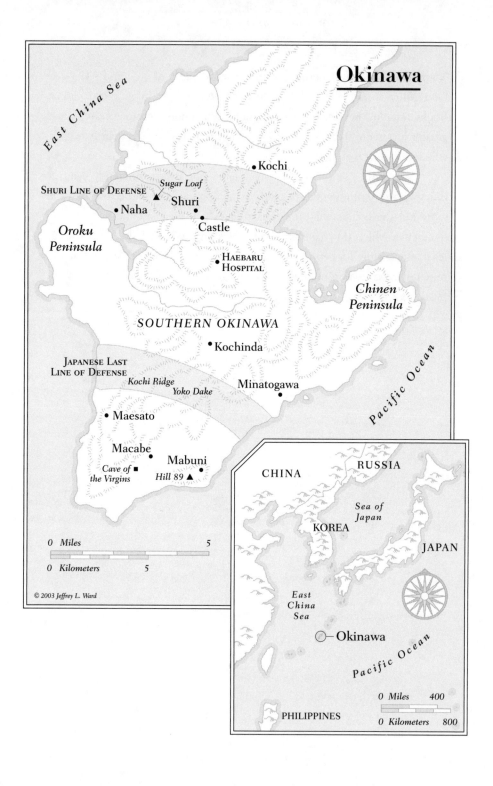

The Wages of Suicide: Okinawa,
April 1–July 2, 1945

Recipe for a Holocaust

Throughout the fall of 2001 and early 2002, the military referents in the West for the war against the Islamic fundamentalists were the fanatical kamikazes of Okinawa of the past—their letters published in newspapers, the Pacific war recounted by columnists, and veterans of the conflict interviewed on television. Suicide bombing by nature is at first horrifying, calling into doubt the notion of a shared human instinct for self-preservation. Suicide killers are purportedly of a creed not of this world, and thus instill despair that such enemies can ever be thwarted and that somehow theirs is a superior ideology by its singular ability to galvanize thousands to kill themselves for the cause. Yet Okinawa reminds us that there are plenty of far more frightening mechanisms to ensure that it fails. Contrary to our own popular doubts and fears, the horror of Okinawa entailed the frustration, not the success, of kamikazes. And with that result there ensued the lessons that suicide warriors are not always willing volunteers, much less superhuman, but themselves just as often unsure and full of doubt. Literature and culture were changed by Okinawa, but the ripples of that battle were also military; after September 11 they lap up as never before to remind us that there remains an array of tactics and long-term strategies by those who fight to live that will ensure failure to those trying to die.

The forces arrayed for the American invasion of Okinawa on April 1, 1945—Operation Iceberg—were gargantuan. The greatest armada of combined naval and land power in the history of the Pacific war was prepared to storm an island not much more than sixty miles in length. In terms of initial troops to be landed, firepower arrayed, and tonnage to be used, the American invasion was larger than the one seen at Normandy nearly a year earlier. Indeed, Okinawa was perhaps the most impressive sea and ground assault since Xerxes' invasion of Greece in 480 B.C.—but then, both those earlier invasions had been directed against the continent of Europe, not an island in the Pacific.

Nearly 1,600 ships carried over a half million Americans toward Okinawa. A quarter million soldiers—infantry, support troops, airmen, and sailors in various branches of the military—eventually hoped to occupy the island. Sixty thousand Marines and army infantrymen of the newly formed 10th Army would embark on the first day alone, supported by bombs from some 40 aircraft carriers of various types and shells from 18 battleships and 150 destroyers. Some 183,000 actual infantry combatants from the army and the Marines were ready to join the fight on the island during the ninety-day campaign. Over 12,000 combat aircraft on the American side could, in theory, be thrown into the fight. The campaign was planned as a textbook American exercise in overwhelming material and numerical power that would simply bury even the most courageous adversaries.

Many of the invading Americans were hardened veterans of the bloodletting on Iwo Jima, Peleliu, Saipan, and Tarawa. If they were successful in capturing the linchpin of the Ryukyu Islands, the Japanese mainland would lie defenseless to American ships, troops, and planes, all to be based a mere 350 miles away. Indeed, after the battle and despite the horrific costs, the official military history of Okinawa declared that "the military value of Okinawa exceeded all hope" as a base for "an even more desperate struggle to come."

But the Americans in their great confidence and careful preparation had also overlooked an essential but bitter truth about their proposed campaign. The enemy would fight this battle in a manner not entirely explicable by the strategic calculus involved in losing Okinawa. Nor did he much care about the Americans' proven tactical and material superiority—much less about the age-old Western idea that the purpose of battle was largely to defeat the enemy, obtain his surrender, advise him of the futility of subsequent resistance, and therein achieve results that mere politics could not.

Indeed, the Japanese did not realistically hope militarily to defeat the invaders on Okinawa at all! Nor did they worry whether their own army, navy, and air forces would survive the conflict. And the defenders may even have accepted that after the fighting, Okinawa, for a time, would—at least for a few months or even years—become American and not Japanese. Col. Hiromichi Yahara, the brilliant architect of the Japanese defenses, wrote after the war that "the fact is that we never had a chance for victory on Okinawa."

Instead, by mid-1945 the desperate Japanese military's aims were quite different from all conventional war wisdom. And so their plans were also very simple: kill so many Americans, blow up or shoot down so many aircraft, and sink so many of their ships that the United States—both its stunned military and its grieving citizens back home—would never wish to undergo such an ordeal again. After the butchery to come on Okinawa, perhaps these rather affluent and soft Westerners would seek a negotiated armistice from Japan— and not tolerate another, greater cataclysm on the mainland in pursuit of an unnecessary unconditional surrender. Okinawa, then, was to offer a suicidal lesson to Americans to stop before they found themselves dying in the millions on the beaches of the Japanese motherland. In the words of the historian Joseph Alexander, the Japanese saw Okinawa as the "England of the Pacific"—a proximate island that would likewise serve as an enormous staging area and supply depot for the eventual foreign annexation of the sacred soil of Japan itself.

In that context, despite the Americans' skill and overwhelming material preponderance, much of the advantage on the island still lay with the Japanese in this new phase of attrition. Because Okinawa was larger than many of the other Pacific atolls of the previous campaigns, because it was a home island of the Japanese empire, because of its unpredictable weather, coral rock, prepared fortifications, and dense vegetation, and because of the number, nature, and leadership of the Japanese defenders, nearly every combatant on the island in theory could resist to the death for a very long time. The commander of the island's defenses, Gen. Mitsuru Ushijima, had written a brief slogan to cheer on his troops that summed up the Japanese strategy: "One Plane for One Warship; One Boat for One Ship; One Man for Ten of the Enemy or One Tank." As it turned out, instead, Americans would kill ten Japanese for every one they lost. Yet even to this day they still feel that something had gone terribly wrong during the campaign. And it had.

Even if, as the planners thought, Okinawa were merely to be conquered, Operation Iceberg had not made allowances for the attacker's age-old and necessary edge in numerical superiority. There were only one and a half, *not* the requisite three, American invaders to match each Japanese defender. Yet to kill *all* the Japanese—110,000 soldiers and thousands more civilians who would resist at their sides, whether coerced or willing—how many American combatants would that gruesome task require? A million? A ten-to-one ratio of offense to defense? Just how many American infantrymen, bombers, and warships would be needed to blast out *every* Japanese in every cave of the island? And did the Americans realize that an entire army of over 100,000 men had become veritable subterranean and nocturnal terrorists—snipers, suicide bombers, and ambushers who would hide beneath coral at day and unleash artillery, mortar, and automatic weapons fire at night? If it cost 6,000 American dead to kill 23,000 Japanese on Iwo Jima, how many fatalities would be incurred in eliminating 110,000 more experienced troops on Okinawa?

In hindsight, Okinawa would prove not that the Americans had marshaled too few troops to take the island, but that its massive armada was in fact *far too small* to eliminate the enemy without suffering catastrophic losses in the process. American field artillery on the island itself would fire 1,104,630 105mm howitzer shells—and another 600,000 rounds of various calibers from 115mm to 75mm—during the course of the three-month campaign. Fifteen of such monstrous shells were fired for every Japanese death—and still such munitions could not save thousands of Americans from being killed. Before the battle was even half over, the Americans had already dropped thousands of tons of explosives on Ushijima's soldiers, without achieving any clear weakening of the enemy's will to resist.

Japanese tactics were for the most part well thought out—given the acceptance of the realities of war in mid-1945 when American bombers for weeks prior had incinerated many of the key factories on the mainland while surface ships and submarines made reinforcement and resupply anywhere in the Pacific island empire almost impossible. Generals Ushijima and Isamu Cho—the infamous rightist who in 1931 had once engaged in a terror campaign of assassination to hijack the Tokyo civilian government—along with the brilliant Colonel Yahara, planned to let the Americans land on the beaches unopposed. Then they would lure them into well-fortified Japanese positions in the southern part of the island before systematically grinding them up. By day there would hardly be a Japanese in sight; at night tens of thousands would shell and attack American lines—small teams infiltrating as often as possible to nullify American advantages in naval and ground gunfire. Although Okinawa is a huge island of several hundred square miles, the convergence of over 100,000 troops of the Imperial 32nd Army into the southern third of the island in a series of fortified lines meant that the Japanese, not the Americans, possessed the high ground and the greater concentration of force.

There, hidden wheeled artillery would pound the Americans, only to be drawn back on tracks into the safety of caves and fortifications. The southern Japanese defenses—a series of sequential barriers anchored by the two great so-called Machinao and Shuri fortified lines—had been diabolically adapted to the hills, gorges, and escarpments. Hundreds of camouflaged concrete bunkers and pillboxes allowed uninterrupted fields of fire, remained almost impenetrable from the air, and ensured mutual support and reinforcement through tunnels, telephone and radio communications, and hidden paths. Troops were dug in on the reverse slopes with the intention of luring Americans up to the crests—only to mow them down as they unknowingly exposed themselves on the ridges.

Other scattered infantry units would fight in almost invisible pockets, popping up to shoot Americans who passed by, slipping into their fortified positions at dark, and using snipers to target officers day and night. Meanwhile, as the Americans on the southern part of the island were being immobilized and slowly ground up, kamikaze planes and "suicide" boats—350 were captured and destroyed on the nearby Kerama Islands—would systematically wreck the American fleet off the coast, ensuring its withdrawal and thus the isolation of the land forces.

Then, without resupply, the fighting would degenerate into a sort of Göt-terdämmerung as Okinawa became a final inferno for friend and foe alike—as the Americans, like the Japanese, would have to make do only with what ammunition and supplies were left on the island itself. The more the kamikazes hit the American navy, the more the pressure would be on the land forces to make costly attacks on the entrenched Japanese, take the is-land frontally and rapidly, and so free vulnerable ships from the deadly range of suicide planes based nearby on the mainland. If there was no chance of escape from the island, then the only hope for Japanese salvation would be to kill so many Americans on land and at sea that they would exit and bypass the island, nursing wounds so grievous that they would not dare repeat the ordeal on the mainland.

The Americans, of course, had very different ideas. General Buckner, who commanded all land forces in the invasion under the rubric of the 10th Army, part of a larger joint expeditionary task force, looked not so much at the nature of the island—tragically so in retrospect—but rather at the un-precedented killing power of the U.S. fleet, the logistical capacity of the American army, and the deadly nature of his Marines who had never yet for very long given ground or failed to capture a fortified Japanese position, de-spite horrific carnage on Tarawa, Iwo Jima, and Peleliu. In his view, the pre-liminary carrier bomber attacks of February and March would immobilize all Japanese airfields on the island, ensuring air superiority over Okinawa itself.

Then on the day of the landing, naval shelling and further saturation bombing could destroy the most formidable artillery and command em-placements—if they had not already been obliterated from continual aerial bombing since mid-February. That bombardment would allow a buildup of supplies—thousands of vehicles, millions of artillery shells, tons of gasoline, food, and small-arms ammunition—guaranteeing overwhelming American firepower against the finite and always dwindling material reserves of the iso-lated Japanese. In fact, on average the Americans unloaded about 200,000 tons of matériel on the Okinawa beaches almost every week of the campaign, as ships (458 in all) streamed in from the Philippines, the Marianas, Hawaii, and San Francisco almost daily.

Once on the island, armored columns—in the manner of successful head-on assaults practiced in the European theater—would plow through concentrations of lightly armed Japanese, as carrier fighters and bombers along with mobile artillery could be directed by radios to strafe and pound islands of resistance. In days the Americans should be able to herd the retreating Japanese into a final noose, where they would face surrender—or annihilation by combined aerial, ground, and naval bombardment. Or so the American generals, who knew nothing of coral, caves, and Japanese tactical genius, believed.

In hindsight, it would have been far wiser for General Buckner first to have pondered the challenges of steep gorges and nearly impassable terrain, the deadly nature of the kamikaze threat, and the frequency of cloudy and rainy weather over Okinawa. Constant rain especially prevented accurate reconnaissance; it hampered bombing and mired armor and infantry alike in knee-deep mud. Caution and better surveillance would have presented a chilling scenario of the true obstacles ahead: Okinawa was protected by 110,000 crack Japanese troops—five times the number found on Iwo Jima— *not* the preinvasion estimates of 65,000.

The defenders had had nearly a year to craft impenetrable fortifications with multiple entries and exits. Nearly a half million native Okinawans were mixed in with the defenders, both as innocents and active combatants. There may not have been a single bulldozer on the island or any three-ton trucks, but nearly a quarter million laborers with shovels and picks had invested over a year in pouring cement, digging underground tunnels—eventually to comprise a vast latticework some sixty miles in extent—carving out coral redoubts, and then supplying the entire fortified maze with nearly unlimited supplies of water, food, and ammunition. Given the terrain, the absence of reliable roads, and the shortage of fuel, day laborers could in the long run be as efficient as fleets of earthmoving machines. Three of the most aggressive and experienced Japanese ground commanders in the Imperial Army were in charge of the opposition. Indeed, as it turned out, the Japanese had a far more accurate estimate of the size, nature, and timetable of the American invasion than the Americans did of the Japanese defenses.

Did the Americans really understand that, whereas their fleet was relatively stationary and well beyond the protection of their own land-based fighters and bombers, the Japanese had use of thousands of fighters less than four hundred miles away on the mainland? That the Japanese could lose their Okinawan airfields and still have plenty of homeland planes reach the American fleet from hundreds of bases in a little over two hours?

Had the American high command anticipated such resistance, then they might have bombed far longer, brought in even more troops, and once on the ground fought an entirely different war—surrounding and isolating but not storming Japanese positions, outflanking lines of resistance through amphibious landings to their rear, accepting a six-month battle of attrition rather than demanding three months of annihilation. But then that was not the Marine way—at least not after a string of Pacific island successes and at a time when American troops and supplies were arriving overseas in unheard-of numbers. How could an American army progress to the final showdown on the mainland after conceding that 110,000 enemy soldiers were to be bypassed out of fear of casualties? And so the Americans indeed pressed on to victory—in the end to be saved not only by their superior fire-power, supplies, and know-how, but also through the innate courage and bloody sacrifice of what was probably the most unquestioning generation of Americans this nation has yet produced.

Somewhere in between General Buckner's and General Ushijima's ideal plans of war making, a quarter million people were to die—often a few inches from each other—in a mere ninety days. Yet for most of the first week the battle for Okinawa transpired almost exactly as each side had anticipated without much loss on either side. On the day of the landings, American ships laid down the greatest barrage in naval history—44,825 heavy, 33,000 rocket, and 22,500 mortar shells. Had each shot killed just one Japanese soldier, the battle would have ended before it started. Most of the shells, however, exploded harmlessly amid the concrete and coral. A few salvos brought death—but more often to civilians who lacked the protective entrenchments of their Japanese overseers.

The fleet's gunnery was joined by waves of carrier planes that strafed and bombed the beach and immediate vicinity. When the Americans landed—again over 50,000 on the first day alone—they lost only 28 men killed and took the first four days' planned objectives by nightfall. Two large enemy airfields were captured within hours. Scattered kamikaze attacks during the first few days had damaged only a half dozen ships, including the heavy cruiser *Indianapolis*, the battleship *West Virginia*, and the carrier *Inde-*

fatigable. Otherwise the fleet was relatively safe. The invasion was making remarkable progress as Marines raced throughout the north and center of the island while the army headed for the enemy defensive lines to the south.

Buckner's senior Marine commander, General Geiger, remarked of the rapid advancement and light casualties, "Don't ask me why we haven't had more opposition. I don't understand it. But now we're in a position to work over the Jap forces at our leisure at the least possible loss to ourselves." Admiring the bombardment and the easy landings, Admiral Turner reported to Nimitz's headquarters, "I may be crazy, but it looks like the Japanese have quit the war, at least in this sector."

That initial optimism after the easy landings continued for a week in the north, as the 6th Marine Division with only occasional hard fighting crushed most of the Japanese resistance by April 12. By April 20 it and other Marine contingents had essentially subdued two-thirds of the island. But on the seas the tempo of the battle had already shifted dramatically on April 6, when an unforeseen and enormous flight of over 200 Japanese kamikazes descended on the American fleet. They sank four ships and damaged ten others—as the prelude to a failed one-way strike by the 70,000-ton battleship *Yamato* and its escort destroyers and cruisers. Then for the next ten weeks the Americans would fight off at least ten organized kamikaze sorties of hundreds of planes, and lose 5,000 sailors in the most costly of any single battle in the history of the United States Navy.

Meanwhile, on the southwestern part of the island, U.S. Army battalions at last reached the formidable defenses at the Kakazu Ridge—coral hills pitted with caves and passageways full of Japanese defenders of the 13th Infantry Battalion under the command of the gifted Colonel Hara. After failed assaults during April 9–12, the GIs suffered nearly 3,000 casualties, killed over 4,000 of Hara's troops, but had still not taken the needed few hundred yards of coral. The Americans at last realized that they had marched into an enormous trap of waiting, dug-in Japanese armed with concealed heavy weapons. And from April 10 to 24, nearly the entire American army in the south made repeated but failed efforts to blast through the Japanese defenses.

The Americans inexplicably failed to modify their initial operational plan in light of the sudden and unexpected Japanese ferocity. Instead, they continued to plunge ahead. No enemy could have made more ingenious use of the naturally rugged landscape or fought harder than the Japanese. Unfortunately, they were opposed by an adversary whose overwhelming firepower and superior technology were not substitutes for martial courage and skill in hand-to-hand killing, but mere ancillaries. Despite Japanese bombardment by ghastly 320mm mortars and an array of 75mm and 150mm howitzers, 47mm antitank guns, hundreds of hidden machine guns, the sudden news of the death of President Roosevelt on April 12, and a massive counterattack on April 13, U.S. Army units regrouped and continued south to be joined eventually later in the month by Marines returning from their conquest of the northern Motobu Peninsula.

The first hills of the Shuri defenses began to fall by April 20. On April 25, General Ushijima had retreated to the even more formidable last bastions behind the Shuri line, where the fighting remained stalemated for much of May. The so-called "blowtorch and corkscrew" method, in which either gasoline was pumped into caves and ignited, or cave entrances were blown up by explosives—or both—ensured that the fighting was increasingly dirty and hand-to-hand. When some Japanese units proved nearly impregnable in their underground redoubts, smoke bombs, phosphorous grenades, and huge amounts of pumped gasoline were used to force their egress.

The struggle on Sugar Loaf Hill between May 12 and 19 was especially desperate as Marines tried to storm the slope in the manner of Japanese banzai attacks while the enemy in the American way relied on superior firepower from entrenched positions. Army brigades reinforced by Marines would slog through mud and rain for weeks on end but find no success until May 21, when Ushijima finally brought what was left of the Japanese 32nd Army back to the last redoubt on the southwest corner of the island. Yet fighting there would still rage on for the remainder of June. General Buckner himself was killed on June 18, the highest-ranking American officer to die in the Pacific theater during the Second World War. Ushijima and Cho would commit suicide a week later.

Okinawa was not considered officially secure until July 2. If the Japanese 32nd Army was annihilated, the American 10th Army was nearly ruined and would need months to reconstitute its shattered army and Marine divisions. Whether because of pleas from the navy to accelerate the offensive to save the fleet from nearly daily kamikaze attacks, or due to growing army

Ripples of Battle   29

frustration at gaining so little ground at such great costs, General Buckner poured in more men to continue the piecemeal frontal assaults and ignored his subordinates' suggestions to starve, surround, or bypass the determined Japanese resistance. Maj. Gen. Andrew Bruce, commander of the army's 77th Infantry Division, for example, argued vehemently for a southern landing behind the Shuri lines to force the Japanese to fight in both directions. He had his plans rejected on grounds that it would divert precious supplies from the main frontal assault and would only result in a double theater of attrition.

Likewise, the redeployment from the north of two Marine divisions in late April also would follow preexisting strategy, the divisions being used solely to replace battered army regiments—some with less than 40 percent combat efficiency and with shattered platoons of five or six men—rather than being employed in amphibious landings at the Japanese rear. The attackers would pay dearly for such orthodoxy for much of May. Postbellum interviews by surviving Japanese—especially the testimony of the brilliant Colonel Yahara—revealed that such additional landings would probably have cracked the tenuous Japanese lines of defense far earlier.

The result was that American ground and naval forces suffered 12,520 killed and another 33,631 wounded or missing in the three months between the invasion on April 1 and the official end of the Okinawa campaign on July 2. Although the naval air forces had fought gallantly in both attacking the island and the mainland, and defending the fleet, they nevertheless lost 763 planes in the air and on carriers in just ninety days—the Japanese purportedly losing *five times* that number. Besides the loss of eight patrolling planes every day, the American navy still suffered its worst damage in its then 170-year history—a staggering 36 ships sunk and 368 hit. For each week of the campaign, three craft went to the bottom and another 30 were bombed or crashed into by the enemy. Indeed, four ships from the fleet on average were hit by kamikazes every day for the duration of their deployment off Okinawa. The Japanese improbably claimed that nearly 10,000 naval planes—the vast majority of them conventional bombers and fighters—had taken some part in the battle between March and June.

The defenders were proud of such mayhem but themselves suffered far worse—at least 110,000 killed, or nearly ten soldiers lost for every American slain, at a sickening clip of fifty men dead every hour of the battle, nearly one per minute, nonstop for three months on end. Perhaps 100,000 civilians may have been killed—how many of them were active combatants is not known. Nor do we have any accurate idea of the number of wounded and missing Okinawans; some estimates put the number of soldiers and civilians who were sealed in caves at over 20,000. Fewer than 7,500 Japanese soldiers were taken prisoner. All in all, nearly a quarter of a million people were killed or wounded in the fighting on Okinawa—over 2,500 humans dying every day, most in a confined area of a few square miles in the southern part of the island.

E. B. Sledge, a 1st Marine Division veteran of the fighting, wrote of the carnage on the Shuri line over thirty-five years later:

> The mud was knee deep in some places, probably deeper in others if one dared venture there. For several feet around every corpse, maggots crawled about in the muck and then were washed away by the runoff of the rain. There wasn't a tree or bush left. All was open country. Shells had torn up the turf so completely that ground cover was nonexistent. The rain poured down on us as evening approached. The scene was nothing but mud; shell fire; flooded craters with their silent, pathetic, rotting occupants; knocked-out tanks and amtracs; and discarded equipment—utter desolation. . . . We were in the depths of the abyss, the ultimate horror of war. . . . In the mud and driving rain before Shuri, we were surrounded by maggots and decay. Men struggled and fought and bled in an environment so degrading I believed we had been flung into hell's own cesspool.

And for what was all this carnage? Plenty of strategic reasons were advanced. Ostensibly the United States had now obtained an enormous base of 640 square miles within a mere 350 miles of the mainland, a staging and supply area for the final invasion to come, a deepwater anchorage for the entire American fleet, and dozens of air bases for both tactical fighters and strategic bombers. Just as important, the Americans felt that with the fall of Okinawa, the Japanese fleet and naval air forces in the Pacific theater for all practicality would cease to exist. The enemy's best army divisions would be obliterated. A future invasion of Kyushu and Honshu (Operations Olympic and Coronet) would enjoy almost complete air superiority—without worry of naval attack and with the assurance that the many veteran Japanese land forces in the immediate area had been long ago wiped out.

To the Japanese generals and their staff who committed suicide in the final days of the battle, it was not altogether clear that they had failed. Colonel Yahara pointed out that the American supreme commander, General Buckner, had been killed by Japanese before any of his own ranking generals on the island died by their own hand. Even the American President had expired during the battle—perhaps in the Japanese view from the sheer shock of the mounting American fatalities. And the original Japanese purpose, after all, had never been to win or even survive, but to cause so much death and destruction that the Americans would think twice before repeating a similar assault on the homeland.

The Japanese might have been correct in thinking that such American losses could be replicated on Kyushu and Honshu, but they were dead wrong about the Americans not invading. The victory on Okinawa taught the Americans that thousands of their own would probably die in conquering Japan, but that the mainland could—and must—be conquered all the same. Fifty more Japanese combat divisions, millions more in the militias, and thousands of trained kamikazes purportedly waiting in arms could kill many, but not stop most, of the hundreds of thousands of Americans who would be determined to end the war off the shores of Japan itself.

Okinawa was not the first occasion for suicide attacks. Americans had seen them earlier on the ground and in the air both at Guadalcanal and Leyte Gulf. Nor for the first time did civilians jump off cliffs or kill themselves in caves. Such horror had also occurred earlier sporadically during the Marianas campaign at Marpi Point on Saipan. And we should remember that thousands of Americans had been killed on Iwo Jima as they wiped out nearly all of the Japanese who would not surrender. But Okinawa was the summation of all the macabre elements of a barbarous three years of island fighting. It was not just the last battle of the Pacific war, but the murderous aggregate of all that had gone on before.

After their bloody victory in July 1945, the Americans searched for ways *not* to avoid another Okinawa, but rather to do what they had done to Okinawa in ways that did *not* exact similar costs. If anything, after defeating the suicide attackers of Okinawa, the Americans felt that they could survive—and do—anything. That was surely true, but in little over a month after the victory on Okinawa, what they came up with as the solution for avoiding another Pyrrhic victory in defeating kamikazes, armed and indistinguishable civilians, bomb-rigged soldiers, and banzai attacks would shock the world.

The Laboratory of Suicide

Fighters who deliberately seek death in battle—whether to end their own misery amid certain defeat, to undergo offensive missions that hold out no chance of their own survival, or as wounded and doomed in the last moments of life to kill the enemy without hope of escape—are ubiquitous in both history and myth. When nearly surrounded, King Leonidas of Sparta sent away thousands of his allied army from Thermopylae (480 B.C.). Then with his remaining 299 Spartans and a few hundred Thespians and Thebans, he prepared to leave the confines of the pass and charge out to fight amid a sea of thousands of Persian troops. "Fight with great courage," the king purportedly told his Spartans hours before annihilation, "for today we will dine among the dead."

During the failed Jewish revolt of A.D. 73, when the last enclave of the zealots at the citadel of Masada was surrounded and before the Roman besiegers could storm the stronghold, the rebels under Eleazar ben Yair killed themselves. By the historian Josephus's count, all but seven of some 960 trapped men, women, and children perished. Hitler's order in January 1943 for the encircled garrison at Stalingrad to shun both escape and surrender, but fight to the last man, was equivalent to suicide for thousands.

But the various elements of the Japanese death brigades were quite different from *any* fanatical suicides seen before in the long history of war. Thousands of Japanese were trained as suicide pilots. Even more suicide bombers commanded ramming-boats or as infantrymen organized death charges. Many foot soldiers fought with dynamite satchels or grenades strapped to their bodies. In all these cases the sole intention was to kill as many Americans as possible before meeting certain death. The acceptance of suicide was state-sanctioned—and very soon after its inception was to be not sporadic, but even planned and organized on a mass scale by the Japanese government. What, then, would make a modern nation turn to such apparently precivilized measures against the enemy?

Desperation in war, of course, is a human constant across time and space that can make the once inconceivable and repugnant act suddenly seem palatable. It is no surprise that the first organized suicide fighters made their appearance in autumn 1944 during the defense of the Philippines. Then most of the Japanese air force and navy was either in retreat or nearly destroyed—and there was little optimism about stopping the American juggernaut through traditional means as it neared the Japanese homeland. What would have been considered foolish and unnecessary on December 8, 1941, was not seen as such in October 1944, as the last defensive line of the once impenetrable Co-Prosperity Sphere was breached. Indeed, Japanese commanders who sent two-man midget-submarine crews into Pearl Harbor on December 7 had gained permission from Admiral Yamamoto for the daring missions only on the assurance that there was at least some chance of rescuing the crews.

But by April 1, 1945, when the Americans landed on Okinawa, Japan was confronted with the most powerful fleet in the history of warfare with no conventional mechanism for either sinking such an armada or turning it away. Japan's best pilots were long dead. Its once legendary Zero was now outclassed by a variety of American fighters; and its capital ships were mostly sunk, in drydock, or without sufficient fuel. More important, with the beginning of the American B-29 fire raids in March 1945, the militarists could make the believable argument to both soldiers and civilians that the enemy meant not to defeat the Japanese armed forces but rather to destroy its very people.

Still, the cornered Japanese military of 1944–45 was hardly unique in its hopelessness. The nature of civilized war in the past three millennia is replete with examples of doomed armies that quietly surrendered or were massacred without their commanders first inaugurating well-organized suicide squads—whether at Cannae, Constantinople, or Tannenberg. Rather, ideology and a fanaticism of sorts are also requisite if a nation is going to embrace the idea of sending its youth on missions of no return. In the case of Japan, well before the Pacific war began to deteriorate, there were long-standing elements within its militarized society of the 1930s and 1940s that could prove conducive to suicide—should the need ever arise for the wholesale adoption of such ultimate sacrifice.

Japanese culture until the nineteenth century was unusually feudal and hierarchical, run by assorted shoguns and their lesser lords, or daimyo, who held power through the employment of samurai warriors. The glue that held together the entire tribal system was a shame culture based on a variety of protocols that ensured absolute obedience to those in power—and a willingness of subordinates to die as part of their sworn fealty.

The samurai code was not eccentric, but rather drew on a number of more traditional Japanese religious beliefs. Confucianism had always inculcated a need for strict loyalty and obedience to authority. Shintoism reminded soldiers that they were, in fact, offspring of divinities. If proven brave in battle, after death they would return to their godly existence. Even more mainstream Buddhism taught that life is tenuous. Death is not the end—merely a manifestation of a new and different sort of existence.

Still, deep-seated confidence in authority, transcendence, and moral sanction, even when coupled with an absence of a Christian repugnance for suicide, by themselves are not incentives enough to create cadres of kamikazes—as the relatively traditional and humane behavior of Japanese soldiers in the 1905 Russo-Japanese War and the First World War attest. To enlist thousands of suicide pilots it takes more than the absence of democracy, confidence in the afterlife, and few taboos against killing oneself.

The destruction of a brief constitutional government in Japan during the 1930s by militarists, of course, also had provided a necessary ingredient for contemplating such drastic measures. The plotters were not merely thugs who wanted power. Instead, the more extreme men like the fiery Isamu Cho of the "Cherry Society" (Sakura-kai)—a prominent butcher in the Nanking Massacre to come—were far more systematic and sinister revolutionaries who sought to craft an entirely new Japanese identity cast in reactionary terms.

In this vein, the armed forces' nationalist ideology added a novel wrinkle to traditionally conservative Japanese culture. The generals now preached that Western technology, when married to spiritual purity, could create a Japanese warrior far superior to his more decadent European or American counterpart—pampered Occidentals who relied on material wealth and machines rather than the primacy of innate courage. This "spiritual mobilization" (*Seishin Kyoiku*)—fed by the resentments of nearby colonialism and nursed by the old slights of racist Western condescension—was then grafted by the new ultranationalists onto traditional emperor worship (*kodo*). The result was an entire citizenry indoctrinated in the belief in racial purity and national destiny that demanded the absolute allegiance of every Japanese.

Youth in schools were now taught by rote—in eerie forerunners to the present-day fundamentalist Islamic *madrassas* that now turn out suicide murderers in the Middle East—that they must make sacrifices in their daily lives for their emperor, the personification of the divine destiny of a racially superior Japanese people. An increasing emphasis was put on the glories of dying in combat—especially the avoidance of surrender and killing enemy soldiers in the bargain. In early 1941, General Tojo issued an official military "code of ethics" that called upon every Japanese soldier not "to fear to die for the cause of everlasting justice. Do not stay alive in dishonor. Do not die in such a way as to leave a bad name behind you." Such sacrifice would ensure that Japanese warriors would become divine, and perhaps live an eternal spiritual existence at "The Patriots' Shrine" (the Yasukuni Temple on Kudan Hill in Tokyo), which had been founded in 1868 as home for the heroic souls of dead veterans.

In this multifaceted context of past Japanese cultural practice, the desperation of 1944–45, and the propaganda of the authoritarian generals in Tokyo, the conditions for suicide attacks on a grand scale arose that would have been impossible in the democratic West or among the totalitarian murderers of Nazi Germany and Soviet Russia. Yet even with all that, the kamikazes might well have been a passing phenomenon. The final ingredient was some sporadic success in sinking or damaging American ships during their first haphazard attacks in autumn 1944 at the battle of Leyte Gulf. Suicide bombing in any era continues only because it is for a time deemed tactically or strategically effective.

Just as important as their actual results, both the zeal and the successes of the kamikazes were always exaggerated. In a society with a state-controlled media and an effective propaganda ministry, Japanese planners could argue to the masses that suicide tactics alone promised salvation from the Americans—or at more bleak times deny their presence altogether. Had the truth of the enormous losses been told, coupled with the reality that not a single American battleship or carrier was ever sunk by kamikazes alone, problems of morale might have thinned the suicide-pilot ranks from the very beginning in 1944.

After all, suicide attacks in any context would soon have ceased if the architects of such special corps had learned that their bombers were doing little long-term harm to the enemy, whether material, psychological, or political. Instead, there were at least some early reports that the kamikazes were achieving results in a way traditional aerial bombing attacks had not. Moreover, the steady attrition in army and naval aircraft by summer 1944 far outweighed the Japanese government's ability to replace planes or train new pilots. So the apprehension grew that if some new tactic was not discovered rather quickly, the dwindling arsenal of resistance was soon to be obliterated altogether. If a pilot was going to be shot down anyway, why not instead take some of the enemy with him—especially since being captured as a prisoner-of-war was a worse disgrace than simply dying without killing the enemy?

Once it crossed the Rubicon of accepting state-organized suicide as a legitimate military tactic, the Japanese command learned that it might well regain some of its lost ability to strike the Americans and perhaps stave off an unconditional surrender. Its frontline bombers and fighters were, of course, too few and outclassed by 1945 to mix it up against the air combat patrols of new Hellcats and Corsairs in conventional attacks on American ships and bombers. And aviation fuel was in such short supply that the inflight training necessary to prepare capable pilots was nearly impossible. But Japan nevertheless still possessed thousands of antiquated Zeros and dive- and torpedo-bombers—26,000 produced in 1944 alone—as well as apparently thousands more eager and patriotic conscripts.

How then might they even the odds? In conventional practice it could take a year to train an effective pilot—two or three more still to produce in large numbers any of the new prototype aircraft that Japan hoped could at least match the latest American designs in conventional dogfights. Thus, the trick was to find a tactic in the here and now of late 1944 and early 1945 to impart to thousands of outmoded planes and green pilots the ability to destroy the most sophisticated military in the world. Suicide bombers seemed to have solved the dilemma quite well. The Zero, after all, was still a relatively reliable plane. If it could no longer be flown by seasoned pilots to even the odds against more advanced Grumman F6F-5 Hellcats, it might nevertheless make a deadly cruise missile—especially in headlong dives from high altitudes in which there was no worry about pulling out. And when Zeros were not available, anything that flew, from lumbering trainers to obsolete dive-bombers, at least would be put to better use in killing Americans than in sitting unused and discarded in hangars, especially when employed in mass attacks—again, as long as the life of the pilot was no longer a paramount concern.

If a man did not plan to live through his attack, then worries about full gas tanks, clear weather on the way home, radio contact with his base, sophisticated aerial tactics, and the top performance of his plane began to fade. By strapping a young zealot to the seat of a bomb-carrying plane, the Japanese had in effect nullified a two- or three-year American edge in technology: what the delivery vehicle lacked in speed and performance, it now gained in near superhuman accuracy. The kamikaze pilot was an early smart bomb—and its guidance system was far more sophisticated than any computer in its ability to hunt down and find a mobile enemy.

Since kamikazes cared only to target the enemy and destroy him, a man's brain was concerned with using all its skill to hit a ship or large bomber—not to protect friends, evade fire, return home, or save his plane. And out of that single-minded concentration on death, the Japanese in their eleventh hour for a time found a mechanism to transform second-rate planes and third-rate pilots into first-rate guided missiles far more effective than German V-1 rockets or any missile weapons in either the American or British arsenal that could not alter their trajectory or general course once launched.

The use of kamikazes in the last months of World War II would result in real but unforeseen ripples both short-term and with us still. As we shall see, the astounding damage they inflicted against the American fleet between April and June 1945 purportedly taught students of conflict that death cadres could be great equalizers for any power that had access to technology and was willing to marry it to an ideology—or religion—that could tolerate or even foster suicide.

The ostensible lesson of the suicides on Okinawa was that a willingness to die might result in military parity for a time against a technologically superior foe; and that Western sophistication in arms—whether that be self-sealing gas tanks, onboard radio and radar communications, armor plating, ejection seats and parachutes, or elaborate sea search-and-rescue infrastructures—was in large part designed to protect the combatant as much as to injure the enemy. But if the life of the warrior was to be sacrificed in the moment of his attack, then much of what was deemed progress in war was rendered instantly superfluous.

Thus it is no accident that well after the defeat of the Japanese off Okinawa, the basic principles of suicide attack are still with us today—giving hope to any militarily backward and technologically inferior foe that with the proper propaganda, ideology, or religion to indoctrinate a cadre of suicide bombers, the supposedly sophisticated and advanced infrastructure of the West could still be vulnerable. If one lacks an F-16 or B-52, a hijacked and fuel-laden jet airliner might be just as effective—as long as the pilot and his accomplices have every intention of steering the plane and themselves into its target. In turn, those who seek to live can be deemed weak by those determined to die in killing them. And better quality weapons that are designed to protect the user as well as kill the target can be neutralized by inferior models employed only to destroy, not survive the ordeal.

What were the long-term lessons of the response to the suicides at Okinawa? As we shall also discover, at Okinawa the use of kamikazes and an entire array of death bombers unshackled the Americans in both their thinking and practice of war. What the Japanese started, the Americans had even more terrifying ways of finishing—then and now.

Divine Wind

A divine wind (kamikaze) twice, in 1274 and 1281, had blown away Kublai Khan's Mongol armada—sudden and unexpected typhoons that saved Japan from sure invasion by an overwhelmingly superior foreigner. Nearly seven hundred years later, man and machine would purportedly do again for Japan against the Americans what nature apparently this time would not.

Throughout the earlier part of World War II, some soldiers and pilots in the Japanese military were prone to near-suicidal tactics in confronting the greater numbers and material edge of the Americans. During the savage fighting on Guadalcanal (summer and fall 1942) and on the Aleutians (May 1943), hundreds of desperate Japanese soldiers rushed heedlessly into entrenched American artillery and machine gun positions in human-wave or so-called "banzai charges." In all cases the sacrifices led to horrendous casualities without changing the course of battle. Japanese pilots—when wounded or on the verge of crashing—sometimes steered their planes into American ships. Such desperate attacks, for example, may have helped sink the aircraft carrier *Hornet* off Guadalcanal in October 1942.

Yet the first organized and successful large-scale kamikaze missions did not take place until the desperate defense of the Philippines as part of the *Sho* ("Victor") plan of integrated air, sea, and ground counterattacks against the American invasion. Vice Adm. Takijiro Onishi purportedly crafted the first successful kamikaze assault of his newly created *Yamato* and *Shikishima* units on October 25, when they damaged a number of American ships and sank the escort carrier *St. Lo.* Just as important, the Japanese felt that the newly formed kamikazes could serve as a frightening terror weapon: once enemy sailors realized that approaching planes meant to crash into their ships and that brave Japanese pilots were willing to die in order to kill them, the Americans would become unnerved and lose heart at fighting such audacious and desperate enemies who would do what they themselves could not. Rikihei Inoguchi and Tadashi Nakajima, who helped command the kamikaze attacks, remarked of the generally held Japanese belief that such corps were absolutely unique:

> History provides many cases of individual soldiers who fought under certain-death circumstances, but never before was such a program carried out so systematically and over such a long period of time. In the case of do-or-die action, however great the risk involved, there is always a chance of survival. But the *kamikaze* attack

could be carried out *only* by killing himself. The attack and death were one and the same thing.

From October 25, 1944, until the April 1945 sorties against Okinawa, the Japanese made a series of suicide attacks on American shipping as they sought to refine their weapons and tactics—the most practicable weapon emerging as a Zero carrying a five-hundred-pound bomb. Sometimes a plane skimmed the waves in order to avoid radar and crashed into the vulnerable waterline of a ship. More often they came in at high altitudes and dived from nearly twenty thousand feet to lessen their window of vulnerability to anti-aircraft fire and enemy fighters. Dawn and sunset were the preferred times to launch the attacks—as the rising and setting sun allowed better identification of enemy vessels than was possible during the night, without the vulnerability of flying in full daylight. In addition, ritual funerals, public ceremony, and occasional media attention romanticized the kamikazes in hopes of increasing recruitment and gaining acceptance among an initially wary Japanese high command and skeptical citizenry at large. Close group interaction, discussion, and constant indoctrination were critical in preventing any faint-hearts from having second thoughts about killing themselves. The result was that during the autumn and winter of 1944 off the Philippines, the kamikazes damaged and sank more American ships than in any three-month period of the entire war since Pearl Harbor. And by early 1945, increased numbers of suicide bombers attacked the Americans off Formosa and Iwo Jima, again damaging dozens of destroyers and light carriers.

Unlike conventional attacks, the destructive power of desperate Zeros involved more than the dropping of bombs. In addition to the power of a five-hundred-pound explosive device, the weight, density, and size of the plane coming in at speeds of up to 300 miles per hour could easily tear apart wooden carrier decks and even their steel superstructures. Then gallons of aviation fuel, in the manner of napalm, would be ignited on impact, spreading fire beyond the explosion. Finally, the architects of suicide felt that terror was an ally as well: they figured (erroneously as it turned out) that American sailors might quickly become disheartened when they learned that their new enemies were not merely bombs and bullets, but entire planes and their pilots as well.

The real test, however, would be Okinawa itself. There the army under the veteran General Ushijima and the fanatical General Cho were resolved to die with their entire commands as the price of killing thousands of Americans. By March hundreds of kamikazes, based on the mainland at Kyushu, organized the so-called *kikusui* force or "floating chrysanthemums," named for the traditional pure flower that would symbolize the combined air-and-sea operation. At Okinawa the Japanese felt that they had much better opportunities to destroy American ships than was true at either the Philippines or Iwo Jima. The island was too far distant for land-based American aircraft to attack. Until bases could be established on the newly conquered island, almost all American air support for the amphibious assault had to come from the carriers themselves—whose limited numbers of floating wooden runways in theory could be put out of commission for days by just a few kamikazes.

In other words, the American fleet more or less was stationary and posted permanently off Okinawa, without the umbrella of the Army Air Force, all the while in easy range of thousands of enemy planes from the mainland. Normally that extended deployment would not have troubled American planners, who were confident that their new carrier fighters and highly trained pilots would make short work of both conventional and occasional suicide attacks.

But the Japanese were planning something on a scale entirely unforeseen in preparing some 4,000 planes for suicide attacks, commencing their sorties immediately after the initial landings. In all there would be roughly ten mass *kikusui* attacks. The most dramatic was perhaps the first on April 6, when for the entire day and early evening some 223 planes dived on Task Force 58, the American invasion fleet stationed off the landing beaches, and various radar picket destroyers northeast of Okinawa. Despite inadequate cover from Zero fighters and poorly trained pilots, the unprecedented number of planes allowed the kamikazes to hit at least fourteen ships. The Americans had never seen anything quite like it.

More important, 15 percent of the original force inflicted some damage—a far higher figure than obtained by past traditional Japanese naval aviators. The only consolation to the Americans was that the bulk of the planes bombed distant destroyers acting as radar pickets. Perhaps the suicide planes deliberately wished to disrupt early warnings to the core of the American fleet; or they were satisfied that they could at least sink a smaller destroyer with one crash; or the Japanese pilots realized they would probably be shot down venturing over the cruisers and battleships on their way to the carriers in the middle of the armada and so attacked the first targets in sight. Although in this first attack the Japanese had hit only the fleet carrier *Hancock* and the light carrier *San Jacinto*, the Americans immediately realized that should they lose their picket destroyers, minesweepers, and supply craft at such an alarming rate, eventually their capital ships could fall prey as well.

The kamikazes returned on April 12 in even greater numbers. Some 350 bombers and fighters took off from Kyushu. They were intermingled with escort fighters and a few more experienced and valuable pilots who planned to make conventional attacks. This time the Japanese dropped "chaff" (thin foil strips) to confuse radar, attacked near dusk, and came in at all altitudes and directions. The Zeros heavily damaged some of the largest ships in the fleet—the carriers *Enterprise* and *Essex*, the battleships *Missouri, New Mexico, Tennessee*, and *Idaho*, and the cruiser *Oakland* as well as dozens of ancillary destroyers, gunboats, and minesweepers.

Shocked American sailors tried everything to prevent such unforeseen mayhem. They bombed the Japanese bases in Kyushu where camouflaged and scattered planes proved difficult to detect. They tried redirecting carrier planes from sorties over Okinawa to fleet defense, and added dozens of antiaircraft batteries to escort ships—eventually naval gunfire would down 70 percent of the attackers. And still the kamikazes came with a third large attack of 155 planes on April 16. Once again they managed to hit a carrier, the *Intrepid*, as well as more destroyers, minesweepers, and tankers. Then for the next three weeks the Japanese were diving continuously, damaging and sinking American ships almost daily before sending another massive concentrated flight on May 3 and 4, when 305 planes—at least 280 were lost—damaged nearly a dozen of the picket destroyers and support ships.

Finally the Americans appeared to be tiring from the daily barrage. On May 11 the Japanese hit Admiral Mitscher's flagship itself, the carrier *Bunker Hill*, and left it a burning wreck, and also hit again the battleship *New Mexico*. American officers by the end of May calculated that if the kamikazes continued to score at the present rates, the entire fleet would have to withdraw by the middle of June—or acknowledge that some of their key capital ships would be crippled and the majority of their destroyers sunk or damaged, and thousands of sailors killed and wounded at an unsustainable rate. American navy personnel by now had been fighting daily kamikaze attacks for nearly two months. They had seen their best vessels hit and their friends blown apart and still were without any sure method of stopping the attackers. Given the nature of the kamikazes' determination, even a smaller sortie of some 30 or 40 planes—otherwise hardly a threat as conventional fighters and bombers—could spell catastrophe.

Perhaps the most disheartening air attack came late in the battle on June 5, nearly sixty-five days after the initial invasion and at a time when the Americans were beginning to believe the enemy had lost his initiative. First kamikazes hit the battleship *Mississippi*, the cruiser *Louisville*, and assorted destroyers and minesweepers. Then later on, an enormous storm caught the recoiling Americans, further damaging carriers and battleships, wrecking 142 planes, and sending dozens of ships back to the United States for major repairs—even as the suicides returned the next day to augment the toll from the weather damage. Fortunately, by mid-June the near capitulation of Okinawa, the destruction of hundreds of Japanese planes in the air and at their bases in Japan, and the first signs of some pilot reluctance in pressing home the attacks caused the suicide bombers to taper off.

Altogether, the combined *kikusui* campaign had sunk eleven destroyers, one minesweeper, and assorted other auxiliary craft, but damaged—and in some cases disabled for the rest of the war—four fleet carriers, three light carriers, ten battleships, five cruisers, sixty-one destroyers, and countless other support ships. Based on exaggerated reports and propaganda, the Japanese high command reported losses ten times the actual American numbers, which had the effect for a time of neutralizing the growing doubt among new squadrons of pilots that they were being arbitrarily recruited to die for a lost cause.

The record of the size and number of actual kamikaze attacks at Okinawa remains somewhat unclear as Japanese and American figures are not in agreement on either the number of planes involved or the precise figure of damaged and destroyed targets. We should assume, however, that at least 2,000 Japanese pilots were lost in sorties that killed almost 5,000 American sailors. The Americans, in fact, believed that they had shot down over 7,000 planes. To obtain some idea of the deadly nature of the kamikazes, contrast the inverse ratio of fatalities of their suicidal army counterparts on Okinawa, who sacrificed 100,000 men to kill 7,000 Americans—2 dead Japanese pilots for every 5 American sailors versus 100 imperial infantrymen needed to kill 7 Marines and GIs. Since prior to the inauguration of kamikaze tactics, neither the Japanese navy nor air force in 1945 had been able to inflict any major damage on the American fleet, the kamikazes represented a counterassault well beyond the expectations of even the most optimistic supporters of the new squadrons. And when the attacks ceased on June 22, a battered American fleet realized that there were supposedly thousands more of such weapons less than four hundred miles away on the mainland ready to renew their attacks.

What, then, is the legacy of the kamikazes—a brilliant and malevolent tactic of neutralizing the edge in material power and technology of the Americans, or a resounding Japanese defeat that only helped prompt a murderous response in the atomic attacks on Hiroshima and Nagasaki? The answer is ambiguous, since the kamikazes in a sense succeeded and failed—by inflicting unimagined damage in their inability either to save Okinawa, destroy the American fleet, or break the will of their enemies. After all, while the Americans suffered dreadful naval losses, *not a single fleet carrier or battleship was sunk.* Planes continued to attack Okinawa daily despite kamikaze targeting of their home carriers. If anything, the Americans proved that they could beat off the suicides, repair damaged craft, and replace their lost ships faster than the Japanese could make up their own losses in planes and fanatical pilots. So the ever more shrill boasts of tens of thousands of suicide killers waiting to attack in planes, boats, and submarines would finally prove hollow—both because of a shortage of delivery systems and the reality that there were fewer suicide volunteers and eager draftees than publicly proclaimed.

The ripples of the "Floating Chrysanthemums," then, were more psychological and ideological—and so remain today as such across time and space. The metaphysics of air suicide attacks only confirmed in the Western mind the fanaticism of the imperial military, making it clear that extreme measures would be necessary to break their hold on the citizens of Japan. If a foe wished to crash himself in order to kill—and had plenty more planes and pilots to come—why worry about the magnitude of the retaliatory response? The American navy left Okinawa convinced that warfare in the Pacific had to continue to be far more harsh and terrible than what had transpired in Europe. They concluded that Asians in their caves, holes, and suicide ships and planes were a different—usually thought to be a more fanatical—foe than Germans or Italians, and so were deserving of even more extreme treatment. And that conjecture would have consequences in American thinking in the decades to come in the bombing campaigns ahead in Korea and especially Vietnam, where massive caves and underground fortifications were eerily reminiscent of Okinawa and likewise virtually impregnable to occasionally mindless American carpet bombing.

But more important, the sacrifice of some 3,913 American-documented successful kamikaze attacks during the war set a paradigm of asymmetrical warfare whose antidotes are also with us still. Airplanes are not merely the carriers of bombs, missiles, and guns, but if piloted by suicides can become forces of sheer destruction themselves. The kamikazes naturally resonated with the terrorists of September 11—and will continue to hold out false hope for future guerrillas to come, by offering to those with less power the specter of destroying enormous assets of American power, whether large ships or urban skyscrapers.

But again, what those who crash airplanes in the past and present alike failed to grasp was also the nature of the deadly repercussions that arose from their explosions. Suicide bombings strike at the very psyche of the Western mind that is repelled by the religious fanaticism and the authoritarianism, or perhaps the despair, of such enemies—confirming that wars are not just misunderstandings over policy or the reckless actions of a deranged leader, but accurate reflections of fundamental differences in culture and society. In precisely the same way as kamikazes off Okinawa led to A-bombs, so too jumbo jets exploding at the World Trade Center were the logical precursors to daisy-cutters, bunker-busters, and thermobaric bombs in Afghanistan—as an unleashed America resounded with a terrible fury not seen or anticipated since 1945. The Western world publicly objected to the Israeli plunge into the Jenin refugee camp in April 2002 and its purported destruction of the civilian infrastructure—but much of it also privately sighed, "Such are the wages for suicide-murderers who blow up children in Tel Aviv." If it is true that moral pretensions at restraint are the ultimate brakes on the murderous Western way of war, it is also accurate to suggest that such ethical restrictions erode considerably when the enemy employs suicide bombers.

The Japanese also had an array of other suicide plans of attack by sea and air that were astounding both in their variety and desperation. As the campaign wore on, the Americans discovered literally dozens of new Japanese suicide weapons, specialized death battalions, and a generally shared commitment among former civilians and draftees to fight to the death. The most sophisticated of the one-way weapons was the so-called *Okha* ("exploding cherry blossom") flying bomb. With the capture of the Mariana Islands in June and July 1944 and the accompanying slaughter of hundreds of Japanese bombers and fighters—445 planes shot down—imperial planners realized that their once unrivaled planes were now too slow, their pilots too inexperienced, and their bombs too light to destroy the American fleet. Out of that desperation arose the *Okha* (called a *Baka*, or "idiot," bomb by the Americans), a one-way piloted rocket that in theory could neutralize all of the Americans' advantages in naval defense.

The missile-planes were cheap to build, constructed of low-quality metal and wood, simply designed, and only twenty feet long, with stubby wings and two vertical stabilizers. The nose cone was filled with an armor-coated charge of 2,640 pounds of TNT, over five times more destructive power as that which was carried in most kamikaze suicide planes. Five small rockets—adapted from German designs—gave a nine-second propellant burst that thrust the descending gliders to speeds of 600 mph.

The rocket planes were dropped a safe distance from their targets by twin-engine Betty bombers at an altitude of twenty thousand feet, ensuring that the *Okhas* roared out of the sky unannounced at unbelievable speeds—while in theory at least requiring little skill to aim them at the large and relatively slow-moving American ships. Without many worries about taking off, landing, or missing such large targets—in these respects the thinking was similar to that of the unskilled pilots who rammed jumbo jets into the World Trade Center on September 11, 2001—the so-called "Thunder Gods" who navigated the *Okhas* could be trained quickly and cheaply.

Still, operational and tactical problems emerged immediately—besides premature explosions, crashes of the bombers, and an inability to transport the rockets to their bases due to American bombing. The short-ranged *Okhas* had to be dropped fairly close to the American fleet. But such requisite proximity ensured that the slow-moving and encumbered mother Betty bombers—that scarcely managed 150 knots when loaded—were then themselves easy targets. Although 56 of the Thunder Gods were killed, 372 Betty bomber crewmen perished just in nearing the American ships. And once sent off, the rocket bombs proved nearly impossible to control with any precision. Altogether only one American destroyer was sunk and another five were damaged—despite the launching of some 185 *Okhas* in the battle for Okinawa alone.

Besides the rocket bombers, the Japanese built a series of suicide midget submarines, one-way motorboats, and human torpedoes—precursors of the suicide boat that nearly sank the USS *Cole* in Yemen on October 12, 2000. Yet the combined results of all such special weapons were the sinking of less than a half dozen American landing craft, oilers, and destroyers. Perhaps the most famous and least successful of all suicide missions was the final voyage of the world's largest battleship, the famed *Yamato* that steamed out of Kure naval harbor on March 28, 1945, on a mission of no return. Along with its escort ships, the *Yamato* planned to plow into the American fleet off Okinawa in hopes that its massive 18.1-inch guns could blast away the thin-skinned carriers before it was spotted and sunk—or at least draw off enemy carrier-based planes so that simultaneous kamikaze attacks might more easily hit their targets. In fact, the *Yamato* never got close to Okinawa. It was blasted apart by American carrier planes on April 7—taking over two thousand crewmen to the bottom scarcely halfway to its target.

But suicide was no stranger to the actual land battle itself on Okinawa and usually occurred on the island in a variety of guises. As had been true of earlier fighting in the Pacific, there were a number of sudden death charges by hundreds of Japanese. In this regard General Cho especially bristled at the continual defensive tactics of Colonel Yahara and was finally given the go-ahead for an offensive on May 4 to coincide with kamikaze attacks on the fleet and proposed amphibious landings behind American lines. Some fifteen thousand of the Japanese 32nd Army struck out at the Americans at

daybreak, small units carrying food and ammunition for ten days of independent operation with orders "to kill one American devil for every Japanese." Convinced that the temporary halt of the Americans at the Shuri line
signaled weakness, the Japanese abandoned the very tactics that had brought
them success and thereby helped accelerate their own defeat.

By midnight of the next day the offensive was proving to be a tactical
disaster. Not only did the Japanese lose five thousand soldiers and over nineteen key heavy artillery pieces, they inflicted just over a thousand casualties
on the American XXIV Corps. Throughout the two-day attack there were impromptu banzai charges, their aim simply to kill Americans. At other times
infantrymen volunteered to infiltrate into American lines at night to slit Marine throats—even though such stealthy actions usually meant death by alert
American lookouts.

Other suicide attackers adopted a different and more dangerous tactic
of carrying satchel charges and grenades—or even wiring such explosives to
their bodies—so that they might get close enough to American soldiers,
trucks, tanks, jeeps, and almost anything imaginable and blow themselves
up, taking dozens with them. Two Japanese soldiers, on one occasion,
strapped explosives to their backs and blew up a footbridge that had been
built to allow the 22nd Marines to cross the Asa River. Such suicide bombing rapidly became the only possible way of fulfilling General Ushijima's initial boast of one man for each tank.

As in the case of the kamikazes, zeal could in theory often make up for
both the dearth of heavy weapons and the inadequacy of lethal antitank
rockets, in effect creating the 1945 equivalent of laser-guided artillery pro-
jectiles. A suicide bomber can be every bit as effective as a "smart" shell, using his senses and intelligence to zero in on the target—with the added
advantage of not being wed to a predetermined trajectory. How many of the
some seven thousand American infantrymen killed on the island itself fell to
suicide attackers is unknown, but the discipline and firepower of Marine
units usually meant that such exposed suicidal charges were in fact often to
be welcomed over more lethal sniper attacks and shelling from well-fortified
caves.

Sometimes Japanese soldiers deliberately holed up in subterranean
chambers, hoping that the attacking Americans would have to descend in

small groups of twos and threes and then be blown up as the defenders killed themselves. In response, the Americans learned to torch such strongholds first and ask for surrender later. In five days, for example, between June 13 and 17, the flame-shooting tanks of the 713th Armored Flamethrower Battalion poured 37,000 gallons of gasoline into Japanese caves and bunkers.

Col. Hiromichi Yahara, who had designed much of the Japanese resistance and was often at odds with his more fiery superiors, recalled after the war a conversation with another officer about the dramatic—but also self-serving—efforts of the militarists to sacrifice thousands of Japanese soldiers:

> I then explained the all-out suicide attack plan in which our soldiers would charge down the hill to Mabuni. The generals would witness this scene just before they died peacefully on the hilltop. I was glad to hear Sunano add, "Our artillery can't contribute much to such a finale, but somehow we should move some guns to Odo village. From there they can contribute to the scene, by firing guns like fireworks. It will be spectacular." I was heartened to hear his plan. We went on to discuss Japan's future, about which we were deeply concerned. It was clear that Japan would inevitably fall after Okinawa. Our leaders had chosen this path to destruction. They did not care that hundreds of thousands of soldiers would die. They seemed to care only about the preservation of their own status, prestige, and honor.

Equally disturbing to Americans, however, were the occasional suicides of Okinawan civilians, who were told by the Japanese that conquering GIs and Marines would torture and kill them upon capture—in the very manner that veterans themselves of the 32nd Army had mutilated Chinese civilians for years in Manchuria. Junkyo Isa, who was treated humanely after falling into American hands, recalls that Japanese soldiers had told her earlier that "women who'd been captured in the central areas of the island were being raped by American soldiers and that these Americans were killing children by ripping them apart at the crotch. Of course these were just tall tales meant to scare us and convince us not to let ourselves be captured by the enemy. But I was still afraid to be caught."

During the capture of the Kerama Islands off the coast of Okinawa, dozens of Japanese civilians killed themselves rather than fall into American hands. The official history of Okinawa records a ghastly scene of when army troops came upon a small valley:

> In the morning they found a small valley littered with more than 150 dead and dying Japanese, most of them civilians. Fathers had systematically throttled each member of their families and then dis-emboweled themselves with knives and hand grenades. Under one blanket lay a father, two small children, a grandfather, and a grand-mother, all strangled by cloth ropes. Soldiers and medics did what they could. The natives, who had been told that the invading "bar-barians" would kill and rape, watched in amazement as the Ameri-cans provided food and medical care; an old man who had killed his daughter wept in bitter remorse.

No tallies exist of the actual numbers of civilian suicides on Okinawa proper during the three-month ordeal; but anecdotal accounts suggest that thousands may have taken their lives. Even so-called civilians remained a danger after capture; one veteran, Thomas Hannaher, remarked, "In the later stages of the campaign, I was assigned to guard a large compound of prison-ers. It was boring duty. The inmates were behind barbed wire. Most were civilians but it was hard to tell. One of them blew himself up with a hand grenade." Frank Gibney, an intelligence officer on Okinawa, who wrote a commentary on Colonel Yahara's postwar memoirs, concluded:

> As Yahara's narrative noted, several thousand perished in suicides or futile last-ditch attacks in a literal battle-to-the-death inside the navy base entrenchments on the Oroku Peninsula near Naha Port. Worst of all were the civilian deaths. Thousands of Okinawan civil-ians, and as many women and children as men, were ordered to stay in caves with Japanese troops who were preparing a last-ditch "de-fense." The flower of the island's youth—teenage girl nurses' aides as well as *boeitai* boy-soldiers—was sacrificed to the directives of the Japanese army command. In many cases they were forced to

hurl themselves from the low southern cliffs into the sea, so they, too, could "die for the Emperor."

Much is made of the unusually "large" number of Japanese prisoners taken on Okinawa—over 7,000 from some 110,000 combatants—as if the presence of any surrendering soldiers marked a radical break in past practice for the Japanese military. True, there were more prisoners on Okinawa than taken elsewhere in the Pacific—but then there also were far more Japanese soldiers to begin with than had been present on Saipan, Peleliu, or Iwo Jima. Still, a mere 7 percent of all Japanese soldiers gave themselves up—tens of thousands either dying or killing themselves in caves below. On June 18, Generals Cho and Ushijima both committed seppuku—ritual disembowelment—before being beheaded by trusty aides, a fate shared by an unknown number of fellow Japanese officers when approaching American Marines were known to be only a few hundred yards distant. Most enlisted men, however, had neither the appurtenances nor the attendants for such rituals and so often blew themselves up by simply putting a grenade to their bodies.

What was the effect on Americans of seeing the sheer variety of suicides among civilians and soldiers alike, which were aimed first at killing GIs and then, in defeat, ending their own lives? At first, confusion and perplexity spread. Up until Okinawa, the invading Americans had fought in two general scenarios—either on islands like Iwo Jima, where there were essentially *no* civilians, or in places such as the Philippines, where the local inhabitants were clearly friendly and welcomed liberation. After Okinawa, no one had any illusions about a third and more difficult situation to come on the mainland itself—where rumor had it that 30 million Japanese elderly, women, and children were arming themselves with guns, spears, and explosives to join in the resistance alongside both regular troops and militias.

In earlier situations there had been little ambiguity in the nature of friend and foe—there were either no locals at all, friendly civilians, or clearly hostile noncombatants. But Okinawa was different even from the less populous Saipan. Okinawans themselves had always been resentful of their treatment by the Japanese, enjoying both a distinct culture and spiritual and material separation from the mainland. The result was that while they were likely to fight alongside Japanese or at least openly aid and abet imperial sol-

diers, they were also eager to flee or become neutrals once the doomed nature of the Japanese resistance was made clear. The trick, then, for Marines
was to determine exactly the changing state of mind of each noncombatant
they discovered in caves and redoubts in the instant before they themselves
might be attacked. Junkyo Isa, an Okinawan native, relates how life and
death hung in the balance when she and her family were rooted out of their
hiding place:

> That evening three American soldiers brandishing weapons arrived
> and forced us out of our hiding place. *"Dete koi!"* (Get out of there!)
> they called out in Japanese. They pointed their guns right at us,
> straight toward our chests! I couldn't believe how big these guys
> were. All I remember thinking was, "Oh, my goodness, this is the
> enemy!" Can you imagine how I felt being lifted up by one of them
> and taken away in a truck? I couldn't speak or understand English,
> so I had to tell them with hand gestures that I couldn't walk. They
> nodded and prepared two bamboo baskets, one for carrying me, and
> the other for my baby brother.

Were those thousands of civilians trapped in caves determined suicide
bombers, stunned noncombatants, or the terrified defeated resolved to kill
themselves in solitude? And should Americans then prevent suicides, encourage them, or simply ignore those who wished to go off alone to kill themselves? Did this desire for death arise out of irrational fear—or trepidation
grounded in the fact that they had killed Americans? All such baffling questions were new to the American combatants, but had the general effect of at
least reminding them that they were up against an entirely novel enemy, of
a type unseen even in Hitler's Europe.

Much has been written about the grudging admiration that the American soldier held for the kamikazes and even the suicidal bravery of doomed
infantry units. But beneath that wonderment at such a determined foe there
remained a deep-seated disgust with suicidal tactics that were never seen as
rational, but rather insane—hence the renaming by Americans of the "exploding cherry blossoms" to "idiot bombs." As the battle dragged on, Ameri-

cans became hardened to the realities that thousands of the enemy wished to kill them more than to save their own lives. That grim knowledge alone resulted in a general feeling toward prisoners and at times noncombatants that could be summed up by something like "Why should we respect their lives, when they don't even respect their own?"

Because the effectiveness of American countermeasures—increased radar, picket destroyers, expanded fighter cover at sea, flamethrowers, dynamite, and night watches on land—neutralized most Japanese suicide attacks, rendering them serious and deadly annoyances rather than decisive tactical moves that might have lost the Americans the island, there arose a disdain and then implacable anger at the continuing assaults. Since the suicide bombers could not overturn the verdict of the battlefield, it became clear that they simply wanted to kill as many Americans as possible, not retake ground or sink capital ships.

The Americans also learned that the defeat of suicide bombers did not require new exotic weapons—albeit flamethrowers against those in caves were critical—as much as a renewed reliance on traditional Western discipline and firepower. So they turned to bombing distant kamikaze bases, coordinating well-trained antiaircraft batteries at sea, and sending out superior Hellcats with better pilots miles from the fleet to shoot down outclassed Zeros. On the island itself tough leathernecks using mortars, machine guns, and grenades learned how to blast apart recalcitrant pockets as the American counterassault was fueled by a steady reinforcement of soldiers, guns, ships, and planes at a rate far greater than they were lost.

So Okinawa proved to the American military that no matter what new weapon or specialized unit the Japanese threw at them—many of them quite out of Dante's *Inferno* in their ingenuity at inflicting terror—it could be defeated through greater firepower, numbers, and training. The only variable in the equation was the number of casualties that the Americans were willing to accept. Otherwise, the eventual result of the ensuing conflict was never in doubt. The Japanese wished for something far greater, far deadlier than Okinawa in the struggle to come on the mainland—suicidal attacks by boats, planes, submarines, torpedoes, rockets, and mass waves of charging infantry in the tens of thousands. The Americans were ready to oblige them—but first contemplated ways of repeating the holocaust of Okinawa, but ensuring that the next time it would be purely a Japanese rather than a shared American nightmare. And so it was.

The Military Lessons

In high school textbooks, Okinawa is now rarely mentioned. Hiroshima, the internment of Japanese in the western United States, the racial segregation of the American military during the war, and the rape of Nanking—all warrant more attention. Even the recent *Oxford Companion to Military History* has *no* entry for the battle—though articles appear on Guadalcanal, Iwo Jima, and an array of far lesser engagements in addition to entries as diverse as "homosexuality and the armed forces," "women in the military," and "African-American troops." Other than the concerns of a new military scholarship that seeks to address the past sins of homophobia, sexism, and racism by diverting emphasis away from tactics, strategy, and pitched battles, what accounts for this relative neglect of the most powerful amphibious assault in history and, indeed, *the single most deadly campaign in the history of the United States Navy?* For all its ghastliness, was Okinawa really of so little historical consequence? Was Winston Churchill alone cognizant of the battle's epic importance, remarking in its immediate aftermath that the skill of American fighting men and the determination and ferocity of the Japanese placed "this battle among the most intense and famous in military history"?

The inattention to the battle perhaps goes back to 1945 itself, when American soldiers complained that few back home knew about their ongoing sacrifice. April and May marked the last days of the Third Reich as most in the United States turned their thoughts to triumphant armies of liberation who raced through a collapsing Germany, capturing thousands of prisoners, grabbing huge chunks of territory, and suffering few casualties in their lightning advances. Okinawa in contrast represented another bloody mess like Guadalcanal and Iwo Jima, where there would be lots of horrors but little maneuver, fluidity, or opportunity for swashbuckling Pattonesque armor.

Because there was no chance of escape for the Japanese from the island, since their fleet and air force were essentially destroyed, the ultimate outcome was foreordained. That reality meant for Americans back home that the battle was not a question of if, but when and at what cost Okinawa would fall. Despite the lethality of the kamikazes and the murderous record of the Japanese 32nd Army, few really believed the massive American fleet would be either sunk or forced to withdraw, leaving the Americans unsupplied and at the mercy of the entrenched enemy. Perhaps there is something both anticlimatic and macabre in knowing that the suspense of battle lies only in the butcher's bill to come, not in its ultimate verdict.

What Americans did learn led only to greater denial and then later apathy. Both the horrific nature of the fighting and the mud and stench of the battlefield environment made grim reading back home. The tragic death of General Buckner just days before the island was declared secure also cast a pall over postbellum commemoration and analysis. Had he lived, there may well have been careful and critical scrutiny of his generalship as planners preparing for the mainland invasions were already questioning the wisdom of Marine and army head-on assaults against a doomed enemy. Such censure of American tactics still today leads to larger and unanswered strategic questions: could Okinawa have been cut off and bypassed altogether, allowing an unsupplied 110,000 Japanese soldiers to die on the vine while Americans looked for other forward bases in Formosa to launch their planned assaults on the mainland? The answer surely is yes—had the Americans wished to prolong the war for a year or two while trading time for lives.

Furthermore, the denouement of the Pacific war cast a further shadow over the importance of Okinawa. Most critics later looked at the battle from the hindsight of Hiroshima, not realizing that in April 1945 it was not at all clear that the Americans would—or should—use some new weapon to prevent a costly invasion of the mainland. Instead, after Hiroshima and Nagasaki, far from regretting the decision, it was more likely that citizens asked in retrospect whether Okinawa had been necessary at all. If atomic weapons had precluded a holocaust in Japan, surely a few months earlier planners could have held off from Okinawa until such super bombs were brought to the front? All in all, Okinawa's great cost, its brutality, and lingering questions about its very necessity weeks before the surrender made it a battle Americans would prefer to forget—and largely ignore to this day. Again, something clearly went quite wrong at Okinawa.

Yet, for all the formal neglect by the media and historians alike, what happened on Okinawa may have changed Americans more than any other battle in their history. The most obvious ripple is, of course, the decision to use the atomic bomb at Hiroshima and Nagasaki. Skeptics have argued for a half century over the pretext for the nuclear attack—given the successful fire raids that had already leveled the major Japanese cities. Many claim that the decision to drop was really based on everything from a purported desire to signal to the Russians both American power and its will to use it, to a grisly desire to try out such an expensive weapon on a live target—or simple racist hatred against the Japanese people. But ultimately the reasons for Hiroshima were surely strategic, and again are inexplicable without remembrance of Okinawa.

The Americans had seen from April 1 to July 2 the damage that a cornered Japanese military—shorn of its navy, air force, and intermingled with civilians—could inflict on Americans. They clearly wanted no more Okinawas. Had the Americans *not* invaded Okinawa, it is more, not less, likely that they would have landed on the Japanese mainland in late summer and thereby suffered far greater casualties.

Veteran of the nightmare of Okinawa and fated to invade Japan with what was left of his Marine division, E. B. Sledge sat in his base camp on the island dumbfounded at the news of Hiroshima and the subsequent surrender. "We received the news with quiet disbelief coupled with an indescribable sense of relief. We thought the Japanese would never surrender. Many refused to believe it. Sitting in stunned silence, we remembered our dead. So many dead. So many maimed. So many bright futures consigned to the ashes of the past."

More precisely, at the beginning of July there were roughly 6,150 combat-ready Japanese planes, with nearly 8,000 pilots trained enough to fly them into targets; those were official postbellum accounts, and the actual number available in August 1945 may well have been far more. The Japanese army bragged that it had available 2,350,000 regular troops, but predicted in its death throes that it could impress up to 30 million to form an enormous citizen militia. The plan of homeland defense *(ketsu-go)* was predicated on the idea that every Japanese civilian and soldier alike would kill as many Americans as possible—resulting in either a fitting genocide for a still unconquered and unoccupied people or such mayhem for the enemy that the Americans, not the Japanese, would seek negotiations.

So the holocaust on Okinawa led to the dropping of the bombs, which led to a surrender rather than a greater carnage for both sides. We should remember that not only were millions poised to battle each other in the streets and countryside of Japan, but the always deadly inventive Gen. Curtis LeMay was ready on his own to use airpower in radically new ways to avoid American casualties. In response to the horrific losses on Okinawa, he was carefully assembling a monstrous fleet of B-29s—perhaps eventually 5,000 in number—to be augmented by over 5,000 B-24s and B-17s transferred from the European theater, with the possibility that over a thousand British Lancaster bombers and their seasoned crews would join the armada as well! That rain of napalm to come from a nightmarish fleet of 10,000 or more bombers on short missions from Okinawa would have made both atomic bombs seem child's play in comparison. The fire raids on March 11, 1945, alone killed more than died at Hiroshima, and were followed by far more destruction—perhaps 500,000 incinerated in all by the subsequent bombing—than occurred at Nagasaki.

LeMay had every intention of carpet-bombing the Japanese countryside in order to reduce the number of American ground-troop casualties on the mainland. So to avoid something one hundred times worse than Okinawa on the mainland, and in the name of saving both Japanese and American casualties on the battlefield, LeMay might well have been willing to inflict something ten times more deadly than Hiroshima and Nagasaki. And the disturbing fact is that LeMay still might have saved more lives than would have been lost on both sides from a land invasion of the homeland.

In addition, hundreds of thousands of Chinese and Japanese were dying in conventional land battles in the last months of the war, a slaughter that was showing no signs of cessation at the time of Okinawa. In that regard the two A-bombs that broke the control of the militarists also saved thousands in China. In only a week of fighting in early August, the Soviets killed some 80,000 Japanese and captured over 500,000—many never to return alive from labor camps. In turn, 8,000 Russians were lost and another 20,000 wounded. Had the war continued for another year, the bloodiest theater of the entire war might well have been Manchuria, where altogether 1,600,000 invading Russian soldiers confronted over a million Japanese defenders. Both sides were battle-hardened veterans and prepared to give no quarter.

Only the ghastly consequences of atomic weapons gave ammunition to the Japanese critics of the imperial government—who could now point to the dramatic annihilation of their own civilians brought on by futile efforts to continue the war to oblivion. So the horrific sacrifices of Okinawa precluded far greater slaughter to come in China and Japan in the fighting envisioned for late 1945 and 1946—not to mention the fate of some 350,000 Allied prisoners who may well have been executed by the Japanese on news that their homeland had been stormed.

If Okinawa had led Americans to concede that something more dreadful than conventional arms would be necessary to avoid a greater bloodbath on the mainland, the sacrifices in vain by kamikazes were having a similar effect on Japanese back home. The abrupt end of the war led to a public backlash against the militarists and especially the architects of suicide—even earlier a few Japanese had begun to question the use of such extreme tactics that failed to halt the Americans on Okinawa. Ensign Teruo Yamaguchi, a naval kamikaze, wrote his parents that "it leaves a bad taste in my mouth when I think of the deceits being played on innocent civilians by some of our wily politicians. But I am willing to take orders from the high command, and even from the politicians, because I believe in the polity of Japan." Literally millions of Japanese civilians and soldiers were willing to die to defend their mainland from an American invasion, both as conventional and suicide attackers, and with full knowledge by 1945 that their militarist government was fraudulent and dishonest.

No discussion of Hiroshima, then, is intellectually legitimate without careful consideration of the events that transpired on Okinawa. In this regard, George Feifer's incisive analysis of the relationship between Hiroshima and Okinawa must remain the last word:

> Okinawa's caves, killing grounds, and anguish ought to be remembered. It ought to be suggested, at least for the sake of the ambivalent human record, that the first atomic bombs probably prevented the homicidal equivalent of over two hundred more of

the same: the twenty million Japanese deaths if invasion had been necessary, in addition to all the other deaths, Western and Asian.

It is difficult to comprehend such figures and to remember the strains of 1945. Focusing on the bomb is easier. But if a symbol is needed to help preserve the memory of the Pacific War, Okinawa is the more fitting one.

The American military and public also came away from Okinawa with a number of perceptions about land warfare in Asia, some of them accurate, some racist, a few entirely erroneous—but all fundamental in forming the American way of war in Korea and Vietnam in the next thirty years. After the startling array of suicides on Okinawa, Americans were convinced that Asians in general did not value life—theirs or anyone else's—in the same manner as Westerners, and when faced with overwhelming military power and sure defeat would nevertheless continue to fight hard in their efforts to kill Americans. Because territory was not really as important on Okinawa as body counts—the fight would end not with the capture per se of strategic ground but rather only with the complete annihilation of the enemy who was trapped on the island—Americans developed a particular mentality that would come to haunt them in both the Korean peninsula and Southeast Asia.

The Japanese quit on Okinawa when they were killed off, not when the fall of a particular ridge or line of defenses forecast eventual tactical defeat. Indeed, even when the Americans reached the southernmost tip of the island and routed the Japanese, they were ordered to spread back out over previously "conquered" territory to root out snipers and pockets of resistance—killing 8,975 more Japanese soldiers in the purported "mop-up." Former lieutenants and captains of the Pacific war, when later promoted to American generals in Korea and Vietnam, assumed again that real estate was not as important as simply killing as many fanatical Asian troops as possible—through bombing, shelling, and frontal assaults. War ended when the enemy was exterminated or faced with certain annihilation. It did not necessarily stop when the Japanese were encircled, outmaneuvered, or shorn of supplies. The caves and night assaults of Okinawa prefigured the tunnels and ambushes of Vietnam—in each case nullifying massive American bombing and artillery barrages. Every Japanese dead or captured, not the fall of the Shuri line, meant a quicker end to the war—just as "body counts" in Vietnam, not the capture of Hanoi, were seen as the key to ending that conflict.

Because Okinawa was the major engagement in the Pacific where civilians sometimes fought on the side of the enemy, Americans experienced the dilemma of determining which woman, child, or old man was harmless, friendly, or a killer. And because Okinawa was out of view, little reported on, and fought against a supposedly repugnant and fascist enemy, Americans left the island with the assurance that when stranded in such a hell, they should blast indiscriminately any civilian in their proximity on suspicion of aiding the enemy—also with disastrous consequences to come in the suddenly televised fighting of the 1960s and 1970s when victory hinged not on enemy body counts alone, but also in winning the hearts and minds of supposedly noncombatant civilian populations in an arena broadcast live around the world. Japanese veterans of the rape of Nanking might murder thousands of Okinawan civilians—40,000 adult males alone were shanghaied into the imperial army. But in such a messy battle, jaded American GIs—as purportedly more liberal Westerners—who either mistakenly or by intent shot a few hundred would incur far greater moral condemnation both at home and abroad.

Similarly, commanding officers came away from Okinawa believing that the American public could stomach the loss of fifty thousand casualties in an Asian theater—failing to grasp that Okinawa was not a typical, but an aberrant, event of the highest order. The end of the war in Europe, the death of President Roosevelt, the news that a Japanese collapse was imminent, all that and more took attention away from the bloodletting on Okinawa itself. Only after the battle was over and the war concluded did it sink into Americans that thousands of their best were slaughtered a few weeks before the armistice by an enemy that was surrounded and cut off.

Yet wrongly interpreting such temporary public acquiescence as solid support for their strategy of annihilation, the military thought that if Americans could kill far more than they lost, defeat the enemy militarily, and gain the stated objective, then the public back home would support its sacrifice of the nation's youth in any similar future Pacific engagement. In fact, had the battle taken place earlier and during a lull in the European theater, outrage over the costs of Okinawa—far greater than either Peleliu or Tarawa, whose tolls of dead stunned Americans—may have been seen as a national scandal and marked the last battle in which Americans would be sent to fight hand-to-hand in Asia against an enemy whose only hope of victory lay in killing GIs in any manner possible.

The American military wanted Okinawa as a closer home for the B-29s and numerous tactical fighters wings, in addition to a deepwater port. But the generals also realized that even had they skipped it, ignoring its value as an air and naval base, 100,000 Japanese would never have surrendered unless they were nearly obliterated—or learned that enough Japanese elsewhere in the empire were annihilated to cause their emperor to concede. So again, corpses, not mere acres, became the rationale of the campaign.

In that same way of thinking, later in both Korea and Vietnam, the occupation of territory—whether the capture and control of Pyongyang or Hanoi—became less the focus of victory than simply killing the enemy. Unfortunately the analogies did not hold. Korea and Vietnam were not islands of conventional troops cut off from supply, but rather proxy wars, in which neighboring communist and nuclear powers had instigated civil strife with every intention of daily resupplying their nearby surrogate insurrectionists.

But not all errors in thinking were to be on the American side. Okinawa also sent to the world other military ripples, mixed signals about the use of suicide attacks that would prove grievous to any who learned the wrong lessons from the battle. The Japanese proved that a militarily inferior and outnumbered force—should it commit thousands of its combatants to suicide tactics—could inflict enormous damage on its more powerful foe. Technological superiority purportedly could be nullified by less sophisticated weapons that made no allowance for the safety or survival of the attacker. Fanatical personal bravery and suicidal group devotion to a cause were supposed to trump massive firepower and the skilled men who enjoyed such calculated material superiority. And since Western military ingenuity presupposed the sanctity of the combatant, a great deal of resources went into defenses, communications, and search-and-rescue missions to preserve the assailant rather than merely kill the enemy. Whether al-Qaeda terrorists, Palestinian suicide bombers, or Iraqi paramilitaries, some overmatched fighters have surmised from the savagery of battles like Okinawa that Western military forces—such as the sophisticated American Air Force of 2001 or the homeland forces of Israel—could be circumvented by even poorly trained pilots and teenagers with bombs strapped to their bodies. Or so they thought.

But careful analysis of Okinawa offers a quite different and far more chilling lesson. For all the bravado of the Japanese bombers, they *failed* utterly to stop the Americans—indeed, failed to sink a single major capital ship. True, some large carriers like the *Franklin* were nearly destroyed—over seven hundred dead—and forced to sail home. The loss of their planes in the Okinawa campaign was, of course, important. But even such spectacular short-term successes were tempered by two stark realizations. The *Franklin* steamed away under its own power unassisted and could be repaired and refitted. More important, unlike 1942 when even the temporary loss of a fleet carrier spelled near disaster, the United States now had over sixteen fleet carriers in the Pacific, with more planned. If the kamikazes were to have any long-term effect in curtailing American tactical airpower against Okinawa or the mainland, then they had to sink, *not* damage, flattops and destroy ten or fifteen, *not* damage two or three.

Five thousand dead sailors is a horrendous figure, but for the Japanese it had to be seen in the context of an enemy that had a million-man navy and sixteen fleet carriers intact after the greatest suicide attack in history. Marine divisions were shattered on Okinawa; yet more Marines were ready to invade Japan after the battle than before. As both a weapon of terror and a conventional means to destroy enemy assets, the Japanese suicide attackers had no long-term strategic success.

Why is this so? Human nature explains much, for the pool of those who wish to kill themselves in service to a lost cause is finite, despite professed fanaticism. There really was only a limited supply of a few thousand kamikaze pilots among millions of Japanese, as large-scale attacks ceased altogether by July. Even by the end of the Okinawa campaign, pilots were being assigned and were no longer exclusively volunteers. Rumors spread that science students were given preferential treatment and were being saved for research duties, while others in liberal, social, and legal studies were drafted for the suicide schools. Some pilots ditched or turned back. Others were intoxicated to the point of stupor. Hatsuho Naito, who wrote a history of the *Okha* squadrons, concluded: "The young men who were actually called on to make mass suicide attacks had nothing to do with the organized insanity. They experienced terrors and trauma that are beyond the imagination of anyone else. I do not believe that any of them shouted, 'Long Live the Emperor' as they dived their bomb-filled planes into the enemy."

There was no disguising the fact that the vast majority of the pilots, like contemporary suicide bombers in Palestine, were between 18 and 24, of lower rank, and ordered on their missions by older and more senior officers. Resentment of the inequity in determining suicide duty, and wonder whether other Japanese were willing to make similar sacrifices, were widespread even among the most fervent kamikaze pilots. After writing in his diary, "What is the duty today? It is to fight. What is the duty tomorrow? It is to win. What is the daily duty? It is to die. We die in battle without complaint," twenty-two-year-old ensign Heiichi Okabe nevertheless added, "I wonder if others, like scientists, who pursue the war effort on their own fronts, would die as we do without complaint. Only then will the unity of Japan be such that she can have any prospect of winning the war."

Heiichi Okabe's officers rarely, if at all, led the suicide attacks in person—and oftentimes survived the war. Again, in the case of the special *Okha* squadrons, tension mounted between petty and reserve officers to such a degree that fistfights broke out on occasion. Even some of the pilots of the mother planes who launched the suicide rockets protested. Not uncommon were the remarks of one bomber pilot, Goro Nonaka: "Do you really think we can do such a thing? Our men, the ones we have been living with, are being escorted to their deaths in the bloodiest and most cold-hearted way possible. Do you think we can leave them and return again and again?" Thus it was no surprise that the organizer of the *Okha* rocket squadrons, Shoichi Ota, went into hiding after the surrender and purportedly lived under an assumed name for years after the war ended.

We shall never know what would have transpired had the United States invaded Japanese home soil, but for some five weeks after Okinawa the American fleet was still in range of land-based enemy planes and thousands of aircraft still remained on the homeland—and yet kamikaze attacks were more or less nonexistent. After Okinawa was declared secure on July 2, only five more suicide attacks were reported before the surrender. Were the

Japanese simply out of willing pilots, saving their reserve kamikazes for the final assault, or perplexed that there were no volunteers to strike the massive American fleet until and unless it landed invading troops on the mainland?

There was a similar chain of events after the terrible autumn of 2001. The West was told that thousands of Islamic fundamentalists were ready to bomb America, Europe, and Israel. In truth, there were only a few hundred from an angry society of hundreds of millions willing to blow themselves up to kill Americans. Romantics may have remembered the kamikazes; realists recalled how they were dealt with. Quite simply, there has never arisen a military culture quite like the West, in its terrifying ability to draw on innate values such as secular rationalism, free inquiry, and consensual government to create frightening weapons of destruction and the protocols and disciplined soldiers to use them to deadly effect—a firepower and material onslaught that can overwhelm the most fanatical and deadly of warriors, whether they be Apaches, kamikazes, or al-Qaeda terrorists.

Much of the collapse of the kamikazes, then, had to do with the American counterresponse. The terror of suicide brought out the greater terror of the Western way of war. Americans not merely devised immediate countermeasures to the kamikazes and suicide banzai charges—everything from picket destroyers to flame-shooting tanks—but also left the island with a changed mentality about the nature of war itself: from now on fanaticism of the human will would be repaid in kind with the fanaticism of industrial and technological power. Okinawa taught the world that the chief horror of war is not the random use of suicide bombers, but the response that they incur from Western powers whose self-imposed restraint upon their ingenuity for killing usually rests only with their own sense of moral reluctance—a brake that suicidal attack seems to strip away entirely.

The official military history of Okinawa quite succinctly summed up the typical confident American attitude to the nightmare of a campaign gone terribly wrong: "The high cost of the victory was due to the fact that the battle had been fought against a capably led Japanese army of greater strength than anticipated, over difficult terrain heavily and expertly fortified, and thousands of miles from home. The campaign had lasted considerably longer than was expected. But Americans had demonstrated again on Okinawa that they could, ultimately, wrest from the Japanese whatever ground they wanted."

The terrorists of September 11 should have learned that lesson of "whatever ground they wanted" from Okinawa. At least in the matter of dealing with suicide bombers and banzai attacks, Japan's enemies surely did have the last word. It was not surprising, but entirely predictable that a nation that sixty years ago produced napalm, flamethrowers—and eventually A-bombs— to combat thousands of suicidal warriors would retain the organization and willpower to incinerate a few hundred suicide bombers and their enclaves of support.

Epilogue: The Men of Okinawa

The consequences of any one battle are far more than the mere political or cultural fallout. As many as a quarter million people died on Okinawa. Yet we have no idea of the aggregate effect of that sudden destruction of energy and young talent on either Japan or America—or the human race. Nor can we appreciate the consequences that those sudden deaths had on a million more of their close family members and friends.

So military history is brutal for reasons other than what it tells us about the grim nature of the fighting. It is callous also in what it does not touch on—the hundreds of thousands of battle dead who are never recalled or commemorated as individuals, whose stories and counterfactual suppositions are never indulged in other than by a few family members themselves without access to publication or wider enlightenment. In that regard, we learn little about what was or what might have been of the Okinawa dead.

By April 1945, Ernie Pyle was not merely America's best-known war correspondent, but the country's most widely read columnist as well. Well before the beginning of the war, as a roving reporter between 1935 and 1941, Pyle had developed a readership of millions through syndicated daily columns that chronicled the average lives of Americans coping with the Great Depression. When the war broke out, he was a natural choice to assume a role as America's premier war correspondent, and his subsequent ground-level dispatches from Europe served as the country's most direct link with the men in the field.

Ernie Pyle, America's journalistic icon, was killed in a so-called safe zone behind the lines on the small island of Ie Shima off Okinawa on April 18, 1945. Reporting on the fighting of the 77th Infantry Division, Pyle was traveling in a Jeep that was forced off the road by machine gun fire from a pocket of Japanese holdouts hidden in the coral slopes. Pyle and a regimental commander scurried to safety in a nearby ditch; but after a few moments the correspondent mistakenly thought the danger was past, raised his head, and received a burst in the temple a few inches below the rim of his helmet.

Enemy machine gunners were not supposed to be behind American lines shooting at traffic. Soldiers usually did not stick their heads out of holes unless they were sure that the coast was clear; and the head itself is a small target, the vulnerable temple and face below the steel helmet smaller still. Yet Pyle died from a head wound from a single Japanese gunner in a secured area, and was buried with the inscription "At this spot the 77th Infantry Division lost a buddy, Ernie Pyle, 18 April 1945." While Pyle's death did not suddenly galvanize attention to the horrific nature of the mostly ignored fighting on Okinawa, his loss nevertheless stunned the nation.

Yet it is rarely noted that Pyle's sudden death in combat in some sense ensured that his own work and populist reputation would achieve a timelessness that his survival might well have otherwise nullified. After years of war in Europe, Pyle himself admitted that he could hardly face combat again. He reported on the eve of the invasion that he simply could not talk, in terrible mute anticipation of mangled bodies and carnage on the invasion beaches. Even after the relief of the deceptively easy American landing— "What a wonderful feeling"—for most of the early part of the Okinawa campaign he stayed to the rear or at sea. Pyle was coping with an increasing drinking problem, his marriage nearly over, with a wife on the verge of suicide. Unfair criticism was arising that he had lost his edge while younger, more reckless reporters were sending back more realistic combat dispatches.

It is a capricious and terrible thing to speculate that a good and decent man's sudden and unearned death has often enhanced his reputation in a way that his continued career might not have. Surely the Lincoln we now venerate is at least in part the man who was saved from the mess of Reconstruction that ruined the administrations of Johnson and Grant. Furies were chasing John Fitzgerald Kennedy when he fell on November 22, 1963—a tough reelection, a dismal record of legislative accomplishment, a reckless personal life whose embarrassing disclosures rested only on the sobriety and ephemeral goodwill of a growing and restless circle of reporters. Pyle, who became famous by sending back dispatches from the frontline fighting in Europe, was forever immortalized on Okinawa as dying pencil in hand during the heat of combat—not embittered and worn out after witnessing too many deaths and so at last content in the last weeks of his life mostly to report on it all from the rear.

In some sense, like Pyle's death, the sudden and equally capricious—indeed, flukelike—death of the fifty-eight-year-old Gen. Simon Bolivar Buckner saved the commanding officer from embarrassing questions and perhaps a military inquiry itself. On June 18, as the battle wound down, Buckner was visiting the Mezado Ridge to see a final advance by the 8th Marine Regiment. After he had observed the assault for about an hour, a sudden Japanese artillery salvo—from a single surviving gun of a decimated battery—zeroed in on the high-ranking Americans. A shell hit a nearby boulder and the flying shards struck Buckner in the chest. The general bled to death in minutes. None of the surrounding officers suffered a scratch.

Thus just days before the fighting was over and the Generals Ushijima and Cho committed suicide, Buckner fell on the front lines—the highest-ranking American officer to be killed by enemy fire in the entire Pacific war. With his tragic death, in an instant the old lingering questions about Buckner's generalship on Okinawa likewise disappeared. Why did the veteran 1st and recently formed 6th Marine Divisions remain nearly idle for weeks in the north while Buckner's beloved army divisions were being annihilated at the Naha-Shuri line? Why did Buckner refuse Maj. Gen. Andrew Bruce's suggestion to land the 77th Division to the rear of Ushijima at Minatoa Beach—or similar and even more imaginative requests by scores of veteran Marine officers concerned at the carnage growing out of Buckner's head-on assaults? Why were not Maj. Gen. Lemuel Shepherd and Gen. Alexander Vandegrift listened to when they proposed taking their Marine divisions around rather than through the Japanese positions? Why instead did Buckner feed piecemeal into the inferno a stream of manpower, in unimaginative corkscrew-

and-blowtorch tactics that simply allowed the Japanese to retreat from one fortified ridge to another? After mid-May, when the Japanese were cut off, could not the Americans have established fortified lines of encirclement, pounded Ushijima's positions through bombing and artillery, and thus forgone the final hand-to-hand fighting necessary to kill every enemy soldier?

Later General MacArthur himself would argue just that—and complain that Buckner's tactics had sacrificed "thousands of American soldiers" in a needless desire to drive all the Japanese off the island when they could have been bypassed. Well before Buckner's death, a host of newspaper reporters, fed by angry Marine and navy officers, were openly criticizing his unimaginative tactics that were tailor-made to the Japanese plan of defense, freely employing pejoratives like "ultraconservative," "fiasco," and "a worse example of military incompetence than Pearl Harbor."

But there was to be no postbellum inquiry that would have besmirched the reputation of a good soldier and a beloved general. His worst critics sighed that he had paid the ultimate price for a battle plan that probably unnecessarily sacrificed the lives of thousands of others. His supporters pointed out that no more could be asked of a general than to die at the front with his men after achieving an undeniably critical military victory. Buckner's tragic and nonsensical death then ended criticism of his costly generalship, and thereby helps explain why there has been no comprehensive reexamination of his tactics on Okinawa to this day—a battle that led to twenty times as many casualties as Pearl Harbor when America was not weak and surprised, but enormously powerful and nearing complete victory.

But the survival, not the death, of Allied soldiers on Okinawa also affected the lives of thousands of Americans who decades later would first read about the battle and gain some idea of what the fighting had been like—and what it had been for. There are two landmark memoirs of the American combat experience in World War II. Both not surprisingly focus on the savagery of the Pacific theater and culminate with the dreadfulness of Okinawa. If the tactics and strategic importance of the battle were forgotten after the war, the awfulness and the horror-induced courage displayed there could not be—and so would resurface later to teach thousands of readers what war and Americans at war were about. William Manchester's *Goodbye, Darkness* and E. B. Sledge's *With the Old Breed* are not merely graphic narratives of combat, but works of literature in their own right comparable to Xenophon's *Anabasis*, Siegfried Sassoon's *Memoirs of an Infantry Officer*, and Robert Graves's *Goodbye to All That*.

Unlike most battle narratives of the twentieth century, both *Goodbye, Darkness* and *With the Old Breed* achieve transcendence in connecting the absurdity of Okinawa with the not so absurd idea of fighting for something quite antithetical to and far better than Japanese militarism. More than just graphic, often sickening accounts of the stupidities and senselessness of war—although they are all that and more—both books convey a rare sense that men really do fight for more than just their colleagues on the battlefield. So, for example, E. B. Sledge ends his account of Okinawa with news of Hiroshima and the war's end. After acknowledging that "War is brutish, inglorious, and a terrible waste," and that "Combat leaves an indelible mark on those who are forced to endure it," he nevertheless ends with, "Until the millennium arrives and countries cease trying to enslave others, it will be necessary to accept one's responsibilities and to be willing to make sacrifices for one's country—as my comrades did." Note his key phrase, *"and countries cease trying to enslave others."*

William Manchester attempted to explain to a subsequent generation the near-mythical world for which his fellow Marines had once fought so ferociously: "Debt was ignoble. Courage was a virtue. Mothers were beloved. Marriage was a sacrament. Divorce was disgraceful. . . . All these and 'God Bless America' and Christmas or Hanukkah and the certitude that victory in the war would assure their continuance into perpetuity—all this led you into battle, and sustained you as you fought, and comforted you if you fell, and, if it came to that, justified your death to all who loved you as you had loved them."

After finishing with a description of the horrors of Okinawa, Manchester then concluded of such lost values of a lost age, "Later the rules would change. But we didn't know that then. We didn't *know*." Somehow the stark paradoxes of Okinawa, the easy beach landings and horrific inland fighting, the suicides on land and kamikazes at sea, the civilian and quasicivilian casualties, the connection of Okinawa to Hiroshima, and the lingering questions over whether the worst battle of the Pacific was really necessary, all that brought out something in both men years later—*Goodbye, Darkness* was published in 1979, *With the Old Breed* reprinted in 1981—that otherwise might have stayed silent. Both books suggest that those few weeks on the island changed their authors in ways hundreds of thousands of events in their later lives decades later did not. And perhaps one reason why America acted so forcefully against the suicide bombers of September 11 was that, consciously or not, their fathers and grandfathers had seen it all—and dealt with it—long before on Okinawa.

Goodbye, Darkness and *With the Old Breed*, of course, along with the death of the famous, are only the more public manifestations of thousands of private sagas that have circulated both here and in Japan since emanating from the killing fields of Okinawa. They are only the tiny visible tip of the far larger proverbial iceberg below, whose foreboding presence has been just below the surface in the collective minds of tens of thousands ever since. How a rural, farming Swedish family found itself linked with the madcap last plans of Mitsuru Ushijima and Isamu Cho a world away I am not quite sure yet. But it happened, and for dozens of us it has made all the difference ever since.

CHAPTER 2

Shiloh's Ghosts,
April 6–7, 1862

Morning: The Birth of Uncle Billy

Shiloh changed the life of William Tecumseh Sherman, even as he would thereafter go on to alter the course of the Civil War—and do so in a manner that still affects Americans to this day. That miraculous chain of events all started on the morning of April 6, 1862.

The surprise Southern charge at Shiloh began shortly before 7 A.M. The Confederates broke first against William Tecumseh Sherman's 5th Division of the Army of the Ohio posted on the extreme Union right wing, farthest away from Grant's base camp at Pittsburg Landing on the Tennessee River. Sherman had little idea that the initial waves of attackers marked the onslaught of the greatest Confederate attack of the year-old Civil War. In fact, the day before, Sherman had assured an equally complacent Grant's staff in written dispatches that the chances of an enemy offensive against the Union positions were virtually nil.

Neither Sherman nor any other officer in the Federal Army realized that Albert Sidney Johnston's army of over forty thousand Southerners had camped undiscovered a mere two miles from their lines. Now in the early Sunday morning of April 6, 1862, it was planning to smash the division, then

The Southern States

ILLINOIS

Mississippi River

Ohio River

Louisville

KENTUCKY

Paducah

Bowling Green

Cumberland River

MISSOURI

Columbus

Fort Donelson

Fort Henry

Nashville

Tennessee River

Murfreesboro

ARKANSAS

Pittsburg Landing

Columbia

TENNESSEE

SHILOH

Savannah

Mississippi River

Memphis

Chattanooga

Corinth

Bridgeport

MISSISSIPPI

Tuscumbia

Decatur

0 Miles   100

GEORGIA

0 Kilometers   200

ALABAMA

© 2003 Jeffrey L. Ward

across the battlefield turn the Union left flank and drive the smaller Northern army into the Tennessee River. "Take your damned regiment back to
Ohio. There is no enemy nearer than Corinth," Sherman barked out to one
of his colonels when he was correctly warned that a large Confederate force
was nearing his lines.

Suddenly the advance guard of two regiments of Gen. Patrick Cleburne's Mississippians and Tennesseans—nearly a thousand men—came
out of the thicket. They quickly overran the front line of the Ohioans—most
were hurriedly finishing breakfast or just waking up—and headed directly for
Sherman himself. They began firing volleys at fifty yards. "Sherman will be
shot!" screamed Adjutant Dawes of the 53rd Ohio Regiment as he saw his
general about to be overwhelmed.

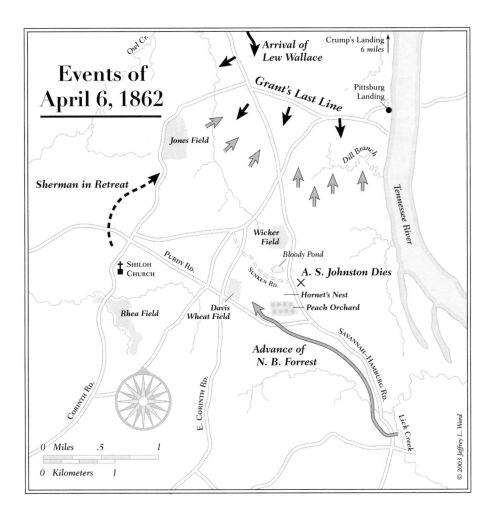

Events of April 6, 1862

Owl Cr.

Arrival of Lew Wallace

Crump's Landing
6 miles

Grant's Last Line

Pittsburg
Landing

Jones Field

Dill Branch

Sherman in Retreat

Tennessee River

Wicker
Field

Bloody Pond

✝ SHILOH
■ CHURCH

PURDY RD.

SUNKEN RD.

A. S. Johnston Dies
✕

Hornet's Nest

Rhea Field

Davis
Wheat Field

Peach Orchard

**Advance of
N. B. Forrest**

SAVANNAH—HAMBURG RD.

CORINTH RD.

E. CORINTH RD.

Lick Creek

0   Miles   .5   1

0   Kilometers   1

© 2003 Jeffrey L. Ward

"My God, we are attacked," Sherman yelled. The first volley cut down several around him. A few feet away at his side a Private Holliday was killed instantly, among the first officially recorded Union casualties at Shiloh. "The shot that killed him was meant for me," he wrote a week later of his miraculous escape. As a mounted Sherman raised his hand in defense, a pellet from a .69-caliber round—each such cartridge contained a single ball and three smaller buckshot—struck his hand and passed through. In seconds a stunned Sherman recovered enough to ride through another hail of bullets back to his nearby headquarters at Shiloh Church, trying to mold some type of defensive perimeter before his surprised regiments—none before the battle had ever fired a shot in anger—were completely overwhelmed.

Just before the 53rd Ohio Regiment collapsed, its final volleys, aided by canister shot from Union batteries, for a time slowed the Confederate juggernaut. The surprised Northerners regrouped to inflict 70 percent casualties among the attackers as the Southerners lumbered uphill over the final five hundred yards of open ground. Although Cleburne's Confederates had surprised Sherman's regiments, by 8:30 A.M. the first line of Confederate attackers had wilted under the increasing fire of the retiring Union division, bending but not yet breaking the Union ranks.

In support of Cleburne's initial assault, Braxton Bragg, with nearly ten thousand men, now brought a massive second line of infantry against Sherman's reeling amateurs. Fortunately for the Union regiments, Bragg's efforts were anything but orderly. Confusion, misplaced orders, and the wait for tardy artillery support had all combined to delay and then interrupt Bragg's planned early morning charge. But by 8:30 the huge Confederate mass was finally bringing its weight to bear against the last two surviving regiments of Sherman's original defensive line. Sherman finally admitted that he was "satisfied for the first time that the enemy designed a determined attack on our whole camp." Yet he still did not yet appreciate his danger: not just his own seven thousand men, but the entire Union Army—from his own right wing all the way to the Tennessee River—were in danger of being crushed in minutes by simultaneous Confederate charges. For one of the few times in the entire war, there were soon to be more Southerners on a single battlefield than Union troops. Sherman was both completely calm and yet—despite later denials—utterly surprised.

As Sherman's division slowly crumbled under the Southern weight, his aide-de-camp, John Taylor, remarked that its general was "smoking a cigar, cool and unperturbed." His complete mastery of fear "soon instilled a feeling that it was grand to be there with him." Even so, by 9:30 A.M. the Union lines were falling back thousands of yards to their support camp at Shiloh Church. Many of their precious batteries were already overwhelmed and captured. And some of the Ohioans had no intention of stopping there to form a new line of defense. Instead, an increasing number headed for the last refuge of the Union base at Pittsburg Landing on the Tennessee River, about a mile farther to the east. By late afternoon some 10,000 to 15,000 Northerners—well over a third of the army—were either missing or congregating beneath the cliffs, trembling in panic. Sherman rode among these collapsing companies, striving to halt the fleeing small groups of terrified soldiers as bullets whizzed in from both sides.

Regiments to his immediate left—belonging to John McClernand's 1st Division—now came up to the front to plug gaps arising between Sherman and Benjamin Prentiss's 6th Division before the second Confederate wave broke the Union line entirely. Then John Taylor saw Sherman go down as his wounded horse stumbled and fell dead. The stunned general himself somehow jumped clear from the horse, leaving his saddle and holster beneath the carcass. He raced over to Taylor, grabbed his aide's mount, and returned to the fray. "Well, my boy, didn't I promise you all the fighting you could do?" Sherman screamed as he rode off. He was in his element.

His efforts to make a stand at Shiloh Church and preserve the divisional headquarters were now doomed, as it became clear that even further retreat was necessary. Both his immediate right and left flanks were crumbling under the pressure. By 10 A.M. Sherman was trying to bring what was left of his division to a new line of defense even farther to the rear at the Purdy-Hamburg road. The general himself was helping to position a battery when his second horse was shot.

Lieutenant Taylor found his stunned superior once more on the ground facing a wave of advancing Confederates. Somehow he helped him catch one of the stricken battery horses. Sherman had mounted three different horses in less than an hour. Now his hand was bleeding profusely, his coat was riddled with bullet holes, and a ball had passed through his hat. Was he trying to get shot? It did not seem that way to observers on the battlefield, who found him collected rather than reckless. One of his artillery commanders, Lt. Patrick White, remarked of the muddy and bloodstained general that he was "the coolest man I saw that day."

And he was. Within minutes yet another bullet hit his shoulder strap. Apparently it was a ricochet and did not penetrate deeply into the flesh. Hand bleeding, shoulder in a sling, bruised from two falls from his horses, and filthy dirty, Sherman still continued to ride his third mount along the lines amid a hail of gunfire, encouraging his green troops to buy time for the

Union Army with their lives. He later wrote his wife of these nightmarish moments, "I did the best I could with what remained, and all admit I was of good service—I noticed that when we were enveloped and death stared us all in the face my seniors in rank leaned on me."

In the heat of battle Sherman realized instantaneously that if his flank could retire without collapsing, there might soon be help from over 25,000 fresh Union reinforcements that were within a ten-mile radius of Shiloh. But for now the battered Union Army on the battlefield was outnumbered by anywhere from 5,000 to 10,000 troops, more so as the Sunday morning wore on and thousands of Northerners fled their positions to find safety at Pittsburg Landing. By noon Grant's wonderful Army of the Tennessee was nearly wrecked.

Fortunately for the Northerners, the Confederates were just as shocked that their initial assaults had caught the enemy completely surprised, unentrenched, and outnumbered. Thus they had no contingency plan for rapidly moving successive waves of reinforcements to finish off Sherman's distraught division before turning to their right to cut the Union Army off from its supply base at Pittsburg Landing.

Such good fortune was rare for the usually outmanned and outsupplied Confederates during early 1862. For the last six months the war in the West had gone disastrously. By February 1862 the losses of Forts Henry and Donelson on the Tennessee and Cumberland Rivers respectively, together with the easy capture of over fifteen thousand Southern prisoners—irreplaceable soldiers who might have turned the tide at Shiloh—were followed by the Union occupation of Nashville, the second largest Confederate city in the West after New Orleans. As Albert Sidney Johnston fled south in retreat, Memphis and the entire Mississippi Valley were now undefended and vulnerable, raising the specter that the critical nexus of the Western states of Texas and Arkansas might be severed by both water and rail connection from the rest of the Confederate nation. Johnston, once thought the savior of the Confederacy, was now bitterly pilloried in Southern newspapers as either incompetent or cowardly.

In response, the march up the Tennessee River to Shiloh was to be the Confederates' grand offensive, as their woefully unprepared armies were hastily thrown together to prevent the coalescence of two Union forces under Grant and Maj. Gen. Don Carlos Buell from finishing the occupation of Tennessee and the upper Mississippi River altogether. The Southerners had a vague sense that, Napoleon-like, they might occupy the central position, destroying Grant and Buell separately before the two combined to crush them through sheer numbers and matériel. For their part, the North vastly overestimated the size of their Confederate enemies. In their nervousness they had no appreciation that a desperate Southern move on either the Army of the Tennessee or the Army of the Ohio could easily prove suicidal, allowing Grant or Buell to reinforce each other under attack. In Tennessee alone the North held at least a two-to-one edge in manpower.

It was, of course, miraculous that a host of squabbling Southern generals finally brought their forty-thousand-man force undetected to within yards of Grant's outnumbered army. Yet once they arrived, there was still no iron-clad agreement concerning the method of assault. Nor was there any consensus on the best way to dislodge the Northerners—and there was little hope that a surprise attack might succeed. Indeed, just hours before the charge, a large contingent of jittery officers favored pulling back to Corinth, Mississippi, to regroup and form a defensive perimeter. Wild rumors were circulating that the armies of Grant and Buell had already united and were in fact entrenched and waiting at Shiloh. Only Albert Sidney Johnston's adamant insistence that there should be no cancellation in plans of hitting Grant held the Southern army together.

In fact, the Confederates were a disparate group of separate forces nominally under the command of General Johnston, who in turn relied heavily on the advice of P. T. Beauregard in organizing four armies totaling around forty thousand men. Although on paper the four corps commanders—Generals Polk, Bragg, Hardee, and Breckinridge—took their orders from Johnston, most operated and were supplied independently. Even within moments of the first shooting they were rarely in direct communication with either Johnston or Beauregard—much less with each other. The Southern army was a microcosm of the loosely organized Confederacy itself, and so its commanders enjoyed no shared mechanism of how to capitalize on the initial astounding success.

Rather than outflank the Union line with two crushing pincers, the armies instead clumsily charged head-on against the Union right in three successive lines, reminiscent of Napoleon's textbook columns or perhaps the old triplex Roman plan of legionary advance. When the exhausted and hungry men finally did overrun Sherman's camps, they stopped to pillage and eat, again wasting critical minutes in which the retreating Northerners regained their composure and scurried to find new defensive positions. Johnston had performed brilliantly in collecting a massive army of forty thousand and marching them undetected to within a few thousand yards of the Union lines. But he was a less competent tactician. And his subordinates, especially Beauregard, lacked even his battle sense. In addition, Johnston's troops were fundamentally ill-equipped, often without training, experience, or the uniformity of organization and cohesiveness of Grant's army.

Sherman's heroic efforts at resistance forced his enemies to commit thousands of men against his right wing. Yet the Confederates' better hope was to focus on the opposite end of the battlefield against the weaker Union left, and therein cut off the entire army's line of retreat to Pittsburg Landing. Consequently, most of the first day, Shiloh was characterized by gruesome but largely detached confrontations. Confederate corps quite independently battered down the Union line without any concentration of force to blow apart Grant's army. The result was that the Southerners were mostly successful in dozens of isolated firefights, slowly cutting off pockets of Union resistance but losing too many men and too much time in the ordeal to achieve the desired general collapse.

Sherman soon had only half a division left. Yet he was determined to stay with his retreating men in hopes of slowing down the Confederate avalanche until Union reinforcements could craft a line of resistance. By 10:30 A.M. he finally reorganized what was left of his command at least a half mile to the rear of his original camp. He would stay there for the next four hours. Grant, who met him in midmorning, found that Sherman's fragmented right wing could hold and retreat in order to form a perimeter around Pittsburg Landing.

By day's end Sherman had linked up with the other surviving Union divisions in a horseshoe line of defense while Grant awaited the arrival of twenty-seven thousand reinforcements from generals Lew Wallace and Buell. Sherman would go on the offensive the next morning. For the rest of the battle he would play a key role in the Union's remarkable reversal of fortune on April 7 and lead the limited Union pursuit of the defeated Confederates on the morning of the eighth—once again nearly to be shot down at the head of his troops by the furious and final rear guard of Nathan Bedford Forrest.

Sherman's remarkable conduct at Shiloh was well recorded by a number of his superiors—Grant especially—and it is described in detail in his own memoirs and letters. General Nelson, a division commander in Buell's Army of the Ohio that entered the battle on the second day, and no friend of either Grant or Sherman, remarked, "If General Sherman had fallen, the army would have been captured or destroyed." After collating eyewitness accounts of the battle, Maj. Gen. Henry W. Halleck later confirmed to Secretary of War Edwin M. Stanton, "It is the unanimous opinion here that Brig. Gen. W. T. Sherman saved the fortune of the day on the 6th instance, and contributed largely to the glorious victory on the 7th. He was in the thickest of the fight on both days."

The usually taciturn Grant was just as complimentary, "I feel it a duty . . . to a gallant and able officer, Brig. Gen. W. T. Sherman, to make a special mention. He was not only with his command during the entire two-day action, but displayed judgement and skill in the management of his men. Although severely wounded in the hand the first day his place was never vacant." Grant added in his memoirs that "a casualty to Sherman that would have taken him from the field that day would have been a sad one for the troops engaged at Shiloh. And how near we came to this!"

Just as William Tecumseh Sherman, alone of the great Union generals, fought at both the first and last battles of the Civil War—Bull Run and Bentonville—so too was he at the front in the very beginning and ending minutes of Shiloh, crisscrossing the battlefield for nearly forty-eight hours, rallying his green Ohio Division that anchored the beleaguered right wing of the Army of the Tennessee. He may well have been among the very first Union officers hit at Shiloh. He tangled with the last man wounded at the battle, the brilliant and infamous Confederate cavalryman Nathan Bedford Forrest. Sherman's biographers usually devote an entire chapter to his astounding heroism at Shiloh, using phrases like "reborn," "transformation," "second-chance," and "never looked back" to mark the battle as a dividing line between his prior disgrace and subsequent greatness.

What then really happened to Sherman at Shiloh? Neither his prominent and well-documented role in the fighting there nor the magnitude and
importance of the battle can in themselves explain his magical and lasting
transformation. Shiloh in itself did not end the war, or even mark an end to
the fighting in the West. And Sherman did not fight at Shiloh as a major general of an army, but rather served as one of at least ten divisional commanders in the field, themselves all subordinate in rank and authority to Generals
Grant, Buell, and Halleck. He had no responsibility for the Union strategy
that led to Shiloh. Nor did he exercise any overall tactical command of the
battle itself. In the aftermath of the fighting, the newly famous Sherman did
largely what he was told.

But a strange sequence of events unfolded at Shiloh around Sherman
that in a few hours altered both his own career and the next decade of his
nation at large. Nothing in his immediate prequel to Shiloh presaged Sherman's astounding success. In fact, his entire career twenty years prior to
Shiloh—he was forty-one at the battle—had been ostensibly characterized
by only an adequate military record. Although sixth in his 1840 class at West
Point, Sherman had held a series of nondescript postings through some fifteen years of military service throughout the South and West in a variety of
commands. He had missed out entirely on the Mexican War by being stationed in California.

In disgust, Sherman finally resigned from the army in 1853 in order to
start up a bank branch in San Francisco. In contrast to the obscure security
of his military assignments, his subsequent seven years in private business
were an unmitigated disaster: regional director of a failing financial institu-
tion, mounting debts, and finally living apart from his family in a series of
low-paying and temporary jobs. Sherman's near decade of ignominy was only
heightened by the contrast with the success and riches of his wife's family,
especially the fame of his father-in-law (Thomas Ewing, the leading barris-
ter in America and also Sherman's stepfather), coupled with the meteoric
rise of his own brother John to the U.S. Senate as a Republican from Ohio.

Worse still, when Sherman at last reentered military life, he experienced
a roller-coaster series of events in the two years directly prior to Shiloh,
capped by devastating failure. He spent much of 1860 as a civilian organizing the new Louisiana State Military Academy (the future Louisiana State

University) as its first superintendent, in charge of hiring faculty, organizing a curriculum, and literally building the infrastructure of a new campus. By all accounts he was enormously successful. In spite of being a Northerner from Ohio and brother of a Yankee senator, Sherman was well liked by his Southern hosts. Indeed, he was later purportedly offered a high command in the Confederate Army at the outbreak of the war. But his academic tenure would end abruptly in February 1861 with the pending secession of Louisiana and the awful knowledge that the arms and cadets of his own military academy would shortly aid the Confederate cause. Consequently, after years of failure, Sherman saw his greatest triumph—he had been well paid as the academy's superintendent and was planning to build an elegant home on the campus when he resigned—vanish after a year, terminated by events well beyond his own control. In desperation and broke, he quietly headed back north in the wake of secession.

The months immediately prior to the outbreak of the Civil War boded no better. Despite the North's dire need for experienced officers and a scarcity of West Point graduates—by far the best of whom had enlisted in the Confederate Army—Sherman was passed over for higher command by both those officers of less rank and politicos who had no military training at all. Finally, his cool performance as a colonel and brigade commander at Bull Run in July 1861, together with his political connections, brought Sherman to Lincoln's attention. Miraculously he was promoted to a large command of the Cumberland theater in the West, in charge of the protection of all Union interests in the border state of Kentucky. Sherman was at last given responsibility commensurate with his innate talent—though not with either his experience or confidence. Hence here in Kentucky catastrophe struck in late 1861.

After a propitious beginning in organizing defenses and raising troops, Sherman found himself utterly exhausted and demoralized. It soon dawned on him that he was obligated to protect a 300-mile front with only 18,000 raw troops, in a border state where the zeal of Southern sympathizers and Confederate raiders grew in reverse proportion to the general neglect of the West by the Union command in Washington. Overworked and suffering from chronic asthma, Sherman grew increasingly pessimistic as he neared physical collapse, unaware that the enemy was probably in worse shape even than he. By October 1861 he was writing gloomy letters to Lincoln, cabinet officers, and his military superiors—and foolishly giving candid and thoroughly depressing lectures to visiting reporters.

Finally, in a meeting in Louisville on October 17, 1861, with Secretary of War Simon Cameron, other Union military leaders, and unidentified newsmen, Sherman poured out his frustrations. To defend Kentucky alone he would need immediately 60,000 troops. And to mount a theater offensive to clear the Confederates from the entire Mississippi Valley at least 200,000 Union recruits would eventually be required! His hearers were astounded. The fantastic numbers bandied about made a most disheartening prognosis even worse. Later events, in fact, would prove Sherman's realistic figures prescient.

The general Union orthodoxy at the time was that a single rather dramatic victory in Kentucky or Tennessee—Grant's "one great battle"—might so demoralize the South as to bring on a general armistice. Now the theater commander was instead predicting years of conflict with armies in the hundreds of thousands that would cost millions of dollars to raise. Not surprisingly, within a month after Sherman's depressing interview, gossip flew that Sherman was at best exhausted and ill, at worse delusional and insane—and either way liable through his defeatist rantings to lose northern Kentucky if not southern Ohio. By December 11, 1861, the *Cincinnati Commercial* printed the alarming headline about their native son: "General William T. Sherman Insane," and then further pontificated about his removal:

> The harsh criticisms that have been lavished on this gentleman, provoked by his strange conduct, will now give way to feelings of deepest sympathy for him in his great calamity. It seems providential that the country has not to mourn the loss of an army through the loss of mind of a great general into whose hands was committed the vast responsibility of the command of Kentucky.

In disgrace, and suffering what seemed to be classic symptoms of clinical depression, coupled with physical exhaustion, Sherman spent much of December 1861 and January 1862 in isolation, relieved of command in Kentucky, and generally discredited. "I am so sensible now of my disgrace from having exaggerated the force of our enemy in Kentucky that I do think I should have committed suicide were it not for my children," he wrote his brother in the midst of exile. Most newspaper observers believed that his briefly resurrected career had now ended in infamy.

Only lobbying efforts by his wife, father-in-law, and brother led Lincoln and Halleck to give a shaky and reluctant Sherman a second chance. By mid-February he received a lowly assignment in western Kentucky, training recruits for the newly appointed general Ulysses S. Grant's proposed campaigns against Fort Donelson and Fort Henry. Without the pressure of running an entire theater and bolstered by reports of Grant's aggressive competence, Sherman slowly began to regain his health and some of his former assurance. When Grant's two victories not only secured Kentucky but opened Tennessee to Federal advance, Sherman was buoyed by the chance to raise his own division of inexperienced Ohio recruits to join Grant's new Army of the Tennessee. So by early April, as a division commander at Shiloh, a steadier Sherman was part of a huge Union effort to pacify southern Tennessee and clear the upper Mississippi River.

Still, on the morning of April 6, Sherman was well aware that his past pessimism about the conduct of the war had been interpreted in the popular press as timidity, if not outright madness. That the real Sherman his entire life had been a cool risk-taker—whether establishing a new California bank branch in the midst of the Gold Rush or a novel academy in Louisiana on the eve of the Civil War—had been forgotten in the hysteria. Instead, this second and probably last chance under Grant had convinced Sherman of the need for dramatic action to recover his own reputation and his family's name among fellow officers, politicians, and newsmen, who were all wary of his mercurial past and ignorant of his prior two decades of steady service. His new Ohio recruits, it was said, still whispered that their general was crazy.

The effect of the topsy-turvy past four months on Sherman at Shiloh was thus paradoxical. In one sense, the newspaper slurs that he was insane freed him from worry over career advancement and preserving his reputation: he had none. Sherman accepted the generally held idea that he was going nowhere in the Union Army—and so had nothing to lose. As a result, at no time did he show the slightest fear of the approaching enemy at Shiloh— to the point on the eve of the battle of recklessly dismissing clear reports that he was about to be attacked by a much larger Confederate force. His general ignominy also led Sherman to be unconcerned with his own personal safety: at Shiloh, he determined, he would be a general always at the head of his army. He would either be killed at the front and so escape the disrepute that he had brought to his family, or he would provide a public display of courage and skill that might squelch rumors of his incompetence—if not resurrect his name altogether as he led his troops to victory.

In consequence, on April 6, the morning of the Confederate attack, a fatalistic Sherman deliberately dismissed clear signs of the impending enemy aggression or at least had no intention of adopting a defensive posture. His vulnerable right wing was neither fortified nor even entrenched—an equally surprised Grant had issued no such orders himself. Stung by past criticism of the prior months that he was overly nervous, Sherman now foolishly but calmly ridiculed solid scouting reports that the enemy was on the move and headed in his direction.

For this he was criticized by contemporaries and faulted by biographers, despite his weak protestations in his memoirs that he was never surprised at Shiloh. He most surely was. But historians sometimes fail to point out that it would have made little difference had Sherman ordered his men to entrench, inasmuch as there was no such order to any of the other divisions of the 35,000-man army that morning. An immobile division behind ramparts on the promontory of the Union line would have been quickly surrounded and cut off. And given his prior reputation, such precautionary measures might well have cost a "crazy Sherman" his command on the eve of battle.

Moreover, given Sherman's vulnerable posting on the extreme right wing, there is no reason to believe his green troops would not have been overrun anyway. Instead, by careful retreats, the use of artillery, and occasional counterattacks, Sherman for most of the day was able to pull his vastly outnumbered division slowly back to the Union base at Pittsburg Landing on the Tennessee River. His own shaky defense for not fortifying his position—that to put raw troops in an offensive campaign behind barricades was to create an aura of defeatism and timidity—has some merit.

In any case, the chief cause for the initial Union collapse was not really surprise or faulty generalship, but poor morale. Inexperienced Union troops were assured that the Confederates, beaten at Forts Henry and Donelson, would be on the defensive and not attack. Somewhat understandably their sudden and unexpected charge shattered that Union complacency and very nearly routed the entire army in the first seconds of firing.

It is also forgotten that Sherman had wisely picked the high ground in the days before the battle. His right flank was well protected by a branch of Owl Creek, his left by a smaller swollen stream. Any attacker would have to run uphill without cover through a narrow meadow into Sherman's guns. And it was Grant's, not Sherman's, idea to disperse the army in the narrow confines surrounding Pittsburg Landing, at a distance from Wallace, Buell, and Grant's own headquarters and yet so near to the Confederate stronghold at Corinth, Mississippi. Strategically Grant's deployment made little sense; tactically Sherman's dispositions there were excellent.

By day's end the Union Army had retreated over two miles to its landing on the Tennessee, lost nearly 10,000 dead, wounded, or missing with another 10,000 to 20,000 scattered, but was nevertheless in an extremely strong last-ditch position. As evening approached, the decimated Union Army, well arranged and awaiting the fresh forces of Generals Wallace and Buell, was oddly in far better shape than the victorious though exhausted Confederates.

The events of the second day of Shiloh on April 7 are famous. Despite the chaos of thousands of terrified Union soldiers at Pittsburg Landing attempting to flee the battlefield, Grant shrugged off his initial surprise and proved unflappable. Both he and a weary Sherman had agreed at 11 P.M. on the sixth that with reinforcements, the Union forces could go on the offensive the next morning. To Grant and Sherman, whichever side took the initiative the next morning would win the battle. The Confederates—through senseless frontal attacks on strong Union positions, especially at the so-called Hornet's Nest, the loss of their commanding general Albert Sidney Johnston, and the clumsiness of their initial deployments—were worn out, unorganized, and as a result unable to press their victory even another hour to annihilate the Union's last pocket. By Monday morning it was too late and the tables were turned. The Southerners were now outnumbered by perhaps more than 20,000 men. Some 25,000 remaining Confederates faced a Union army of 50,000—over half of them fresh troops who had not endured the trauma of the first day's carnage.

If it is true that prior disgrace propelled Sherman to downplay the Confederate menace before Shiloh, and past accusations of anxiety and paranoia led to forced calmness under fire, his cool and reasoned conduct in the battle proper largely ensured at least a tactical standoff for the Union Army. His division—made up exclusively of Ohio natives who had never been in battle—was the first attacked and the last to disengage. It anchored the entire right wing in its steady withdrawal; and Grant's right was the scene of some of the harshest fighting during the first day.

Had Sherman given in to the growing hysteria, precipitously withdrawn his forces, or insisted on a glorious last stand at his original position, the Confederate Army would have destroyed the Union right and poured into the rear of an unprotected army. Others at Shiloh—especially the stubborn General Prentiss at the Hornet's Nest—were equally responsible for the salvation of the Union Army on the first day of Shiloh. But no one covered so much ground or had such a psychological effect on the troops as the blood-spattered Sherman.

We can engage in counterfactual speculation that had Sherman either been killed on April 6—and he almost was on at least five or six occasions—or not fought in such a frenzied manner, contemporary observers were quite correct that the Union would have lost Shiloh before the arrival of either Wallace or Buell. Grant's entire Western campaign would then have stalled—Grant himself disgraced and relieved for being surprised—and the Mississippi River may well have remained in Confederate hands until 1864 or 1865. The North might still have recovered after a defeat at Shiloh, but probably not soon enough to close the war by 1865, nor with Abraham Lincoln reelected in November 1864, nor under terms of a general unconditional surrender of the South. Yet Sherman's remarkable hours at Shiloh also had even greater ramifications far beyond the salvation of the Union offensive in the West in 1862. In at least three other ways, Sherman's performance at the battle changed not only the course of the Civil War, but perhaps ultimately the very practice of modern war itself.

The fighting of the Civil War ended in spring 1865 for two reasons: Robert E. Lee could not free his Army of Northern Virginia from the death grip of Grant's Army of the Potomac, and General Sherman's Army of the

West was rapidly approaching Richmond from the rear. Sherman's was now a monstrous veteran force of over one hundred thousand seasoned Mid-westerners who had destroyed Atlanta, ransacked Georgia, and humiliated the Carolinas in a devastating circular march northward from the interior of the South. In some sense, Lee surrendered not only because his army was on the verge of defeat by Grant, but because thousands of his own veterans were deserting to their families on news that Sherman was loose among homes to the rear. Even those who stayed on the line against Grant realized that they were soon to be caught between two enormous pincers and so likely annihilated.

Key to that finale was the unbelievable three-year campaign of Sherman between Shiloh and Appomattox—and the creation of a strange personal symbiosis between Grant and Sherman. Both developments saved the North and owe their geneses to Sherman's bravery at Shiloh. Again, other generals were critical to the Union battle victory—Prentiss, McClernand, and Buell—but unlike the fate of Sherman, *terribile dictu*, it mattered little to the eventual Northern effort whether they were killed or captured at Shiloh or removed from command in the battle's aftermath.

Sherman never looked back after Shiloh. "I have worked hard to keep down," he wrote his wife of his promotion to major general after Shiloh, "but somehow I am forced into prominence and might as well submit." In the months that followed the Union victory, he assumed martial control of Memphis. There he began formulating a general Union blueprint of occupation for Southern cities: generosity to compliant Southerners who disengaged from the Confederate war effort, no quarter for guerrillas and citizens who actively aided the Secessionists. Then, for most of spring 1863, Sherman proved invaluable in Grant's successful campaign against the Mississippi stronghold of Vicksburg. By early 1864, deeply ensconced in the South, commander of all Northern armies in the West, and causing havoc in Mississippi, Louisiana, and Georgia, he was known as "Uncle Billy" to his fast-moving troops.

Sherman's capture of Atlanta in autumn 1864 saved Lincoln the presidential election. The March to the Sea in November and early December—entirely Sherman's own plan and implemented over the objections of his superiors—humiliated the South and wrought an estimated $100 million in damage to the infrastructure of the Confederacy. The even greater trek through the Carolinas in the winter and early spring of 1865—again, initially opposed by Grant—devastated much of what was left of the Confederate economy and proved to the world the impotence of the Southern resistance. Sherman's vast and seasoned Army of the West that approached Lee's rear— at war's end it far overshadowed the rival-but-decimated Army of the Potomac—had become the most terrible modern military force in the history of warfare. While the doggedness of both Generals Grant and Thomas was critical to the Union effort, it was Sherman's odyssey through the South that turned the tide of the war—a spiritual journey as well that began with his wounds and lost mounts at Shiloh.

Equally important was Sherman's critical relationship with Grant, which likewise was cemented during the firestorm of Shiloh. In the very worst moments of the fighting, a cool Sherman reported to Captain Wiley, Grant's aide-de-camp, "Tell Grant, if he has any men to spare I can use them; if not, I will do the best I can. We are holding them pretty well just now—pretty well—but it's as hot as hell." The two generals were to meet twice during the battle's critical first day. At 10 A.M. Grant himself hurried over to his collapsing right with cartridges for Sherman's Ohioans. There he found his subordinate calm amid his fallen regiments. "In thus moving along the line," wrote Grant of his morning inspection, "I never deemed it important to stay long with Sherman."

They bumped into each other again during the evening. Most officers of the Army of the Tennessee were expecting a general retreat across the river; those who were not were clamoring that only the arrival of Buell and Wallace offered a chance for a draw at Shiloh. In the midst of such panic at Pittsburg Landing, Sherman approached Grant. "Well, Grant, we've had the devil's own day, haven't we?" "Yes," Grant offered, "lick 'em tomorrow, though."

After the fighting, when Grant was determined to resign under General Halleck's trumped-up insinuations of laxity and drunkenness, it was a reenergized (and now a national hero) Sherman who convinced him to stay. Of their meeting in the aftermath of Shiloh, when Grant was close to quitting, Sherman later wrote:

I begged him to stay, illustrating his case by my own. Before the battle of Shiloh, I had been cast down by a mere newspaper assertion of "crazy"; but that single battle had given me new life, and now I was in high feather; and I argued with him that, if he went away, events would go right along, and he would be left out; whereas, if he remained, some happy accident might restore him to favor and his true place. He certainly appreciated my friendly advice, and promised to wait awhile.

The ensuing trust from "that single battle" ensured Sherman's command of the Western theater when Grant went east to assume control of all Union armies. Consequently, throughout 1864 and 1865 the two worked independently and yet harmoniously, in dire contrast to the previous destructive rivalries fostered by generals Halleck, McClellan, Buell, Hooker, Pope, Rosecrans, Burnside, and most of the other generals of Lincoln who had nearly ruined the Union cause in the first two years of the war. Throughout the war Sherman defended Grant in print; for the next twenty years he counseled both Generals Buell and Wallace and their numerous supporters not to pursue their vendettas against Grant and to withdraw charges of Grant's culpability for the atrocious losses at Shiloh. In short, Sherman's heroism at Shiloh created the Grant-Sherman trust, without which the North would certainly not have won the war within four years.

Yet the most profound ripple from Shiloh was Sherman's remarkable transformation in his own views concerning the nature and purpose of modern warfare in the new industrial age. Unlike Grant, who was not directly fighting at the front during Shiloh, Sherman was nearly killed so often and saw such carnage about him, that Shiloh's carnage made a lasting and haunting impression in this first great slaughter of the Civil War. His memoirs and letters are quite clear about his metamorphosis: Shiloh, one of the earliest of all his Civil War experiences, was also his most horrific and remained for the rest of his life the most nightmarish. Four days after the battle he wrote his wife, "The scenes of this field would have cured anybody of war. Mangled bodies, dead, dying, in every conceivable shape, without heads, legs; and horses! . . . I still feel the horrid nature of this war, and the piles of dead Gentlemen & wounded & maimed makes me more anxious than ever for some hope of an End, but I know such a thing cannot be for a long long time." Grant concurred with Sherman's assessment, and later wrote that on the day after Shiloh it would have been possible to walk across the battlefield "in any direction, stepping on dead bodies, without a foot touching the ground."

Nearly a quarter century after Shiloh, the memory of the grotesque dead and wounded continued to haunt Sherman. In an address to the Army of the Tennessee in 1881, he somberly began:

> Who but a living witness can adequately portray those scenes on Shiloh's field, when our wounded men, mingled with rebels, charred and blackened by the burning tents and underbrush, were crawling about, begging for someone to end their misery? Who can describe the plunging shot shattering the strong oak as with a thunderbolt, and beating down horse and rider to the ground? Who but one who has heard them can describe the peculiar sizzing of the minie ball, or the crash and roar of a volley fire? Who can describe the last look of the stricken as he appeals for help that no man can give or describe the dread scene of the surgeon's work, or the burial trench?

After that personal nightmare of Shiloh's mangled bodies, Sherman was determined *not* to fight a battle in the style of Grant in which men charged en masse through open fields of point-blank rifle and cannon fire, the victors guaranteed to lose nearly as many as the defeated. Southerners had vulnerabilities, but bravery under fire was not one of them.

Grant, however, learned a quite different lesson from the second-day reinforcements at Shiloh: the North could win through superior manpower in head-on assaults—trading vicious blows with the Confederates in an effort to kill one Southerner for every two Northern fatalities. Sherman, however, left the battlefield convinced that there had to be a better way for a modern army to defeat its adversary than twenty thousand combined casualties in the space of forty-eight hours. In nearly all of his subsequent fighting there would be almost no repeats of the frontal crashes at Shiloh—Sherman's misguided head-on charge at Kenesaw Mountain in June 1864 is about the sole exception.

In the next three years Sherman would craft the successful strategy of the Union war effort against the South—a call for total war against the entire infrastructure of the enemy that need not entail the killing of innocent civilians or even the destruction of Confederate armies. What enabled the enemy to charge at Shiloh, Sherman saw, were not mere weapons and matériel, but equally the soldiers' sense that the heart of their Confederacy was impregnable and their homes safe. Should he destroy that myth—and wreck the foundation of land and slaves that fueled the plantationists' Confederacy—Southern armies would melt away as surely as if their soldiers had been shot down. Let Lee in Virginia fret about the sanctity of his beloved home ground; meanwhile Sherman would ruin the economy of his Confederate states to his rear. In a series of astute letters to Lincoln, to his adversary John Bell Hood at Atlanta, and to Grant, Sherman outlined this remarkably prescient understanding of the new morality of modern war and the rapidly expanding theater of battle.

War was rightly "hell"; yet Sherman did not come away from Shiloh as a pacifist, but as an angel of moral retribution who would wreak vengeance on the higher powers who had sent those poor boys on both sides to their slaughter at Shiloh. "I propose to demonstrate," he announced before leaving Atlanta, "the vulnerability of the South, and make its inhabitants feel that war and individual ruin are synonymous terms." To the civil authorities of the Confederacy who demanded that he not deport civilians from Atlanta, Sherman later scoffed, "You might as well appeal against the thunder storm as against these terrible hardships of war. They are inevitable and the only way the people of Atlanta can hope once more to live in peace & quiet is to Stop the war, which can alone be done by admitting that it began in Error and is perpetuated in pride." In rejecting John Bell Hood's claim to a higher moral ground in the fighting around Atlanta, Sherman lectured, "If we must be Enemies let us be men, and fight it out as we propose to do, and not deal in such hypocritical appeals to God and humanity. God will judge us in due time."

To Sherman it was wrong to fight a Shiloh, in which his Midwesterners—themselves no abolitionists—were blasted apart while shooting down poor Southern boys who owned neither slaves nor much property. Far more humane, he grasped, was to burn the estates of the rich and the buildings of the rebel statesmen who had voted for secession; free the slaves who were critical to the Southern economy and whose enslavement had prompted the rebellion; and demonstrate that no Confederate soldier could charge a Union line with the certainty that his government and homeland far to the rear were safe from fire and ruin. As he wrote Grant, "We cannot change the hearts of the people of the South, but we can make war so terrible that they will realize the fact that however brave and gallant and devoted to their country, still they are mortal and should exhaust all peaceful remedies before they fly to war."

In Sherman's words, Southerners, while they "cannot be made to love us, they can be made to fear us." The result was that between November 1864 and spring 1865, Sherman suffered almost no casualties in his enormous Army of the West. He killed very few Southerners and made it terribly clear to the ruling minority in the South that their reckless decision to secede would cost them their livelihoods. Sherman not merely destroyed the South, he humiliated it in the process. No wonder that the property destroyer and liberator of slaves, not Grant, the butcher of Confederate manhood, was to be the far more hated by diehard Southerners. Yet Sherman's bitter truths about modern war neither Grant nor Lee really grasped: the real immorality of war was not the March to the Sea, but the battles to come after and like Shiloh—Antietam, Gettysburg, Cold Harbor, the Wilderness—where the young and innocent were massacred while the old and culpable were safely hectoring or even profiting to the rear.

Grant, who won Shiloh through superior manpower, likewise would send thousands to their deaths in Virginia—convinced that Lee's army might likewise collapse before his own stream of bodies was exhausted. Yet he was often less aware of the larger lessons of the war: the heartland of the South still lay untouched, its citizens unrepentant, while the North would lose more of its precious youth in battlefield "victories" than did the South in "defeats."

Lee too never really understood Sherman's strategic notion of war. He went northward in 1863 in search of a head-on collision with the enemy, ruined his army at Gettysburg, killed thousands of Northerners, and prolonged the fighting for another two years. In contrast, Sherman went into the "bowels of Georgia" in 1864 to destroy an economy and an idea, killed few, and lost almost no one—and the war ended in less than a year. Lee perhaps at last realized that Grant could stop his army; but he and his generals never quite understood how and why Sherman had defeated their culture.

Had Sherman been in charge of Lee's army in June 1863, the Army of Northern Virginia would have sidestepped Meade at Gettysburg, may well have burned Washington, D.C., and crippled the economy of southern Pennsylvania and Maryland—before returning intact to the South and the likelihood of a brokered peace. In contrast, had Lee been Sherman in fall 1864, his army would have sought out Hood, Hardee, and Bragg and never reached Savannah.

Contrary to popular opinion and hysterical slurs, Sherman's legacy of destroying civic property and morale was not Dresden, Hiroshima, or My Lai. His Army of the West never deliberately killed civilians, raped, or murdered. Rather, Sherman's war against property and civic infrastructure has now been ingrained as the unofficial policy of the United States military at war—as the recent conflicts in Iraq, the Balkans, and Afghanistan attest. Like Sherman, we prefer to attack the will of a nation to resist through the destruction of its communications and the property of its government and elite without aiming either to kill all its soldiers or randomly target civilians. Sherman alone of nineteenth-century generals understood that wars of the industrial age were fueled by a sophisticated but increasingly vulnerable infrastructure—transportation, communications, manufacturing, government—whose destruction could stall troops in the field and instantaneously strip a newly found affluence away from the promulgators of conflict. Even more brilliantly, he realized that with material progress came at least the pretense of enlightened humanity: eventually the wages of victory in liberal and affluent Western democratic societies would entail that the victor kill few and lose fewer still, an ideal more practicable when the property and capital rather than the lives of the enemy were targeted.

Finally, Sherman developed the idea of collective guilt, or the controversial concept that no population that broadly supports a war should be entirely free of its bitter consequences. The only way to disabuse Southerners of their trust in chattel slavery and secession was to show that eventually such ideologies would lead to the March to the Sea. In the same manner, the Afghans were not entirely blameless for either the Taliban or al-Qaeda, and turned on both only when they saw that the logical wages of their tacit support led to B-52s rather than polite remonstrations from American diplomats and an occasional cruise missile. Whether we like it or not, the multifaceted war conceived by William Tecumseh Sherman between Shiloh and Appomattox is with us Americans today—and it is *not*, as alleged, simply one of "terror."

Fortunately for the fate of the Union and the career of Grant, the dozens of Shiloh shots aimed at Sherman hit his flapping coat, hat, shoulder strap, hand, and horses, and not his chest. Unlike Albert Sidney Johnston—who on the other side of the battle line was braving fire at the front after also being unfairly castigated in the press on the eve of the battle—enemy bullets missed Sherman's arteries and vital organs.

So, unlike the fate of the supreme Confederate commander, Shiloh did not kill, but empowered a once "crazy" and powerless officer. In turn, a now heroic and self-assured Sherman would save Grant both by his conduct at the front and his loyalty in the battle's postmortem. And the two of them would go on to save the Union and destroy the South. Quite early in the Civil War, Shiloh taught the introspective Sherman—and Sherman alone of all the Civil War generals—how *not* to wage war, and so the poor South would soon come to learn in Georgia and the Carolinas the real consequences of that awful battle of April 1862.

Afternoon: The Myth of the Lost Opportunity

While the Confederate left battered Sherman, the right wing finally began the long planned sweep to the Tennessee River. It was here that Albert Sidney Johnston—perhaps the most experienced and best known American officer on either side at the battle—had originally envisioned cutting off

Grant's army from its base of supplies at the river. Then he would drive it back toward Owl Creek, where it would then be surrounded and annihilated.

But late in the morning there was something awry with the once promising Confederate blueprint. All morning Johnston rode along the crest of his Confederate wave, worried that his planned critical right advance was lapping around, rather than overwhelming, a last center of resistance anchored by the Union divisions of Generals Hurlbut, Prentiss, and W.H.L. Wallace. Johnston grew increasingly concerned that his victorious troops were plundering Union camps, straggling to the rear with booty, and often charging haphazardly in the wrong direction. They were already dissipating their remarkable initial successes and giving critical time for the stunned Federal troops to retire and regroup!

Protected by a peach orchard and a sunken road, the desperate and surrounded Northerners to the right in the so-called Hornet's Nest were slaughtering wave after wave of Confederate attackers, and thereby upsetting the entire Southern battle plan at Shiloh. Around noon Johnston himself rode over to inspect the source of enemy resistance and then to direct personally the Southern charges. The attempted destruction of the Union pocket had now taken on a surreal life of its own. Rather than bypassing or outflanking the nest, Johnston and Braxton Bragg began to send hundreds of men to their deaths in vain assaults against Union artillery and sharpshooters—as if the capture of the tiny Federal salient had become a sudden referendum on Southern manhood and courage! Meanwhile precious time was being lost; fleeing Union regiments were reforming defenses to the rear around the Union camp at Pittsburg Landing. The Southern generals were suddenly fighting the wrong battle in the wrong place at the wrong time.

As the Confederate charges withered, it began to seem as if the Southerners themselves had had enough. About 2 P.M., General Breckinridge rode up to Johnston to confess that a regiment of his Tennesseans refused to make any more suicidal attacks. To his plea that he could not make his men budge, Johnston replied, "Oh, yes, General, I think you can." Finally an exasperated Johnston told an insistent Breckinridge that he would lead the charge in person. He then approached the recalcitrant Tennesseans, touched their bayonets from his horse, and exclaimed, "These will do the work. Men, they are stubborn; we must use the bayonet." Johnston turned his trusted mount Fire-eater around and rode out at the van, calling to his foot soldiers, "I will lead you." In the heat of battle, few seemed to note the absurdity that the supreme commander of some forty thousand men, who alone had collected the army and brilliantly brought it undetected to Shiloh, was now leading a near-suicidal charge of a few hundred soldiers—trusting in the bayonet against the mass fire of rifled muskets.

At some point in the onslaught, Johnston faded back through the ranks. Although his men broke their immediate adversaries and sparked the beginning of the collapse of the Hornet's Nest, Johnston himself uncharacteristically sought relief from the fire. At first he seemed elated that he had escaped death from the murderous Northern broadsides. He even slapped his thigh, remarking of a spent ball that merely stung him and of another that sliced his boot-sole in two, "They didn't trip me up that time."

But, in fact, they did. And minutes later the general suddenly seemed hesitant. Had he, in fact, been wounded during his ride into the peach orchard? Fire-eater had tired and seemed to have been hit in at least two places. Besides the boot-heel being shot to pieces, Johnston's overcoat was now riddled with bullet holes. He sighed to a staff member, Gov. Isham G. Harris of Tennessee, "Governor, they came near putting me *hors de combat* in that charge." Moments later Johnston went pale and nearly fell out of his saddle. Harris demanded, "General, are you wounded?" Johnston gasped, "Yes, and I fear seriously."

A series of further mishaps now transpired that ensured the death of Albert Sidney Johnston. He had been shot during the charge in the popliteal artery, just below the knee on the inside of his right leg—usually a serious but nonlethal wound that could be treated in the field with a simple tourniquet, which Johnston, like many soldiers, carried with him. But unfortunately the general had probably been hit several minutes before he informed Harris, perhaps as much as a quarter hour earlier than his first acknowledgment of injury. In the excitement of battle he had felt little pain. In the meantime he had probably lost over two quarts of blood, enough to send him into irreversible shock. Later it was found that a .577-caliber minié ball had entered behind his right knee, the leg where years earlier he had suffered a serious bullet wound in a duel that had left him with bouts of nerve pain and leg paralysis. Due to the prior (and more serious) injury, had he now simply felt nothing when the stray bullet nicked his artery? Or had the ebullition of the victorious charge dulled the pain? Or finally, was a suffering Johnston simply being stoic even as he bled to death?

Still more unfortunate, the blood from the wound had stealthily oozed down the side of his leg, inside his pant on into the boot. So when his staff—among them Col. William Preston, his brother-in-law—carried the general down from Fire-eater, they saw little trace of bleeding on his person and thus at first could not find the source of Johnston's fainting. Instead of tourniquets and bandages, they wrongly administered brandy to revive the comatose Johnston.

His own personal physician, Dr. D. W. Yandell, who was nearly always at the general's side and could have stopped the bleeding in seconds, had a few hours earlier been ordered by Johnston to attend to Union prisoners. "Look after these wounded people, the Yankees among the rest. They were our enemies a moment ago. They are prisoners now." When Yandell objected about leaving the general, Johnston ordered him to stay with the wounded and dying. In short, Albert Sidney Johnston's own inability to notice the wound, the misfortune of a major artery being nicked, the fact that the blood had pooled undetected in his boot, the sudden absence of his personal physician, and the panic of his staff who missed the wound, all conspired to ensure his death—and in such a fashion to prompt second-guessing for decades afterward.

The officers around the lifeless Johnston were horrified that their commander, fresh from a successful charge into the Hornet's Nest, had now mysteriously died within minutes without a visible trace of trauma. They quickly sought to conceal his death from the rank and file to avoid a general panic—especially the knowledge that their beloved leader had died from a wound that need not have killed him. It was now announced that the corpse of a "Colonel Jackson of Texas" was being brought back from the front. Only when Johnston's remains were taken into the Confederate headquarters did Dr. Chopin, General Beauregard's personal surgeon, finally discover the source of the fatal blood loss—as well as three other minor wounds and dozens of holes in his uniform and coat.

Beauregard himself was in near shock. The battle was at a critical phase. The supreme commander and architect of the Confederate advance was now gone. What should the staff do? For well over an hour, between 2:30 P.M.—the approximate time of Johnston's death—until sometime before 4:00, a lull descended upon the Confederate army. No one on the right wing—neither Generals Cheatham, Withers, nor Breckinridge, or Jackson— had stepped up to replace Johnston to coordinate attacks against the reeling Union troops inside the Hornet's Nest. Johnston's final charge had rattled the Union line, and in the Northerners' confusion a free lane directly ahead of the Confederates seemed to have opened up all the way to Pittsburg Landing.

Yet there was to be no sustained follow-up, at least until Braxton Bragg belatedly and unimaginatively began to send units once again head-on against the Union line. Instead of encircling the Hornet's Nest, some South- erners had turned obliquely to the northwest, allowing the Union troops in the pocket even more critical time to regroup. In fact, even after Bragg at last regained some semblance of order in his attacks, General Prentiss's men would not surrender for another hour, sometime around or after 5:00 P.M., nearly three hours after Johnston was carried from the field.

Prentiss capitulated only after some sixty-two Confederate cannon had pulverized his position. But by then it was nearly dusk. As the victorious Southerners at last swarmed over the captured Union left wing, there was lit- tle daylight left to complete the annihilation of Grant's encircled and totter- ing army. True, dozens of Confederate units were streaming forward. Some were plundering the rich Union camps. Others fired away at the panicking enemy runaways; still more were involved in the mop-up of captives. The feeling among the rank and file was that Bragg and his subordinates could still piece together a final twilight coordinated assault and that way sweep the last remnants of Grant's army into the river.

But around 6:00, Beauregard abruptly ordered a general withdrawal! Dozens of Confederate officers were aghast—most notably Col. Nathan Bedford Forrest, who was nearing the bluffs above the trapped Union army, convinced that a final dusk charge could scatter the Federals before they could be reinforced during the night by Wallace and Buell. Here was born the idea of the "Lost Opportunity."

Did Johnston's sudden demise account for the delay in capturing the last Federal pocket and therein perhaps explain why the Confederates now called off a final assault at Pittsburg Landing? All veterans of the battle agreed that for some seven hours, Prentiss had held his command against overwhelming odds. In the process he prevented the Confederates from nearing Pittsburg Landing until nightfall. The assumption then spread that if only the Union salient had collapsed earlier in midafternoon—at about the time of Johnston's death—Grant's camp would have been in enemy hands by 5:00 P.M. Who, then, after the noble sacrifice of the supreme commander, was to blame for allowing a few hundred men to stall the entire Confederate advance? And why was the battle called off when the Union Army was in ruins with its back to the Tennessee River?

Almost immediately, Johnston's sudden death conveniently answered both those queries and in the process created a Confederate legend that fit in so well with the known Southern affinity for romance and chivalry. In this tradition—I heard a popular version of the story in the early 1960s from my own maternal grandmother, Georgia Way Johnston, whose family claimed to be cousins of Albert Sidney—the Confederacy was on the verge of a momentous "victory" at Shiloh. Then suddenly Johnston, architect of the entire campaign, went down with a minor wound. His unexpected death brought the attack against the Hornet's Nest to a standstill, giving the Northerners a precious hour or two to regroup, rearm, and be reinforced. By the time the demoralized Southern staff had assembled a new assault group, it was so late in the day that only inspired generalship could have crafted a final winning pursuit. Instead, far to the rear a confused Beauregard ordered a cessation of the advance, and therein for the second time within a few hours threw away the martyred Johnston's hard-won victory on the first day of Shiloh. Despite Union numerical superiority in the Tennessee theater of at least two to one, overwhelming Federal logistical support, arms, matériel, and the presence of top officers in the West like Grant, Sherman, and Thomas, the South had lost the war due to the chance trajectory of a single stray bullet—itself perhaps ricocheted from a friendly musket.

Had the determined Johnston lived, the Confederate lore further maintains, in a few more minutes he would have blasted apart the Hornet's Nest. Then he would have ordered a massive charge down the bluffs in the late afternoon, racing forward on Fire-eater to send the last pockets of Northern survivors—less than 10,000 of Grant's 35,000-man army were still in any organized formation—into the Tennessee River. Then, with Grant's army destroyed, Buell would never have ventured across the Tennessee. He would have either retired into Kentucky or found himself annihilated by a much larger and victorious Confederate force. And Lew Wallace's reinforcements of some 7,000 men would have had to retreat back to Crump's Landing or find themselves colliding in the dark with an enemy army four times their size.

Given the shocking novelty of Shiloh's carnage at this juncture in the war and the strategic importance of the battle, Johnston's untimely death only led to even larger "what ifs." With Grant's army wrecked and captured at Shiloh, Southerners maintained that the entire course of the Civil War would have been radically altered. An enormous and victorious Confederate army loose in the border states—perhaps reaching 50,000 men when reinforced by Van Dorn's late-arriving Arkansas divisions—would have forced the North to evacuate Tennessee. Consequently, the story goes, there would have been no assault on Vicksburg for months, if at all. Grant would have been disgraced, Sherman perhaps as well—when it was learned that an entire Federal army had been surprised and then annihilated by Johnston in a few hours. The tottering border state of Kentucky would have returned to its Southern roots and joined the Confederacy. What was left of Union forces would be in the hands of Buell and Halleck—hardly the type of aggressive commanders to ward off a victorious Albert Sidney Johnston. Had only Johnston not fallen at the critical moments of Shiloh!

More sober historians downplay the ultimate significance of Johnston's death. They attribute the pause in the assault of the Hornet's Nest more to exhaustion and an absence of ammunition. Scholars also emphasize the earlier tactical blunders of Johnston, who at least sanctioned, if not ordered, wave after wave of Confederate charges against the Union pocket without attempting an early flanking maneuver. Skeptics add that even had the fiery Johnston lived and ordered a general assault on Pittsburg Landing at dusk, Grant's last line was well organized, occupied the high ground, and was bolstered by artillery and gunboats—making it impossible to be scattered in a mere hour before darkness. Moreover, by nightfall the Confederates were so disorganized and depleted that they may well have been stalemated the next morning by Buell and Lew Wallace, even without Grant's help.

In any case, we will never know the exact effect or ultimate significance of Johnston's death on the Confederate cause. The truth perhaps falls well between the Southern claim of catastrophe and Northern insistence on irrelevance. Grant, for example, criticized Johnston's generalship severely and called him "vacillating and undecided in his actions"—apparently due to the earlier losses by his subordinates of Forts Henry and Donelson, and the inability to move his army rapidly from Corinth, Mississippi, to Shiloh. Whether that harsh verdict reflects sober military analysis or Grant's own embarrassment at having Johnston maneuver an army of forty thousand undetected to within yards of his lines is still a matter of debate.

In some sense, however, it does not matter what the actual facts were concerning the exact ramifications of Johnston's demise. Instead, it was the *perception* in the South about Shiloh's effect on the Civil War after the battle that was Johnston's true legacy. Despite what Grant, Sherman, and others maintained, within a decade of the battle, the notion became orthodoxy that Johnston's sudden death had in a few minutes robbed the Confederates of their success at Shiloh. In turn, that defeat, snatched from the jaws of victory, had allowed a beaten Grant to press on to open the Mississippi and sever the Confederacy. Had Johnston just lived, the war would have ended quite differently.

The first promulgators of the myth were the suspect generals themselves at Shiloh, specifically Braxton Bragg and other subordinates who in retrospect excused their dubious performances by claiming they could have stormed Grant's redoubt before darkness if not called back. Stung by postbellum criticism of their own unimaginative advance and failures to coordinate piecemeal attacks—and furious over the self-interested efforts of the scapegoat of Shiloh, P. T. Beauregard, to defend his tarnished reputation at their expense—they insisted that the Union survivors in the Hornet's Nest were given a critical reprieve when Johnston fell. One of the first formal canonizations of "the Lost Opportunity" appeared almost immediately after the battle in July 1862 in the *Savannah Republican* under the caption "A Lost

Opportunity at Shiloh." The author, Peter Alexander, was one of the South's foremost military correspondents and drew his evidence from interviews with Southern generals to argue that Beauregard had thrown away Johnston's hard-fought victory.

> General Bragg himself had written that explicitly not long after the battle: In spite of opposition and prediction of failure, Johnston firmly and decidedly ordered and led the attack in the execution of his general plan, and, notwithstanding the faulty arrangement of troops, was eminently successful up to the moment of his fall. *The victory was won.* How it was lost the official reports will show, and history has already recorded.

Bragg, whom most historians fault for unimaginatively ordering frontal charges against the Hornet's Nest and thereby dissipating critical time and Confederate strength, had, in fact, advanced two claims. The first was that Johnston's death had delayed the Confederates' sure defeat of Prentiss—with fatal ramifications:

> But no one cause probably contributed so greatly to our loss of time, which was the loss of success, as the fall of the commanding general. At the moment of this irreplaceable disaster, the plan of battle was rapidly and successfully executed under his immediate eye and lead on the right. For want of a common superior to the different commands on that part of the field, great delay occurred after this misfortune, and that delay prevented the consummation of the work so gallantly and successfully begun and carried on, until the approach of night induced our new commander to recall the exhausted troops for rest and recuperation. . . .

Bragg also later argued that without Johnston's personal leadership at the front, his trademark aggressiveness, and zeal for total victory, a sickly Beauregard, ensconced at the rear, lost control of the battlefield. Beauregard was no Johnston, and so allowed the Union Army a reprieve by not finishing off the base camp at Pittsburg Landing—with tragic results for the ultimate fate of the Confederacy itself. Johnston, Bragg maintained, alone had mustered the army and insisted on the fight—and alone could have brought his plans to fruition:

> Had the first shot of the 5th, on the skirmish line, killed Sidney Johnston, the battle of Shiloh would not have been fought and won by the Confederates. Had the fatal shot which struck him down on the 6th not been fired, Grant and his forces would have been destroyed or captured before sundown, and Buell would never have crossed the Tennessee.

Almost every ranking Confederate veteran of Shiloh, except Beauregard, seconded Bragg's assessment. Sherman himself acknowledged that he detected a slackening of intensity from his vantage point at about the time Johnston fell. General Gibson, after swearing that the Confederate Army had plenty of light and was ready to charge the Union camp, focused on Beauregard's failure to finish off Grant's camp:

> My conviction is that, had Johnston survived, the victory would have been complete, and his army would have planted the standard of the Confederacy on the banks of the Ohio. General Johnston's death was a tremendous catastrophe. There are no words adequate to express my own conception of the immensity of the loss to our country. Sometimes the hopes of millions of people depend upon one head and one arm. The West perished with Albert Sidney Johnston, and the Southern country followed.

Gen. J. F. Gilmer summed up the consensus best in a letter to Albert Sidney Johnston's son, "It is my well-considered opinion that, if your father had survived the day, he would have crushed and captured General Grant's army before the setting of the sun on the 6th. In fact, at the time your father received the mortal wound advancing with General Breckenridge's command, the day was ours."

Gen. Basil W. Duke sketched out even larger counterfactual claims had Johnston survived, alleging that his victorious army would subsequently have been invincible after Shiloh:

> The army remaining upon the banks of the Tennessee for a few days, would have been reorganized and recovered from the exhausting effects of the battle. The slightly wounded, returning to the ranks, would have made the muster-role full thirty thousand effectives. Price and Van Dorn, coming with about fifteen thousand, and the levies from all quarters which were hastening to Corinth, would have given General Johnston nearly sixty thousand men.

As the tradition of a stolen victory grew, former critics of Johnston reexamined his generalship before and during Shiloh and found the posthumous hero for the first time blameless! It was Beauregard, not Johnston, who had made the critical errors. A jittery Beauregard had opposed fighting on the first day at Shiloh; now it was Beauregard who had insisted on the clumsy attack with three successive lines, an impractical formation that had delayed bringing on the battle by a critical day; and Beauregard had ignored Johnston's original orders of outflanking the Union left and cutting them off from the Tennessee River, by instead pouring men against Sherman on the enemy right.

Nor, the revisionists argued, was Johnston to blame for the prior catastrophe in the West. Even the earlier losses of Fort Henry and Fort Donelson, and the precipitous surrender of Nashville, were hardly due to any error on Johnston's part. General Tighman had been lax in his preparations at Fort Henry. Generals Buckner, Floyd, and Pillow had cowardly given Donelson away—despite plentiful arms, provisions, and men, and a proven record of repelling the Union besiegers. Especially regrettable were the fifteen thousand frontline Confederates needlessly surrendered at Donelson, veterans who a few weeks later could have turned the tide at Shiloh.

Johnston's plans to defend Tennessee, recapture Kentucky, and keep the Mississippi secure were in fact inspired; his subordinates' were not. The proof of the pudding was in the eating: on Johnston's first chance to command himself, he had almost single-handedly and unnoticed created a massive force of resistance at Corinth, Mississippi; brought it in secret to within yards of the Union Army; and then in some eight and a half hours nearly destroyed the illustrious Ulysses S. Grant before falling to a chance wound from a spent bullet. Gen. Richard Taylor, son of President Zachary Taylor, concluded, "Albert Sidney Johnston was the foremost man of all the South; and had it been possible for one heart, one mind, and one arm, to save her cause, she lost them when he fell on the field of Shiloh."

But the belief in the Lost Opportunity soon grew well beyond the circle of Southern generals, for it tapped something inherent in the Southern psyche itself: despite the guns and numbers of the North, the courage of Southern soldiers and the genius of their generals really could have nullified the odds—if only fate had not intervened. Thus the Lost Opportunity of Shiloh spread widely, especially in the decade and a half between 1866 and 1880 when defeated and impoverished Southerners latched onto any explanation to make sense of their present humiliating predicament. A year after the war, Edward Pollard, a Virginia newspaper editor, published *The Lost Cause* and wrote of Johnston's death at Shiloh, "Alas! The story of Shiloh was to be that not only of another lost opportunity for the South, but one of a reversion of fortune, in which a splendid victory changed into something very like a defeat!"

To accept the reality that the Southern elite had waged a precipitous and unwise war—one poorly conducted against a far stronger, far larger, and far wealthier industrial nation, fought with limited resources in defense of African slavery—would have been an admission of either rashness, amorality, or abject stupidity. Far easier it was to praise Southern manhood and blame fate. So Pollard concluded his *Lost Cause*: "Civil wars, like private quarrels, are likely to repeat themselves, where the unsuccessful party has lost the contest only through accident or inadvertence. The Confederates have gone out of this war, with the proud, secret, deathless, *dangerous* consciousness that they are THE BETTER MEN, and there was nothing wanting but a change in a set of circumstances. . . ."

Fewer still wished to acknowledge that the Union had, in fact, adopted a brilliant strategy of blockading Confederate ports, tying Lee down in Virginia, splitting the South asunder at the Mississippi, and turning Sherman loose behind the lines—resulting in the invasion and complete conquest of a country the size of Western Europe within just four years. The North not merely had defeated the Confederacy on the battlefield and obliterated her military forces, but also had killed one-quarter of her white men between age 20 and 40, cut down a fourth of her officers—many of them in the high echelons of Southern aristocracy—and completely ruined her economy. Rarely in the annals of military history has one power so utterly demolished its adversary in so short a period.

But to account for an Armageddon rather than mere military defeat, Southern society spread the myth that the moral crusade against the Northern invader was nearly won on the home soil at Shiloh—until Fate and Chance, not Confederate incompetence coupled with Northern skill and multitudes, doomed the Cause. In 1878 an article published in the *Southern Historical Society Papers* argued, "Shiloh was a great misfortune. At the moment of his fall, Sidney Johnston with all the energy of his nature, was pressing on the routed foe. Crouching under the bank of the Tennessee River, Grant was helpless. One short hour more of life to Johnston would have completed his destruction."

Johnston's son, in a widely read biography of his father written in 1879, seventeen years after Shiloh—*The Life of Albert Sidney Johnston: Embracing His Service in the Armies of the United States, The Republic of Texas, and The Confederate States*—displayed how attractive the myth of the Lost Opportunity had now become. Writing of the failure to attack immediately after the fall of the Hornet's Nest, William Preston Johnston waxed eloquently about what might have been.

> All was shattered by one word. "On!" would have made it history; but the commanding general said, "Retire." Oh, the power of a general-in-chief. It was all over. That bloody field was to mean nothing in all time but a slain hero, and 25,000 soldiers stretched upon a bloody field—and another day of purposeless slaughter with broken bands of desperate men mangling and slaying to no visible end in all God's plan of setting up the right. The great forest tract was sinking into darkness, stained, trampled, and echoing with groans. But the victory—its very hope—was gone. "They had watered their horses in the Tennessee River," but, when he fell who spoke the word, the prediction had lost its meaning.

As the specter of a humiliating Reconstruction spread, the myth grew from Johnston's death causing the loss of the single battle Shiloh to being responsible for the *entire* Confederate defeat itself! Jefferson Davis, ever eager to justify secession and his own mediocre direction of the resistance, was to maintain to the end of his life that Johnston's tragic demise had lost his Confederacy: "When Sidney Johnston fell, it was the turning-point of our fate; for we had no other hand to take up his work in the West." As early as 1866, Johnston's home state of Texas rallied to Davis's notion that their adopted son had nearly won Shiloh before falling at the head of his men—and thus in a few seconds doomed the Confederate cause. A joint resolution of the Texas legislature passed in 1866, a year after the conclusion of the war, remarked of the battle fought four years earlier:

> In the saddle, with the harness of a warrior on, the chieftain met the inevitable messenger of Fate. The pitiless musket-ball that pierced him spilled the noblest blood of the South. When he fell, all was from that moment lost! Victory no longer perched on our flag. Less competent hands guided the strife, and a genius of lesser might ruled in his stead. . . . From the fatal hour when the life-blood of the gallant Johnston moistened the earth—from that hour, sir, may be dated that long series of disasters, relieved, it is true, by heroic effort, and brightened from time to time by brilliant but barren victories—but reaching, nevertheless, through the darkness of successive campaigns, until the southern Cross descended forever amid the wall of a people's agony behind the clouds upon the banks of the Appomattox.

Grant himself at last grew tired of such speculation. In his *Memoirs*, published in 1885, he scoffed:

> Some of these critics claim that Shiloh was won when Johnston fell, and that if he had not fallen the army under me would have been annihilated or captured. *Ifs* defeated the Confederates at Shiloh. There is little doubt that we would have been disgracefully beaten

if all the shells and bullets fired by us had passed harmlessly over the enemy and *if* all of theirs had taken effect.

Had any others of the notable Confederate generals fallen at Shiloh—Bragg, Beauregard, Hardee, or Polk—few would have claimed any monumental significance in their deaths. But Albert Sidney Johnston was a different case altogether—an ideal subject for mythmaking for a variety of reasons that went well beyond his special status as supreme commander of the Confederate forces at Shiloh.

First was the manner of Johnston's death. In very significant ways both its timing and nature lent credibility to the idea that a great Southern hero was within minutes of ensuring the lasting victory of the cause. Johnston seemed to have expired almost magically. Unlike the thousands of Shiloh dead who went into the night screaming, with ghastly holes to the head and intestines, or lingering for hours with entire limbs blown apart, Albert Sidney Johnston's wound was nearly invisible and almost instantaneously lethal—no suffering, disfigurement, or last-minute moaning. Few of the Shiloh dying in the arms of friends were politely asked in their last minutes on earth if they were wounded, only equally solicitously to answer, "Yes, and I fear seriously." Albert Sidney Johnston left the living at Shiloh with dignity, both spiritually and in the flesh. The circumstances of his end only cemented a previous reputation for innate humanity and courage; he had truly earned an immaculate demise through near divine dispensation.

Unlike Beauregard or Grant, Johnston was not merely at the immediate rear; he was, like Sherman, at Ground Zero of the killing. At this early juncture in the war, Lee and Jackson were not yet in the pantheon of Southern heroes. Johnston was better known than both and was considered until the weeks before Shiloh the savior of the Confederate cause. His miraculous escape from Federal agents to join the Confederacy in a long trek from California to Texas was already the stuff of legend. That he had not fought in a major engagement only fueled the fable: no one could deny that, when he fell, Johnston was winning his first and last battle against enormous odds.

Moreover, Southerners in general had special empathy for cavaliers, and so the idea that the ranking general of the entire Confederate Army would fall while mounted, leading his men against fixed positions, was seen as an especially heroic demise, one that likewise tended to overshadow all of Johnston's prior difficult six months. Pericles, after all, two and a half millennia earlier, had told a grieving Athenian crowd that a soldier's heroic death tended to wash away all of a man's prior shortcomings. By some accounts, Johnston's last charge of his life was the most successful—the wizened general, resplendent in black hat with nodding plume perched on the magnificent, Kentucky-bred Fire-eater. In contrast, had he been decapitated by a cannonball in a sea of shredded horseflesh as his men fled, failure coupled with grotesqueries would have been fatal to the creation of the Johnston romance.

There was also a certain logic to the simplistic Confederate assessment (everything good at Shiloh while he lived, everything bad after he died). Beauregard, remember, sent a telegram claiming in the late afternoon of the first day that the South had obtained a great victory. True, most disinterested students of the battle have made the case that Johnston wasted precious hours in vain assaults against the Hornet's Nest that depleted Southern manpower and made the final assault on Pittsburg Landing impossible. And they have argued that while Johnston may well have ordered a twilight attack had he lived, it would most likely have been disastrous—given Grant's concentration of batteries, gunboats, condensed lines, and the general Confederate exhaustion and confusion at dusk. Consequently, it was Albert Sidney Johnston's good fortune to have perished quite literally at the Confederate high tide of the battle, before a sober realization had set in that already by midafternoon thousands in his army were dead, wounded, missing, or straggling, and that those left were probably too few and too tired either to finish off Grant's army or survive the inevitable Northern counterattack to come. His previous eight and a half hours of fighting had not cracked the Union Army when he perished—and this ordeal proved that Union morale was not shattered, but often as resolute as the Confederates'.

Second, key to the growing legend was Albert Sidney Johnston's demeanor and unshakable sense of honor and fairness—attested to well before his death during a lifetime of service for the United States, the Republic of Texas, and the Confederacy. In the bleak weeks before Shiloh, Johnston himself took full responsibility for a series of Southern disasters. When told by his staff that he was unjustly being attacked by the Southern press for his subordinates' loss of Forts Henry and Donelson and the evacuation of Nashville, Johnston reported to Jefferson Davis, "With the people there is but one test of merit in my profession, that of success. It is a hard rule, but I think it is right." Because the lesser ranked Beauregard arrived at Corinth with greater forces than those under Johnston, he selflessly offered him command of the entire Southern army at Shiloh. Beauregard later wrote, "I positively declined, on his account and that of the 'cause,' telling him that I had come to assist, not to supersede him, and offering to give him all assistance in my power. He then concluded to remain in command. It was one of the most affecting scenes of my life."

Although his earlier career had been marked, like Grant's and Sherman's, with a string of professional and financial failures, Johnston had a well-known propensity to be magnanimous and charitable. He had resigned from the army to nurse his ailing first wife as she died from tuberculosis, and for a time attempted to raise his two children in isolation on a Missouri farm. His decade of politicking in Texas was characterized by repeated rejections of offers to run for state political offices. Despite distinguishing himself in the Black Hawk and Mexican Wars, his seeming lack of careerist ambition meant that he was without major commands until well into middle age. His dreary tenure as a Federal paymaster on the Texas frontier was known chiefly for his courage and honesty in safeguarding the transit of thousands of dollars—but offered little chance for acclaim or advancement. In the meantime his unattended plantation in Texas was nearing bankruptcy. When he was asked to lead an expedition against the Mormons in late 1857, Johnston led Federal forces safely through horrendous winter conditions, hostile Indians, and suspicious Mormons, and then avoided a shooting war through firm but reasoned patrolling outside Salt Lake City.

When the Civil War broke out, Johnston was the United States military commander of the Western theater, stationed in California. Some rumors circulated that he might be offered command of all Federal forces in the field. Yet he did not resign his commission until Texas had at last seceded from the Union—and then he refused to use his position in California to transfer Federal arms to Southern sympathizers. His "escape" to Texas across the deserts of the Southwest was a feat of courage and endurance, more so in that he deliberately sought to avoid conflict with Federal pursuers.

In short, the fifty-nine-year-old Johnston had a wealth of friends and contacts but had found almost no money or fame—suggesting that he had never used his offices for personal profit or notoriety. He was as well respected as Lee, but came across with a frontier accessibility and charm that was without aristocratic distance and formality. Southerners from all classes and regions—Johnston was born of New England parents, grew up in Kentucky, was educated for a time in the North, and lived variously in Missouri, Louisiana, and Texas—were enamored with him despite his propensity to resign jobs, lose money, fail in farming, and pass up promising political and military advancements. Just as martyrdom would later fit well with the pious Stonewall Jackson, and the nobility of the Lost Cause would characterize the long-suffering and noble Lee, so the Lost Opportunity found birth with the much admired Albert Sidney Johnston, in a way impossible with the others at Shiloh—the somewhat shady Nathan Bedford Forrest, the martinet Braxton Bragg, or the vainglorious Beauregard.

Third was Johnston's intimate relationship with Jefferson Davis, who did much to protect his own record of ineptness by later attributing Confederate setbacks to the tragic loss of Johnston at Shiloh. On Johnston's death, Davis announced to the Confederate Congress, "Without doing injustice to the living, it may safely be said that our loss is irreplaceable." The two had known each other since adolescence when they were roommates in the medical school at Transylvania University in Lexington, Kentucky, in 1821, been familiar at West Point, and subsequently served together during the Black Hawk War of 1832 and then again at Monterrey, Mexico, during the successful American invasion. Davis, as secretary of war in 1855, had appointed Johnston as a colonel and commander of the 2nd United States Cavalry Regiment stationed in Texas. On the eve of the Civil War, when Johnston arrived in Richmond after his miraculous escape from California, Davis made him full general and commander of all Confederate forces in the West, outranking Joe Johnston, Beauregard, and Robert E. Lee. "I hoped and expected that I had others who would prove generals; but I knew I had one, and that was Sidney Johnston," Davis wrote, when he learned that Johnston had left Federal service and joined the Confederacy.

There was no doubt that Davis also stuck by Johnston out of long friendship and genuine confidence in his abilities. Shiloh, in Davis's eyes, confirmed his original trust, proved his sniping critics wrong about Johnston, and of course became the subsequent basis for explaining away much of his own later ruinous conduct of the war. Because the postbellum Davis was an accomplished polemicist, prolific and long-lived, the Lost Opportunity at Shiloh garnered an important voice. Hours before he passed away, Davis still insisted to the end that he had to finish his memoirs and provide more detail about the noble character of his idol, Albert Sidney Johnston. Had Beauregard perished in Johnston's place at Shiloh, it is more than likely that Davis would have remained silent about the consequences of his demise. Indeed, he probably would have been relieved that his flamboyant subordinate was at last gone.

A fourth reason for Johnston's apotheosis was his own genius at repartee and impromptu speech, especially appreciated in a romantic society that valued wit and elegance. An entire corpus of Johnston's aphorisms survives from his few hours at Shiloh. Many draw allusions from classical literature and reflect his earlier education—he read Latin well enough—and his love of dramatic adages. In the minutes before the battle, legend had it that he rode across the army yelling, "Look along your guns, and fire low." When the first shots were heard overhead, Johnston calmly remarked, "Note the hour, if you please, gentlemen." And as the army approached the battlefield, he shouted to his staff, "Tonight we will water our horses in the Tennessee River." To Colonel Marmaduke, he shouted, "My son, we must this day conquer or perish!"—perhaps a spin on King Leonidas's admonition to his Spartans at Thermopylae that on the evening of the battle's last day they would dine in Hades. A few minutes later he advised General Hindman, "You have earned your spurs as Major-General. Let this day's work win them." As he rode down the line before the initial charge, he paused at the Arkansas contingent: "Men of Arkansas! They say you boast of your prowess with the bowie-knife. Today you wield a nobler weapon—the bayonet. Employ it well."

More formally, his last proclamation before the battle resembled something from Napoleon or perhaps an oration from Caesar's *Gallic* or *Civil Wars*, with its references to family, honor, and the homeland:

With the resolution and discipline and valor becoming men fighting, as you are, for all worth living or dying for, you can but march to a decisive victory over the agrarian mercenaries sent to subjugate you and to despoil you of your liberties, your property, and your honor. Remember the precious stake involved; remember the dependence of your mothers, your wives, your sisters, and your children, on the result; remember the fair, broad, abounding land, and the happy homes that would be desolated by your defeat. The eyes and hopes of eight millions of people rest upon you; you are expected to show yourselves worthy of your lineage, worthy of the women of the South, whose noble devotion in this war has never been exceeded in any time.

In the moments before he was killed, he shouted to his officers, "Those fellows are making a stubborn stand here. I'll have to put the bayonet to them." Earlier in the morning he had rebuked an officer burdened with Union booty: "None of that, sir; we are not here for plunder!" Then taking up a worthless tin cup, he added, "Let this be my share of the spoils today." Perhaps his last words to the rank and file were, "I will lead you." Unlike the unlettered Forrest or the pretentious Beauregard, Johnston revealed a noble eloquence in speech that had the effect of remaining with Confederates for decades after Shiloh—and thus also contributed to the foundation of the martyred hero.

Yet a fifth contributing factor to the miraculous reinvention of Johnston was his physical beauty and rugged physique, which characterized every contemporary description of the general. More than any other commander, North or South, the imposing Johnston looked the part of a general. He had none of the foreboding massive brow of Bragg, nor the dapper almost effeminate appearance of the diminutive Beauregard—much less the suspect shabbiness of the dour Grant and nervous Sherman. As elegant as Lee, he lacked the former's sense of frailty, and possessed the physicality of Forrest without his sinister stare. Rather at six feet two inches, 200 pounds, and square-jawed, he appeared the epitome of Southern manhood.

Contemporary descriptions, while hagiographic, nevertheless reiterate that common consensus. Veteran of Shiloh Colonel Munford wrote that Johnston "was tall, square-shouldered, full-chested, and muscular. He was neither lean nor fat, but healthily full, without grossness, indicating great bodily strength. His bust was superb, the neck and head mounting upward from the shoulder with majestic grace." After continuing with a detailed description of Johnston's mustache, chin, nose, forehead, eyes, skin, and posture, he summarized Johnston as looking near-divine. Munford claimed that while mounted, Johnston was "centaur-like" as if his horse "had grown up part of him."

Nor were such encomia mere postbellum mythmaking. Well before the war, on the eve of his Mormon command, the Northern *Harper's Weekly* reported:

> Colonel Johnston is now in the mature vigor of manhood. He is above six feet in height, strongly and powerfully formed, with a grave, dignified, and commanding presence. His features are strongly marked, showing his Scottish lineage, and denote great resolution and composure of character. His complexion, naturally fair, is, from exposure, a deep brown. His habits are abstemious and temperate, and no excess has impaired his powerful constitution. His mind is clear, strong, and well cultivated.

Later, another contemporary of the general confirmed the view:

> General Johnston reminded us of the pictures of Washington. He was very large and massive in figure, and finely proportioned. He measured six feet two inches in height, and had flesh to give him perfect symmetry. His face was large, broad, and high, and beamed with a look of striking benignity. His features were handsomely molded. He was very straight, and carried himself with grace and lofty and simple dignity. . . . His whole appearance indicated, in a marked degree, power, decision, serenity, thought, benevolence. We thought him then at first flush, and thought it unvaryingly afterward, and think now, in the hallowing memory of his noble manhood, made sacred by the consecration of his thrilling and heroic death for the Southern cause, that he was one of the sweetest and most august men we ever met. His character was enhanced by pure nobility. We thought him an object of deep veneration; and, whenever we look at the familiar and majestic features of the great *Pater Patriae*, we always think of Albert Sidney Johnston.

Like Washington, Johnston looked the part of a heroic general. His appearance complimented the majestic manner of his death, his long career, and his nobility in speech, thus also contributing to the spread of the myth of the Lost Opportunity.

After the initial hysteria over the losses of Forts Henry and Donelson waned, Southerners began to appreciate—and more often exaggerate—Johnston's almost single-handed efforts to force the issue at Shiloh. He alone had marshaled the army. He had overridden the objections of Beauregard, who panicked on the eve before Shiloh and urged a general withdrawal. In words reminiscent of Don Juan on the eve of Lepanto, who had similarly quashed the prebattle jitters of his generals with a brief admonition, Johnston, it was said, broke up the late-night parley with, "Gentlemen, we shall attack at daylight tomorrow."

In reply to worries about Grant combining with Buell before he could attack either, he was said to have remarked to Colonel Preston, "I would fight them if they were a million." Moments before the firing started, Johnston broke up yet another meeting of his wavering generals with, "The battle has opened, gentlemen; it is too late to change our dispositions." And when Johnston learned of the inability of his poorly trained divisions to form up in Beauregard's clumsy three-line plan of attack, he scoffed, "This is perfectly puerile. This is not war!"

The Johnston legend had both immediate and long-term effects on the Southern acceptance of their own dilemma. Few appreciated in the weeks after Shiloh that with the loss of Kentucky and Tennessee, the Mississippi was ultimately defenseless to a relentless and determined man like Grant. He, along with Sherman and quite unlike other Federal generals, thought in terms of strategic conquests rather than tactical victories. Southerners seemed blind to the fact that the grubby-looking pair—complete failures in antebellum civilian life—cared little for manners or tradition, or the gentlemanly conduct of war. Both instead counted heads and bullets, and then in tandem planned to kill off and wreck as much Southern manpower and capital as their ever-growing resources would allow under the guidance and sanction of a realist like Lincoln, who lived in a pragmatic universe very different from the mythic realm of Jefferson Davis. There was rarely a serious and sober Confederate assessment that concluded with the depressing truth that vast advantages in manpower, supplies, political leadership, and talent among generals gave the North an insurmountable edge in the West—and that ultimately the war was to be won or lost there. No Southerner ever thought to ask why an entire people might believe that their own salvation hinged on the survival of a single near-sixty-year-old man like Johnston, who had never led a large army into battle.

The death of the general that created the Lost Opportunity fed into the even more attractive—and far more pernicious—Lost Cause, or the larger Southern notion that a tragic mishap had ruined a majestic Confederacy, not the vast superiority of Union arms, soldiers, trained officers, and the moral edge of eliminating rather than championing slavery. Instead, losing for a noble crusade of self-defense was seen as morally preferable to using industrial might to devastate an outnumbered enemy. The postbellum emphasis on Johnston's character, appearance, and witticisms was entirely in line with this even larger mistaken credo that in the Civil War, chivalry, traditional gallantry, and heroic romanticism should have meant something for the "better men" in a contest against the likes of the rough-looking Lincoln and his equally odious and suspect pair of Grant and Sherman. The former calculated his edge in men and matériel, and then systematically wore down Lee, while the latter envisioned a new war that had nothing to do with battlefield heroics but everything to do with economic power, food, transportation, and the heart of a nation's spiritual and psychological resistance. Southerners apparently found comfort that their martyred Johnston was a better looking, kinder, more mature, and gentlemanly commander than anyone the North might offer—as if all that should have somehow translated into military advantage in a new war of the machine age.

The tragedy of Albert Sidney Johnston dying "at the moment of victory" at Shiloh established a dangerous precedent, and was soon followed by the corollary of Stonewall Jackson being accidentally shot at the climax of Chancellorsville, therein robbing Lee of his "right arm" in the weeks ahead at Gettysburg and allowing a dilatory Longstreet to "lose the war" on Gettysburg's second day. Ultimately, the embrace of such "second day" scenarios, where victory won was turned into defeat only by a chance event along with a predictable refrain of "almost," "what if," and "if only," made it difficult for the postbellum South to accept, or perhaps even understand, the verdict of the

Civil War—with unfortunate ramifications for the ensuing century. Since chattel slavery was outlawed at war's end and the Union restored, the South often took refuge in the Lost Cause myth that the war had been fought solely over the remaining disagreement and principled issue of states' rights. The perceived harshness of Reconstruction only added a patina of victimhood: with the Union reunited and all Americans free, what more did the North really want from a prostrate South?

Central to that fable of an aggrieved better people suffering for their principles was the requisite military side of the equation: the Lost Opportunity that in postbellum analyses of defeat swept away all rational social, economic, and military considerations and substituted instead the gallantry and genius of a few irreplaceable Southerners at a few key minutes. If the South, but for fate, could have defeated the North militarily, then perhaps its Cause was the more just after all. Yet if Confederate survival really was contingent on one landmark event, then a single Nathan Bedford Forrest put in independent command of a large army—something easily in the prerogative of Jefferson Davis—would have had far greater consequences on the war's outcome than the tragic death of Johnston at Shiloh. But that "what if" of not utilizing Forrest properly involved the institutionalized stupidity that actually transpired rather than the romance that did not. Albert Sidney Johnston created a vast ripple at Shiloh that had a marked effect not only on the Civil War, but upon Southern culture itself. Yet it had far more to do with what was imagined than with what really did happen at 2:30 in the afternoon of April 6, 1862.

Albert Sidney Johnston and the Lost Opportunity still survive today. The last page of Wiley Sword's well-researched and sober history of the battle, *Shiloh: Bloody April*, nevertheless ends with the death of Albert Sidney Johnston: "Like Johnston's lifeblood, the Southern Confederacy's hopes also began to ebb rapidly following the momentous events of Shiloh." Nor is the Lost Opportunity confined to texts alone. Frederick C. Hubbard, sculptor of the Confederate monument at the battlefield, explained how he tried to couple the fall of the angelic Johnston with the accompanying ruin of the entire Confederate cause. "My underlying idea was to have the monument represent Victory defeated by Death and Night. Death took away General Johnston, and Night ended the battle just when Victory was in sight. The woman in the center, who represents the Confederacy, reluctantly relinquishes to Night and Death the wreath of Victory she holds in her hand."

Albert Sidney Johnston in a single second at Shiloh had at last become something in death that for all his labors he had never been in life. And so the general who in the flesh had delivered not a single victory for his beloved Southerners, brought to their minds the everlasting reassurance that they had never really been beaten at all. Many today would still agree.

Evening: *Ben-Hur*

Albert Sidney Johnston's death at 2:30 P.M. had stunned but not stopped the Confederate juggernaut—at least not yet. When the last defenders inside the Hornet's Nest were finally overwhelmed by late afternoon, the Union Army had less than a third of its original strength—about ten thousand exhausted men—still on the battlefield. In fact, by evening Grant's army spanned not much more than a semicircle of a few thousand yards surrounding the base at Pittsburg Landing. Where, a nervous Grant wondered, was Gen. Lew Wallace and the seven thousand men of his reserve 3rd Division?

That very morning on his way up the Tennessee River to Shiloh, Grant had stopped to warn Wallace at Crump's Landing to be prepared to support his engaged army. But Grant's verbal orders to Wallace from his gunboat *Tigress* at about 8:00 A.M. were given at least two hours *after* Sherman had first been attacked. Only when Grant himself finally arrived at Shiloh and saw the state of his crumbling armies did he send a second, stronger message back to Crump's Landing sometime around midmorning: Wallace was immediately to march his division the six miles south to Shiloh and join the rest of the Army of the Tennessee.

That hurried summons must have reached Wallace sometime around 11:30 in the morning—several hours after his restless men had first heard the firing. Had Wallace departed at once, Grant later surmised, he should have been on line and pouring in critical reinforcements by 2:00 P.M.—at precisely the time that the Northern center and left came under the most intense attack by Albert Sidney Johnston. But when Wallace failed to show up on the battlefield in the early afternoon, Grant sent another desperate message to no avail. He finally dispatched his most trusted subordinates, Colonel McPherson and Captain Rawlins, to ride over and personally escort Wallace along the river road to the killing fields.

But when the two messengers made it back to Grant, they brought back incredible tales of wrong roads, time-consuming countermarching, and cumbersome wagons and caissons. Wallace was no nearer Shiloh than when he had started, and thus Grant's battle was about to be lost without help! The Union commander was completely dumbfounded: it was now near dark, indeed well past 7:00 P.M.; his army was nearly annihilated—and thousands of his critical reserves mysteriously had disappeared a mere few miles from the battlefield! Where exactly had Lew Wallace taken his men?

Grant had reason to be worried. He had been caught unaware at Shiloh. On the morning of April 6 he was miles downstream at his headquarters to the north in Savannah, Tennessee, and without a clue that Johnston's enormous Confederate army had surprised his unprepared divisions. Now his forces had been retreating all day. Nearly half his regiments were no longer in existence. Hundreds of his men were dying. Many were shot down while running away. Rumors circulated that Union soldiers had been bayoneted in their sleep. Without reinforcements he was likely to lose the first great pitched battle of the war in the West—and with it his own future in the Union Army. Although he had sent word to General Buell on the other side of the Tennessee River to march immediately with his supporting 20,000-man Army of the Ohio, Grant was not convinced that those critical divisions could cover the five miles to the river, be ferried across, and fall in line before his own army collapsed. And an earlier midafternoon advance meeting with a grumpy General Buell had not given him confidence about getting any salvation from that quarter.

There was also bad blood between the Armies of the Tennessee and the Ohio. Both generals knew that their near-independent commands within the Western theater were impractical and could not last. The older Buell resented the astonishing rise of the younger and once obscure Grant after his victories at Forts Henry and Donelson. And his doubts about his reckless rival were now apparently confirmed as he crossed the river at about 1:00 P.M. for a preliminary inspection of the growing mess at Pittsburg Landing. What he saw was shocking: thousands from Grant's shattered army cowering in fright under the cliffs next to the water, apparently after running pell-mell from the battlefield. Terrified men yelled out, "We're whipped! The fight is lost! We're cut to pieces!"

If the now smug Buell were to be late with his twenty thousand men, Grant would be finished both at Shiloh and for good. Yet if the Army of the Ohio pranced in that evening to stave off a Confederate victory, the salvation of the first day's disaster at Shiloh might be Buell's alone. Some even wondered whether Buell was worried about putting his men at the rear of a collapsing army with the river at their backs—throwing good men after bad as it were—and thus despaired he just might not cross the Tennessee in time after all. In any case, the roads from Buell's headquarters to the west bank of the river opposite Grant were in terrible shape. That meant no reinforcements until the evening at the earliest. So now Grant desperately turned to Lew Wallace, his own division commander, to march the six miles from Crump's Landing and save the tottering Army of the Tennessee.

Yet Grant had problems with Lew Wallace as well. At thirty-five he was the youngest general in the Union Army. Wallace was a political appointee without much military experience and no formal training at West Point, who nevertheless was enjoying a meteoric career of his own, beginning with proven gallantry at Bull Run. As a major general, in theory he had no real superiors in rank. The dashing Wallace also had a tendency to be theatrical. At Fort Donelson he had magnified his role to reporters and claimed key responsibility for much of Grant's victory. He bragged to his wife, "I saved the whole army from rout."

Among the West Point generals, the amateur but cocky Wallace was hardly popular, due to his innate talent as well as his self-serving dispatches to reporters, his airs of intellectual superiority—he was said to write and paint—and his hypersensitivity to any perceived slight. Recently in his official report concerning the fighting at Fort Donelson, Wallace had left out mention of two of Grant's personal aides, who were furious about the oversight.

Who knew where the flamboyant Wallace had gone, Grant steamed. It was nearing nightfall, nearly seven hours after his first message must have reached Crump's Landing, a mere six miles away—and still no Wallace!

If Shiloh resurrected the professional life of a down-and-out Gen.

William Tecumseh Sherman and ended the worldly existence of Albert Sidney Johnston, it simply ruined the army career of an ascendant Gen. Lewis Wallace. In fact, April 6 would turn out to be the worst day in Lew Wallace's long life. At dawn he was confused, by early morning somewhat annoyed, and now in later afternoon incensed.

It was bad enough that when the battle started, his battle-ready division was left isolated and without communications, guarding the army's supplies down the Tennessee River at Crump's Landing. Now with the sound of fire a few miles away, it was apparently to be held in reserve and out of the fighting altogether. At 8:00 A.M. a shocked Grant had steamed by Crump's Landing on his way to the battle without even disembarking to give Wallace any clear-cut directions. He had merely yelled to Wallace on the deck of his riverboat to get his division ready should the early morning sounds of firing turn out to be a real battle:

"Well, hold yourself in readiness to march upon orders received."

A disappointed Wallace answered, "But, general, I ordered a concentration about six o'clock. The division must be at Stoney Lonesome [the point of departure for the inland route to Shiloh]. I am ready now." Grant, Wallace reported later, hesitated and did not take up the offer to order an immediate march. Instead the supreme commander finished with a cursory, "Very well. Hold the division ready to march in any direction." Then he steamed in the *Tigress* on to Shiloh.

Wallace's 3rd Division had heard gunfire at daybreak and been ready to march in that direction for at least two hours prior to Grant's brief appearance. Now it would wait in readiness for *another critical three hours* for further orders—while a mere six miles away Sherman's men were being slaughtered. At 11:30 a Captain Baxter, Grant's quartermaster, finally arrived with the anticipated command to move. But for some reason the commands were not signed. Stranger yet, the orders had simply been poorly copied in pencil on lined paper:

> You will leave a sufficient force at Crump's Landing to guard the public property there; with the rest of the division march and form junction with the right of the army. Form line of battle at right angle with the river, and be governed by circumstances.

After asking Baxter a few more details about the murky, unsigned orders, Wallace was wrongly told that the Union forces were "repulsing the enemy"—when, in fact, the Union Army was in retreat!

It was now nearly noon. Wallace quickly was forced to make a decision about these strange ad hoc mandates from his commander. Did his superiors realize that there were not one, but *two* roads to Shiloh? True, the one course along the Tennessee River was the quickest to Grant's base at Pittsburg Landing. But it did *not* end up at the "right" of the Union Army, where Wallace thought he had been ordered to deploy his reserves. And in many places that river path was swampy, nearly impassable for wagons and caissons, and indeed sometimes underwater altogether. In contrast, the inland route—the so-called Shunpike—led directly to Sherman's right wing. It was also at least two miles shorter to that destination and a much better road. Wallace himself had previously repaired and reconnoitered it in the weeks before the battle just for the purpose of reinforcing the Union right wing should a crisis arise.

So now Wallace wondered about this vague order scrawled on ordinary ruled paper: was he to take the shortest route to Grant's camp or the most direct way to the right wing of Grant's army? After all, he had positioned his army at Stoney Lonesome in between the two roads to be prepared to depart to Shiloh in either direction. Was he to march thousands of men and their guns along a partly submerged road or over a route he had previously corduroyed and knew to be passable? Was he to arrive to join a victorious army in pursuit, as Baxter had (wrongly) implied, or to save a defeated force from annihilation? Which leg of the triangle was he to follow to its base of the Union battle line?

Wallace gave his men a mere half hour to eat. At noon he ordered them to set out to Shiloh along the *inland* route to join Sherman's right wing: "So, to save the two and three-quarter miles," Wallace wrote of his fatal choice, "and because it was nearer the right and in better condition, I decided to go by the Shunpike." That decision in and of itself changed the life of General Wallace and ensured that the Union Army could *not* win the battle outright on the first day.

Be this as it may, Wallace's division was nevertheless making record time along the Shunpike. To Grant he may have been lost and marching along the wrong side of the battlefield, but at least Lew Wallace was getting to Shiloh via the quickest route. In a mere hour and a half the 3rd Division had covered some five miles, and its advance guard was at last set to cross Owl Creek a few thousand yards from Sherman's last reported position. In fact, in terms of ground covered, he had made much better time than any of General Buell's generals, who were still on the wrong side of the Tennessee River. By 2 P.M., Wallace was at last about to send at least five thousand of his men to the Union right when a dispatch rider galloped up from his rear. "General Grant sends his compliments. He would like you to hurry up."

Hurry up? Wallace was dumbfounded. Had he not left on first notice of Grant's order? Was he not as they spoke almost at the battlefield? His army was marching in perfect unison, formed to fall in proper battle array next to General Sherman on the right of the Union battle line as ordered. Wallace dismissed the confused messenger. But then a second rider, a Captain Rowley of Grant's personal staff, brought even worse news: "Where are you going, anyhow?"

"To join Sherman," Wallace answered.

"Sherman! Great God! Don't you know Sherman has been driven back? Why, the whole army is within half a mile of the river, and it's a question if we are not all going to be driven into it."

Instead of coming to the rescue of the Union right wing, Wallace was now on the verge of arriving behind the Confederate Army! "Fortunately for me," Wallace later recalled of his stunned surprise, "the eclipse of my faculties did not last long, and I was able presently to comprehend that, with my division, *I was actually in rear of the whole Confederate army!*"

Why, Rowley wondered, had Wallace taken the inland route when Grant must have told him to march roughly along the river to what was left of the Union base camp? Incredibly, almost in sight of the battlefield, Wallace was now ordered to turn his army completely around, march back up the Shunpike the way he had come, cross over to the river route, and then go back around to Pittsburg Landing! This meant a circular route entailing perhaps another ten miles—in addition to the four to five he had already traveled. "Grant," Rowley exclaimed to Wallace, "wants you at Pittsburg Landing— and he wants you there like hell."

Somehow Grant's earlier unwritten orders had become copied wrongly and perhaps disastrously garbled. Later in the battle's aftermath the commanding general felt sure that he had ordered Wallace explicitly to use the river road and meet him at the Union base camp, a five-mile march that would have had the reserves arrive at Pittsburg Landing sometime around 2 P.M., just prior to the furious charges of Albert Sidney Johnston. As the afternoon wore on and the Union Army crumbled, a desperate Grant was irate that Wallace's reinforcements had not arrived—completely ignorant of the fact that Wallace was nearly already at Shiloh, but out of sight, on the opposite side of the battlefield, and about to march into the enemy's unexpected rear. It was a chance of a lifetime in some sense to send a fresh Union division at the backside of a tired Confederate wing.

Yet Grant later grumbled, "I never could see, and do not now see, why any order was necessary further than to direct him to come to Pittsburg Landing, without specifying by what route. His was one of three veteran divisions that had been in battle, and its absence was severely felt." Grant finished with a sneer, "I presume his idea was that by taking the route he did, he would be able to come around on the flank or rear of the enemy, and thus perform an act of heroism that would rebound to the credit of his command, as well as to the benefit of his company."

A taken-aback Wallace now wondered what to do. In sight of the battlefield, he was without warning ordered to retrace his steps to his original camp miles away and then turn back again to follow a marshy and nearly submerged road. Worse, to keep the proper order of his division, Wallace did not order an about-face, the rear now becoming the front. Rather he countermarched the entire division brigade by brigade! The complicated turning maneuver required a painful delay of nearly an hour as the confused army sorted itself out. Unfortunately, Grant's latest frantic messengers, Colonel McPherson and Captain Rawlins, caught up with Wallace just as he reached the crossroads that morning, and turned to make his way over to the river road—not far from the very spot he had departed over three hours earlier.

Thousands of Union soldiers were wounded and dying, and Lew Wallace's relief division was no closer to the battlefield than when it had first left hours earlier. Grant's panicky messengers demanded that Wallace now abandon his batteries and march his division the rest of the way on the double to Pittsburg Landing. He refused, insisting that his division must arrive fully armed, in close order, and ready for battle. The panicked McPherson and Rawlins rode back in disgust—with wild tales of Wallace's incompetence and insubordination. His army was marching in circles!

Wallace finally arrived at the landing in the rain after dark and groped his way through the mess of Union fugitives, wounded, and dead. No one from Grant's staff even met him; he spent most of the night getting his division to the right of Sherman on the Union's last-ditch circumference. Rawlins later wrote to Grant of his encounter that afternoon with Wallace, when the division had finally turned on to the river route:

> Colonel McPherson and I came up to him about 3:30 o'clock P.M. He was then not to exceed four or four and a half miles from the scene of action; the roads were in fine condition; he was marching light; his men were in buoyant spirits, within hearing of the musketry, and eager to get forward. He did not make a mile and a half an hour, although urged and appealed to, to push forward. Had he moved with the rapidity his command were able and anxious to have moved after we overtook him, he would have reached you in time to have engaged the enemy before the close of Sunday's fight.

To Wallace nothing was further from the truth. The first day of Shiloh had been a complete frustration. He had been ordered far too late to advance to the battlefield. Grant's written orders were unintelligible, poorly copied, and unsigned. A succession of messengers brought contradictory and often inaccurate reports of the fighting. His poor men had been forced to march in a near-circle *over fourteen miles* in a wild goose chase to arrive late at a battlefield a mere six miles away. His army arrived wet, cold, and in the dark—an object of derision rather than celebration.

Grant apparently had no idea that just days before the battle his own division commanders had communicated with each other via the Shunpike and planned to use that route if mutual reinforcements were necessary. Due to Grant's ignorance of the Shunpike, Wallace's division had now marched nearly seven hours and covered over fourteen miles in the worst of conditions—and was still not in line against the Confederates. Even if Grant had wanted him at Pittsburg Landing, Wallace had nevertheless managed hours earlier to approach the opposite end of the battlefield, and was almost close enough to engage the enemy's rear when ordered instead to withdraw, retrace his route, and march closely parallel to the river. Had he been allowed to continue, he might have crossed over the Owl Creek bridge and theoretically could have appeared behind the Confederate Army with 7,000 fresh troops, slowing their assault before the collapse of the Union resistance at the Hornet's Nest. In any case, when he finally arrived at Grant's confused command post at Pittsburg Landing, Wallace was determined to forget the day's fiasco and make amends the next morning.

At 6:30 A.M., Wallace's 3rd Division counterattacked with the rest of the Union army—his fresh 7,000 soldiers and General Buell's 20,000-man Army of the Ohio meant that Grant's army had suddenly doubled in size. Indeed, it now outnumbered the tired Confederates by two to one. Wallace performed adequately on the second day, although his troops were not pitted against the main resistance, suffering only 41 killed and 251 wounded in the steady Union counterattack.

On the evening of the seventh, with the retreat of the Confederate Army, Wallace, as he had at Fort Donelson, once more proclaimed himself a near hero. After all, he and Buell had purportedly turned the tide, lost few men, and chased the rebels off the battlefield. The mixup the day before was quickly forgotten: the now victorious Union Army no doubt would rapidly chase General Beauregard's defeated army back to Corinth, destroy what was left of it, and then storm the city, opening all of Mississippi to the advance of a huge force of nearly 100,000 troops. There would be enough laurels for all involved. Wallace was sure that his own timely reinforcement at Shiloh meant that his division would play a prominent part in the final kill. Two days after battle he was near ecstatic, and wrote his wife, "My whole command behaved like heroes, never yielding an inch."

At first, a relieved nation bought it and agreed that Wallace's appearance on the second day had indeed helped turn the tide. He was featured in national magazines like *Leslie's* and *Harper's Weekly*, which prompted floods of congratulatory letters and gifts from his friends and admirers back home. It was Fort Donelson all over again for the dashing young general. Wallace made no effort to hide his pride, predicting a quick pursuit and, with the destruction of the fleeing Confederates, an early end to the Civil War itself. Yet four days after the battle ended, a strange sequence of events began to unfold that would destroy Wallace's career. And within weeks of Shiloh the purported hero would find himself in disgrace and removed of major command!

Wallace's disaster perhaps began on April 12, with the arrival of the punctilious General Halleck. The latter removed Grant from active control of the Army of the Tennessee, apparently on the grounds that Grant had been negligently surprised at Shiloh. As the new commanding officer of all Western forces, the bookish Halleck was at last ready to lead from the field. Now that the terrible battle was over, he would personally manage the final Union pursuit of the defeated.

Yet Halleck proved disastrous for the Union effort and ruinous for Wallace himself. At first, the plodding Halleck disingenuously boasted that he had been the mastermind of the entire Western campaign and tried to take credit for the strategic victory of Shiloh. Then he faulted Grant for the high casualties of April 6, only to waste weeks in moving his ponderous army a mere thirty miles to Corinth—to find the Confederate Army long gone and the city largely deserted. What was won at Shiloh by Grant was thrown away by Halleck in the days that followed.

Demanding that his generals erect breastworks and fortifications each night, the jittery Halleck often made less than a mile's progress a day—a slow-moving Albert Sidney Johnston had covered the same distance from Corinth to Shiloh in the April rains in little more than three days. Alexander the Great or Julius Caesar had often marched their armies of the preindustrial age thirty miles in less than ten hours. In contrast, Halleck's progress was almost comical, as his huge confident army timidly crept toward a demoralized and numerically inferior beaten force.

The dawdling Union pursuit, the escape of the defeated Confederate Army, the inexplicable removal of a popular Grant, the mounting criticism of the dilatory Halleck, the final tallying of the horrific Union losses at Shiloh—12,217 casualties with over 1,700 killed—all set the stage for months of controversy and mutual recriminations as Shiloh was reexamined as no American battle before. The press and the War Department in Washington seemed to forget that Shiloh was a tactical victory and a strategic bonanza; instead, both demanded heads for the appalling losses and the escape of the defeated Confederates. Shiloh would have been seen as nothing novel by summer 1864; but in spring 1862 the very idea of well over 10,000 casualties in a single engagement was appalling to the Northern populace and demanded punitive measures. Had Halleck destroyed the vulnerable retreating Confederates, the mistakes of April 6 would have been forgotten; instead, the Northern public gradually was told that its youth had been butchered without a sure victory or indeed much discernable change in the immediate strategic picture in the West at large.

Worse still for Wallace, the mounting tension between Halleck and Grant would soon make his own position nearly untenable. After Halleck's laggard generalship eventually led to his transfer back east, Grant by midsummer was returned to command of the Western theater—with the endorsement of Lincoln ("I can't spare this man, he fights"). Although Grant had survived Halleck's efforts to sabotage his career, he was nevertheless still shocked by the fury of public criticism of his conduct at Shiloh among the Northern press and politicians. Especially galling were the often wild charges that he had been absent from the battlefield when the shooting started, may well have been drunk, was completely surprised, had ordered no entrenchments, and thus was responsible for the first day's shocking casualties.

In reaction, slowly Grant directed his wrath onto Wallace and subtly began to suggest a scenario that might account for the near fiasco of the first day: had his orders only been followed by Wallace, the Union losses were entirely avoidable. Seven thousand reinforcements, as he had planned, would have arrived by 2 to 3 P.M. at the latest. Their surprise appearance would have stopped the Confederate onslaught cold. The Hornet's Nest would not have fallen. General Buell's help would not have been necessary. If any general was responsible for the shocking butchery, perhaps it was the young, amateur, and flamboyant Lew Wallace, not himself.

Three other events conspired to aid Grant's defense. First, Halleck, who had come off the worse in his duplicitous efforts to besmear Grant, was wary of tangling further with the hero of Fort Donelson—and was only too happy to join in to deflect Grant's wrath from himself onto Wallace. Thus he would henceforth prove deaf to all of Wallace's appeals for an inquiry into the battle. So too, Sherman, the newfound hero of Shiloh, was not eager to enter the controversy. He also had been surprised the first day and had no wish to reexamine the issue of culpability in any great detail. Moreover, he was now a friend of Grant's and owed his resurrection in part to Grant's support; in turn, Sherman had been instrumental in persuading Grant not to quit after Halleck took command of his army in the battle's aftermath. Neither Halleck nor Sherman then had any desire to defend the mercurial Wallace against a national hero. Wallace somehow had found himself without a friend: of the three most powerful men in the Union Army, two were openly hostile, and one at best neutral.

Third and most grievously, Wallace's own obstreperous character and reckless talk now cemented his demise. In his official report after the battle, Wallace was careful to defend his actions, but in a way that only made Grant look worse, especially through his emphasis that he was not ordered to the battlefield until 11:30 A.M. By whatever route he took, Wallace reasonably pointed out, Grant's initial delay ensured that seven thousand men would miss the critical first eight hours of the fighting. And even if he had taken a route different from what Grant purportedly ordered, his own march was nearly completed and had resulted in placing his army unknown at the enemy's rear—and perhaps poised for a critical counterattack that might have saved the Union forces.

Grant was furious over Wallace's implications, and especially any public suggestions that Wallace had played a key role in the victory when he had missed the tough fighting the first day and lost hardly any men the second. Contradicting his first official report written on April 9 that had praised Generals McClernand and Wallace—both "had maintained their places with credit to themselves and the cause"—most of Grant's numerous later accounts of the battle painted a damning portrait of Wallace's incompetence. In fact, Grant claimed that he had ordered Wallace to move at 11 A.M., not 11:30—and not once but three times! While his official orders were not written but copied by a messenger, his own staff could "vouch" that he had expressly commanded the use of the river route. Furthermore, common sense should have convinced anyone that a Union general in earshot of the fighting should not have marched in circles for seven hours to cover a mere six miles. Grant's final account of the battle, reiterated in his memoirs two decades later, would prove Wallace's undoing.

Wallace's shrill counterefforts only made things worse. Earlier during the Donelson campaign he had attacked Gen. Charles F. Smith, Grant's now-martyred mentor, and took undue credit for the victory. Now in Shiloh's aftermath, he once again complained publicly that General McClernand, his equal in rank, was wrongly given priority of future action. Worse still, he harped to aides of General Halleck that their commander's slowness in pursuing the Confederates threatened to throw away the victory gained at Shiloh—astute though unwise criticism that got back to the hypersensitive Halleck within hours. Wallace soon gained a reputation for troublemaking and second-guessing his West Point betters. Before he knew it, by late June, a mere three months after Shiloh, Wallace found himself back home in Indiana and without a division.

He turned frantic. Desperate to get back into the war, shamed by the sudden reversal of fortune, and near paranoid about the mere suggestion that he was in any way culpable for the hundreds of Union dead on Shiloh's first day, Wallace now became obsessed with clearing his name. He went first to the papers. But his old friends at the *New York Tribune* and the *Cincinnati Gazette* either declined to get involved or offered only meager defenses of a Wallace now out of favor with the powers that be.

He mailed further accounts to Halleck and the War Department in Washington, replete with maps and detailed exegesis. Halleck, ever the intriguer, simply showed them to a furious Grant, who was further irate and responded with more affidavits from his loyal subordinates "proving" Wallace's negligence. Wallace in turn applied to Secretary of War Stanton for a formal court of inquiry. He finally approached Sherman, who at least spoke on his behalf to Grant, but to no avail. Yet Sherman ended up giving Wallace the best advice yet: forget the matter, keep quiet, and hope that an increasingly famous Grant would be magnanimous enough to give him a second chance.

Wallace dropped the formal inquiry but ignored the rest of Sherman's advice, and seemed to think that the momentous events now unfolding in the war were secondary to a proper audit of a battle long past and better put to rest. He now enlisted surrogate apologists in the popular press, as he himself wrote tirelessly for the next ten years to reporters, editors, biographers, and historians in hopes of restoring the proper picture of Shiloh—one sensitive to his own dilemma with Grant and absolving him of any responsibility for the Union dead. He even published a short treatise, "General Wallace's

Military Record," in which he claimed with some exaggeration that Grant himself had always found Wallace "blameless." Unfortunately, Wallace could not help but add that "If my march to the battlefield as I began it had not been countermanded, we would have done more than win a victory the first day—we would have captured a large part of the Confederate Army."

That admission—a boast that in theory might well have been true—undermined Wallace's position in various ways. He now shifted from defense to the attack: Grant's first order that was garbled by subordinates was not the real problem, but rather his subsequent and quite clear commands to reverse Wallace midroute on the Shunpike. The effect was to allege that the soon-to-be President of the United States had thrown away a decisive Union victory. Second, Wallace's brag in turn weakened his earlier defense that he took the Shunpike from a natural desire to join Sherman's last reported position. Now *post facto* he seemed to be suggesting that all along he might have taken the overland route not merely to bolster the Union line, but rather *deliberately* to hit the Rebels unexpectedly from the rear. Was Wallace, then, insubordinate the entire time in quests of glory?

Third, few students of the battle would believe that a single division of less than 7,000 men could have stopped the Confederate advance that was sweeping toward Pittsburg Landing—especially when on the second day of the battle all of Buell's 20,000, and Wallace's 3rd Division, joined with Grant's battered forces, took hours to push the Confederates back without shattering their cohesion or ruining their army. Moreover, Confederates later claimed that they knew of Wallace's arrival and were prepared to bar his passage over the remaining bridges. In any case, Wallace's zeal to clear his name more often had the opposite effect of antagonizing far more powerful rivals who were not about to accept any culpability for Shiloh. At the same time he was showing a certain shrillness if not inconsistency in his own purportedly principled defense—all at a time of Grant's rising power and a general American desire to forget the horrific losses of the recent war.

Gen. Lew Wallace never recovered from the ignominy of Shiloh nor regained Grant's confidence. "I could manage him if he had less rank," Grant wrote back in rebuke of Halleck's inquiry about bringing Wallace back to frontline command. Although Wallace would later play a key role in the defense of Cincinnati, assume the influential military command of Maryland, help defend Washington from Jubal Early's raid of July 1864 at the critical battle of Monocacy, and serve on commissions investigating everything from Lincoln's assassination to the Confederate prison wardens at Andersonville, he could not and would not let go of Shiloh. Before April 6 he had been a rising star and a savior of Union lives; after the battle he was unfairly discredited and blamed for thousands of dead Americans. Others could forget Shiloh, but Lew Wallace would not.

We shall never know exactly what happened the first day at Shiloh. But the preponderance of evidence, both written records and drawn from later interviews, in fact favors much of Wallace's account. Most likely, Grant sent an unclear order through an aide without specifying the exact route of advance. He was also probably ignorant of the Shunpike route, and then became so immersed in the chaos of the Union disaster that he felt no need—and had no time—for specifics. The more reflective and occasionally fussy Wallace at the rear logically assumed that he was to take the shorter inland road to arrive at Sherman's right. Perhaps he also entertained private hopes that his sudden appearance on his "secret" road might surprise the Confederates and gain him renown. In any case, Grant should have ordered Wallace to march much earlier in the day and should have given him precise written orders about the direction and purpose of his mission. His aides should have allowed Wallace's veteran division in transit to enter the battlefield from the Shunpike and hit the Confederates from the rear.

All that being said, neither general had accurate information during the confused melee of the first hours at Shiloh, and there were plenty of far greater blunders on both sides during the battle that affected the eventual outcome every bit as much as Wallace's late arrival on the first evening. Grant, remember, was over ten miles away from his army when it was attacked. He had ordered no entrenchments or even rudimentary precautions, and had allowed an army of forty thousand Confederates to get within rifle shot of his forces without being noticed. And, far worse, Halleck had allowed an entire defeated army to flee.

Lew Wallace would live for another forty-three years after Shiloh. He became heavily involved in Mexican politics, served as a territorial governor of New Mexico, and was appointed by President Garfield, another Shiloh veteran, as United States minister to the Ottoman court at Constantinople.

Yet throughout his long and near storybook career—he dealt on numerous occasions with Billy the Kid, the Apache renegade Victorio, and Abdul-Hamid II, the sultan of the Ottoman Empire—Wallace continued his obsession with Shiloh, all the more desperately so as his chief nemesis, Ulysses S. Grant, grew in stature from General of the Army to President of the United States. In some sense, Lew Wallace's entire life between 1862 and 1906 is a chronicle of his efforts to pursue the ghost of the Shunpike.

After Wallace's victory at the battle of Monocacy that helped save Washington, D.C., he found himself for a time on somewhat better terms with Grant. The latter even purportedly admitted to him in August 1864, "If I had known then what I know now, I would have ordered you where you were marching when stopped"—a belated admission that Wallace would often repeat but could not corroborate. But for all Grant's talk of bringing Wallace back to frontline action with the Army of the Potomac, Wallace was more or less ostracized and left alone back in Baltimore until the war ended, a general without an army. Shiloh was simply too large an albatross.

In 1868 he stumped for Grant's election and two years later was poised to enter politics as a Republican loyalist congressman from Indiana. Unexpectedly, he lost the election of 1870, in part due to his reluctance even to reply to Democratic attacks on his record at Shiloh. Throughout the 1870s several of Grant's enemies—rightly critical of his scandal-ridden presidency—returned to Shiloh to attack the President in print. In response, Grant dug his heels in as pro-Republican Washington newspapers instead turned their invective on Wallace as a way of absolving the President. Such would be the sad turn of events until Grant's death: private assurances to Wallace that Grant himself had erred or at least felt that there was no culpability on Wallace's part, juxtaposed with Grant's public defense of Shiloh by blaming Wallace and others. This ambiguous relationship with Grant would characterize Wallace's efforts for the twenty-three years after Shiloh until Grant's death in 1885: a doomed and often sad passive-aggressive effort to win over the President.

When Grant was assigned to write of Shiloh for the influential *Century Magazine*, which was running stories on the war's famous battles—later to become the authoritative *Battles and Leaders of the Civil War*—Wallace wrote him at length. At one point he simply begged for exoneration. As he put it, Grant should put to rest "the anxieties natural to one who has been so bitterly and continuously criticized in the connection." He further reminded Grant, "The terrible reflections in your endorsement of my official report of the battle, and elsewhere, go to the world wholly unqualified. It is not possible to exaggerate the misfortune thus entailed upon me."

Twenty years after the battle, as Grant ailed, Wallace made a final, even more desperate written request for a formal absolution:

> Finally, general, did you ever ask yourself what motive I could have had to play you falsely that day. It couldn't have been personal malice. Only a few weeks before I had been promoted Major-General on your recommendation. It couldn't have been cowardice. You had seen me under fire at Donelson, and twice the second day at Pittsburg Landing you found me with my division under fire. It couldn't have been lack of resolution. I certainly showed no failing of that kin at Monocacy Junction. The fact is, I was the victim of a mistake.

Wallace then pressed his case by visiting the near-bankrupt and dying Grant in the fall of 1884; in the company of Mark Twain, Mrs. Grant exclaimed of her illustrious company, "There's many a woman in this land that would like to be in my place and be able to tell her children that she once stood elbow to elbow between two such great authors as Mark Twain and General Wallace." To no avail—the enfeebled Grant, tired of Wallace's constant nagging of the last quarter century, in both the *Century* article and his posthumously published memoirs, wrote in the text:

> General Wallace did not arrive in time to take part in the first day's fight. General Wallace has claimed that the order delivered to him by Captain Baxter was simply to join the right of the army, and that the road over which he marched would have taken him to the road from Pittsburg to Purdy where it crosses Owl Creek on the right of Sherman but this is not where I had ordered him nor where I wanted him to go. I never could see and do not know why any order was necessary further than to direct him to come to Pittsburg Landing without specifying by what route.

Wallace sought other allies where he could find them—too often other disgraced officers like Col. Charles P. Stone, who had been blamed for the Federal fiasco at Ball's Bluff and imprisoned for 189 days, or General Buell, who was faulted for the Union disaster at Perryville in late 1862 and forced to retire the next year. With friends like these, Wallace hardly needed enemies like Halleck and Grant. Wallace also turned to the public and spoke constantly to civic groups and military reunions alike, often giving spirited defenses of Shiloh and blasting Halleck: "The only one of all our Generals who never even saw a battle. . . . Chief of a nameless and unknown staff."

After Grant's death, the general's old enemies were more apt to come forward and use Wallace as a club to beat their now dead nemesis. General Buell, for example, authored a version of Shiloh for the *Century Magazine* series that savagely attacked Grant's characterization of Wallace, concluding of his performance that there "must be added that a presumption of honest endeavor at Shiloh on the 7th, and on no other occasion have his [Wallace's] zeal and courage been impugned." In the oddest twist of all, the widow of Gen. W.H.L. Wallace (no relation), killed on the first day of Shiloh, had sent the dying Grant a letter recovered from her husband's body, concerning communications between him and Lew Wallace *before* the battle. The letter proved that the two General Wallaces had made prior arrangements to use the Shunpike route to reinforce each other should trouble arise. Apparently Grant had no idea that his own independent subordinates had crafted an effective tactic to unite via an inland road should the Confederates attack either Union landing on the river.

That newfound piece of evidence prompted Grant to have his publisher at the last minute add a small footnote to the text of his memoirs:

This [the letter of W.H.L. Wallace] modifies very materially what I have said, and what has been said by others, of the conduct of General Lewis Wallace at the battle of Shiloh. It shows that he naturally, with no more experience than he had at the time in the profession of arms, would take the particular road that he did start upon in the absence of orders to move by a different road. If the position of our front had not changed, the road which Wallace took would have been somewhat shorter to our right than the River road.

Wallace himself visited the battlefield almost every year. In 1903, just two years before his death, he made a final journey to inspect the official commemoration and monuments, urging changes in the manner in which his march was presented in the official guide and tourist literature. Earlier he had vehemently lobbied the Shiloh National Military Park Commission to adopt all his own maps and reports as the basis for the park guide sold to visitors. But for all of Wallace's frantic efforts in his last years to set the record straight to generations of Americans, his diplomatic and government posts in themselves never allowed him either the power, much less the money, to regain his good name.

Instead, it would be his writing career, not high government service or political patronage, that would restore his reputation to the American public in a way that all his impassioned briefs and pamphlets, his obsequious letters and visits to Grant, and his continual tours of Shiloh could not. Because of, rather than despite, his gift for dramatic romance, his occasional exaggeration and exuberance, and his wide experience, Lew Wallace could write what people wished to read. His disaster at Shiloh had spurred the disconsolate Wallace to vent through writing. And he was not just to write, but to publish what he had written—and to publish with the intent that thousands of Americans would read what he wrote and at last know who he really was!

Wallace turned out to be quite prolific, publishing dozens of poems, articles, plays, and novels, among them two moderately successful epics, *The Fair God* (1873), which retold the historian William Prescott's story of the Spanish conquest of Mexico, and *The Prince of India* (1893), a swashbuckling account surrounding the conquest of Constantinople. But Lew Wallace today is not associated with either novel, which are now rarely read, or even with his ambiguous role at Shiloh. Rather he is known solely as the author of *Ben-Hur*—and thus the creator of the entire *Ben-Hur* popular phenomenon that has swept America for the past 120 years since the novel's first appearance in 1880.

What was the exact connection between Shiloh and *Ben-Hur*? There were, of course, the superficial influences of the battle upon the novelist Wallace. The fighting experiences of Shiloh's second day proved critical in the writing of Ben-Hur's martial and equestrian excellence. Many characters in the novel mirror Wallace's own interests in battle tactics, the intricacies and jealousies of military command, and the thrill of leading men into combat:

> No one performed his part as well as Ben-Hur, whose training served him admirably; for, not merely he knew to strike and guard; his long arm, perfect action, and incomparable strength helped him, also, to success in every encounter. He was at the same time fighting-man and leader. The club he wielded was of goodly length and weighty, so he had need to strike a man but once. He seemed, moreover to have eyes for each combat of his friends, and the faculty of being at the right moment exactly where he was most needed. In his fighting cry were inspiration for his party and alarm for his enemies.

Wallace may have written of the leper colonies endured by Ben-Hur's mother and sister out of his own horror of briefly running a detainee center after his removal from command, and then serving on the board of inquiry over the horrendous conditions in the Confederate prison at Andersonville. And by his own admission Wallace claimed that a debate with an old Shiloh acquaintance, the agnostic Col. Robert G. Ingersoll, prompted him to explore the idea of presenting through *Ben-Hur* a counterdefense of Christianity. President Garfield, another veteran of Shiloh, wrote Wallace an ecstatic fan letter of thanks, which had the effect of markedly increasing sales: "With this beautiful and reverent book you have lightened the burden of my daily life—and renewed our acquaintance which began at Shiloh." A facsimile of that letter was wisely used as a frontispiece to the famous 1892 "Garfield" edition of *Ben-Hur*, which became the most successful and expensive two-volume set of any novel in nineteenth-century America.

Far more important, in some sense the entire plot of *Ben-Hur: A Tale of the Christ* eerily resembles much of Wallace's own sad odyssey following that disaster of April 6, 1862. For all its subplots revolving around Christ, *Ben-Hur* is mostly the saga of a young, brilliant Jewish hero whose adult life is devoted to seeking revenge for an injustice done him and his family—by no less than a friend who knew better and would benefit from his duplicity.

Judah Ben-Hur, a prosperous Jewish aristocrat, while watching from his veranda a triumphal procession below, accidentally loosens a roof tile that nearly kills Gratus, the Roman procurator of Judea. In response, the evil Roman official Messala conspires to turn the misfortune into an "assassination" attempt, thereby condemning Judah Ben-Hur to the galleys, and his mother and sister to the dungeons. At one low point, Ben-Hur philosophizes, "Death was preferable to shame; and believe me, I pray, it is so yet." Before his final acceptance of Christ, Ben-Hur is presented as a volatile and crestfallen hero, desperate at any cost to regain his lost reputation. "The face gave back nothing to mar its youthful comeliness—nothing of accusation or sullenness or menace, only the signs which a great sorrow long borne imprints as time mellows the surface of pictures."

Because of this blow of fate (the loose roof tile turns out every bit as disastrous to Ben-Hur as the missed road was to Wallace, and the ancient Gratus, like the contemporary Grant, was nearly ruined by the innocent accident of a young protagonist), the hero suffers a series of horrors and indignities until he proves his mettle in a sea battle and so regains his freedom. Wealth—he becomes one of the richest men in the Roman Empire—and fame follow. And at last he triumphs over all his enemies and gets his revenge on his rival Messala—only at the climax of his ordeal to accept the power of Christ through witnessing the Crucifixion. The novel ends with Ben-Hur's determination to devote his life and treasure to Christianity, by rejecting the power and authority of Rome. Throughout the narrative, Rome's ruling elites appear arrogant, predatory, conniving, and imperialistic—in many ways analogous to Wallace's own experience with high American officials in the aftermath of Shiloh. The tale illustrates that despite jealousy and the machinations of an evil rival like a Messala (or Halleck), innate talent and goodness can eventually provide enough fame and money to settle old scores—with war and politics being the arena of reckoning.

Far more important, however, *Ben-Hur* was not just an allegory of Shiloh and its principal characters; Wallace's own sense of injustice following the battle may well also have been the larger catalyst for his writing career. He reiterated often the direct connection between his efforts to succeed with *Ben-Hur* and the need to wipe clean the Shiloh stain. Even after the conclusion of Wallace's successful tenure as minister to the Ottoman Empire and when sales of *Ben-Hur* were reaching unbelievable levels, Wallace could still write in 1885 that his wildly successful fiction had almost eclipsed the setback of Shiloh: "I have letters from publishers on both sides of the sea, and so, may the end of life be swift or slow, I may be found at this work. Into such pleasant life but one hurt—the old wound at Shiloh."

An exasperated Wallace also wrote his wife in 1885 that the fame of *Ben-Hur* had almost trumped the ignominy of Shiloh: "Shiloh and its slanders! Will the world ever acquit me of them? If I were guilty I would not feel them so keenly. Ending by finding solace in *Ben-Hur*, I can bear it." He added, "I have a reputation in another sphere sufficient to keep me afloat."

At least writing and the accompanying fortune and fame of a best-seller might allow Wallace to have his own study and hence some relief "to play the violin at midnight if I chose. A detached room away from the world and its worries. A place for my old age to rest in and grow reminiscent, fighting the battles of youth over again." Yet, even in 1900, thirty-eight years after the battle, Wallace could still lament, "That awful mystery known as the Battle of Pittsburg Landing comes home more directly than to most of those engaged in it. O, the lies, the lies that were told to make me the scapegoat to bear off the criminal mistakes of others. . . . Think of what I suffered."

For all his theatrics, in some sense Wallace was reacting to real rather than merely perceived animosity. In 1888, for example, a Milwaukee newspaper maliciously wrote of rumors surrounding a possible offer to Wallace of a cabinet position in the Harrison administration, "Wallace may be a good literary man, but it wants a soldier for secretary of war who can get his men into a fight five miles away without marching all day."

Wallace constantly used his fame as the author of *Ben-Hur* to reopen the old wounds of Shiloh. Well into the twentieth century and in his seventies he requested that the Society of the Army of the Tennessee reexamine the forty-year-old controversy of the Shunpike march; he sought to obtain a military commission during the Spanish-American War that might bring him final military renown to absolve the old charges; and he persisted in sending copies of his acclaimed fiction to aged officers like Generals Garfield, Grant, Howard, Hayes, and Sherman, so that they might in turn finish their memoirs with favorable assessments of Wallace's march at Shiloh.

But if the obsession with Shiloh helped prompt Wallace's literary career and shaped the very plot of *Ben-Hur*, did the novel itself have any lasting effect on American culture? Quite a lot, in fact. *Ben-Hur* turned out to be the most popular work of fiction written in nineteenth-century America; indeed, its aggregate sales were not surpassed until the success of *Gone With the Wind* in the late 1930s. While elite critics and intellectuals often scoffed at the novel's Victorian pretense, cardboard characters, stilted prose, and thinly veiled allusions to Wallace's own life, the turn-of-the-century public adored *Ben-Hur* and made its author one of the most famous men in America. Lew Wallace found the celebrity status of a Stephen King or John Grisham—a hundred years earlier.

After a slow start in 1880 (its first year of publication), *Ben-Hur*'s popularity soon spread by word of mouth. By 1883 it was selling 750 copies a month, by 1886, 4,500. The American publishing industry had never seen anything like it. In just nine years the novel had sold 400,000 copies in thirty-six editions, and surpassed the phenomenal totals of *Uncle Tom's Cabin*! It was also by far the most requested book in America's public libraries.

A mere ten years after the appearance of *Ben-Hur*, Lew Wallace was the most successful novelist in the history of America. But the novel would turn out to sell even more rapidly in the next half-century of its publication. A million copies were published by 1911; the next year alone Sears, Roebuck printed another million copies to sell at thirty-nine cents each in the largest single-year print edition in American history. The last official recorded sales figures in the 1940s put the total copies purchased at somewhere between two and three million; in fact, the true total was probably millions higher. By 1936, *Ben-Hur* had earned the greatest financial returns of any single novel in American history.

Americans were fascinated by Wallace's exotic descriptions of the Holy Land, the singular mission of Ben-Hur to exact revenge, the multicultural milieu of ancient Rome and Jerusalem, and, of course, the message of divine salvation through faith. Even as the Boston Brahmins of the literary elite—James Russell Lowell, Oliver Wendell Holmes, Thomas Bailey Aldrich, and William Dean Howells—snubbed Wallace and scoffed at the amateur's clumsy efforts at fiction, the American public bought the book in droves. For many, it became the first—and only—novel they ever read. Whether Wallace realized it or not, godly and self-made Americans identified with Ben-Hur's singular quest for revenge and redemption. Hundreds more readers wrote to Wallace that the novel had in fact convinced them to convert to Christianity. In that regard, *Ben-Hur* marked a radical change in American letters, as millions of Americans for the first time felt that reading fiction was neither sacrilegious nor the sole esoteric pursuit of intellectuals, but was rightly intended for the secular enjoyment and edification of common people. Lew Wallace, as it turned out, introduced more Americans to reading than any other author of the nineteenth century. He in essence had invented popular American fiction—and behind it all was the spur of Shiloh.

The plays and movie versions to follow reached millions more. The stage production alone—requiring thirty tons of machinery with horses and chariots on a treadmill—was performed six thousand times before 20 million Americans, touring almost every major city in the United States during the first two decades of the twentieth century. In short, the play was the most successful in American history, and to this day has drawn a greater aggregate audience than any dramatic presentation of an American author. It gained rave endorsements from Billy Sunday to William Jennings Bryan. Thousands of derivative books, songs, toys, and ads followed, the popular avalanche only to be surpassed by the (four) motion picture versions to come. Hollywood had seen nothing like the December 1925 release of the long-awaited film starring Ramon Navarro as Ben-Hur, with gigantic sets for the galley battle and chariot race that cost hundreds of thousands of dollars. And while the silent movie set a record of expenditures at over $4 million, it also proved the most lucrative moneymaker in Hollywood's then brief history—earning over $9 million in its first two years.

William Wyler's monumental 1959 remake with Charlton Heston as Ben-Hur (and another 365 speaking roles) was even more successful—nominated for twelve Academy Awards, winning eleven (including Best Picture and Best Actor). The panoramic film grossed over $40 million its first year alone; its primetime television debut in February 1971 (shown over four nights) achieved the highest rating of any movie presented on television up to that time. The Hollywood extravaganzas in turn reignited book sales nearly sixty years after Wallace's death. By 1960, *Ben-Hur* had appeared in over sixty English-language editions—and is selling well in its third century of publication.

Ben-Hur radically affected American popular culture. Everything from bicycles and cigars to toys and drinks—and even towns—were named Ben-Hur. Chariot racing became an American folk spectacle at rodeos and fairs. The modern idea that historical epics—*Quo Vadis, Spartacus*, or *Gone With the Wind*—can appeal widely to supposedly ahistorical Americans we owe largely to the popularizer Lew Wallace. But more important, Wallace's novel began the strange nexus in American life, for good or ill, between literature, motion pictures, advertising, and popular culture. The novel led to the stage and then to the movies, but in the process it spun out entire ancillary industries of songs, skits, ads, clothes, and fan clubs, ensuring that within fifty years of its publication, nearly every American had heard the word "Ben-Hur" without necessarily ever reading the book.

In that sense, *Ben-Hur* prefigures the world of *The Ten Commandments* to *Gladiator* (the latter's movie script is hauntingly similar to Wallace's own play *Commodus*) and established the now predictable evolution of successful novel to movie blockbuster to advertising gold mine to permanent place in the popular folk tradition of America. Wallace's brilliant adventure tale accounts for most of the larger *Ben-Hur*'s mystique—but not quite all. At least some of the novel's inexplicable popularity was due to the tireless plugging of the author himself, who for two decades made it a point to tour, appear in public, give lectures and signings, oversee dramatic adaptations, answer fan letters, and promote his book with influential Americans (like Garfield, Grant, and Sherman) in a frenzied effort to become known, rich—and so perhaps at last taken seriously in wiping away the stain of Shiloh.

While America had long honored its gifted men of letters like Longfellow or Twain, the Wallace phenomenon was something entirely different. Wallace's apotheosis presaged the twentieth century in its transmogrification of the acclaimed writer to popular icon, a literary celebrity whose fame rested not with book reviews in literary journals, but entirely as a result of popular readership and sales figures—and mostly oblivious to the opinion of intellectuals, academics, and other novelists. At his death Wallace had become a national folk hero, one mobbed by the American public, called on tour for an endless series of *Ben-Hur* lectures, hounded by devoted fan clubs, and canonized by politicians (his likeness sits in Statuary Hall in the Capitol building in Washington).

Such were the strange wages of the missed road on April 6, 1862. If today most Americans are ignorant of Lew Wallace, it is equally true—and perhaps just as regrettable—that they are far more likely to know something of his *Ben-Hur* than anything at all of the battle of Shiloh. "My God!" Wallace remarked in 1899 when first examining the stage sets to *Ben-Hur*. "Did I set all this in motion?" He did—but Shiloh had as well.

Night: The Klansman

As Sherman braved fire to reform his perimeter, as Albert Sidney Johnston was bleeding to death in the early afternoon of the first day of the battle, and as Lew Wallace was reversing course and returning to the river route to Pittsburg Landing, Col. Nathan Bedford Forrest joined his cavalry regiment in the furious Confederate assault against the surrounded Union troops in the Hornet's Nest. Prior to his late entry into the melee, Forrest had become increasingly restless with his assigned minor supporting role. Shiloh was certainly not the colonel's type of war. He much preferred fluid skirmishing between rapidly moving mounted columns of intrepid rangers. Instead, the morning's fighting had turned into a static, ugly infantry slugfest. At Shiloh numbers and firepower, not cunning and audacity, were more likely to bring success amid deep mud, thickets, and ravines.

When the shooting had started, the lowly and mostly unknown Colonel Forrest had been given the ignominious task of protecting the Confederate flank at Lick Creek—largely a safe assignment to the rear and at the periphery of the battlefield. For the first five hours of fighting Forrest waited patiently, obedient to his orders to watch the right flank should any Union reservists come up the river to land at Hamburg and turn the Confederates' rear. Finally, Forrest had had enough of his inaction. He remarked to his men, "Boys, do you hear that rattle of musketry and the roar of artillery?" When they shouted, "Yes, yes," he bellowed in reply, "Do you know what it means? It means that our friends and brothers are falling by hundreds at the hands of the enemy and we are here guarding a damned creek. We did not enter the service for such work, and the reputation of the regiment does not justify our commanding officer in leaving us here while we are needed elsewhere. Let's go and help them. What do you say?"

When his men roared back in the affirmative, Colonel Forrest rode into the first major pitched battle of his career. Before that decision to disregard orders and gallop toward the firing, Forrest had been relatively ignored among the Southern high command. His sound advice either to defend the garrison or break out en masse was ignored at Fort Donelson, whose timid commanders instead surrendered thousands of valuable soldiers to Grant. Forrest also had no formal, much less military, education. In fact, he was nearly illiterate. He had not been sought out by the new Confederate government, but instead had raised his own brigade of Tennessee horsemen and supplied them with his own weapons. Most likely, his own shady past in slave trading made him suspect among the aristocratic Southern officer corps.

Yet his dramatic entry into the Hornet's Nest would mark the first of three remarkable acts at Shiloh, which over the next twenty-four hours would magically transform the Memphis slave trader into the legendary icon Gen. Nathan Bedford Forrest. Just as Sherman's near-death experiences at Shiloh would resurrect his professional life with untold misery to come for the South, and as Wallace's missed route would lead to the creation of the cultural phenomenon of *Ben-Hur*, so too Forrest's day at Shiloh would prove the catalyst for a remarkable military career that had consequences for the entire nation well beyond his Civil War years.

Nothing could have offered a more drastic change of landscape from his previous sentry duty. Forrest's cavalrymen now went from the quiet of Lick Creek into the inferno of the Hornet's Nest. Major General Cheatham's efforts, like most of the previous Confederate piecemeal attacks against the frenzied and surrounded Northerners, had been repulsed with heavy losses. Desperate Union artillerymen firing from the protection of the sunken road continued to rain canister across the approaching Southerners. When Forrest rode up, hundreds of Confederates were reeling backward from another failed charge. The rambunctious Forrest could not find any superior to order him forward. He was instead forced to rely on his own initiative. "I will charge under my own orders," he told General Cheatham. His nearly five hundred men abruptly galloped into the fire, making their way to within fifty yards of the Union lines before faltering in muddy ground and rough thickets. Yet Forrest's audacity had emboldened another effort from the exhausted Cheatham's infantrymen. The latter sensed that the Union circle was at last shrinking ever smaller and on the verge of collapsing altogether. Cheatham's own subsequent charge, joined in anew by Forrest's men, helped crack the Union circle.

For the next three hours Forrest helped in finishing off the Hornet's Nest and pursuing hundreds of Prentiss's men who fled toward the refuge of the Tennessee River. And after General Prentiss surrendered the remaining two thousand trapped men in the late afternoon, Forrest pressed his way still forward with other scattered forces to the cliffs above Pittsburg Landing, marking the high-water mark of the Confederate advance of the first day of Shiloh. It was a spectacular sight! Below, thousands of Union soldiers were rushing to the river in panic, gunboats steaming up to provide some desperate support for thousands more milling around—even as some fifty batteries rushed into position to form a last-ditch perimeter before Grant's entire shattered command was pushed into the river.

Time was now critical. The rambunctious Forrest was adamant that there was only a window of a few minutes to crush the dazed Northerners before darkness—and before reinforcements from across the river, and the increasing fire of dozens of Union cannon, would put an end to the Confederate advance. But by the time Forrest's request to storm Pittsburg Landing was forwarded to Maj. Gen. Leonidas Polk, it was nearly dark, and the advanced Confederate companies on the ridge were coming under steady artillery assault.

Still, as he retreated for the night to safer ground, Forrest was even more convinced that the landing had to be assaulted sometime that very evening, before reinforcements swelled the Union army at sunrise. At the very outset, Albert Sidney Johnston and his generals had envisioned crushing Grant's army through a flank attack on the right aimed at the Union base at Pittsburg Landing, a sudden stroke designed to finish the Army of the Tennessee before it united with the Army of the Ohio. Now it seemed that a nondescript colonel alone of the Southern command wished to follow the original intent of the Confederate tactical and strategic plan by sweeping down to the river before Buell's army crossed.

Unfortunately, Forrest's request to crash into the last Union position was rejected by Polk. The general countered that the night, the exhaustion of his men, the sudden arrival of Union batteries and gunboats at the landing, and the apparent expectation of an easy final assault the next morning, all that made such a risky assault unnecessary, if not unwise. Forrest was dumbfounded—but still convinced that Union reinforcements during the night might the next day nullify all of the Confederate gains. Below—even as Grant was meeting Sherman to assure him of a victorious counterattack the next morning, as Lew Wallace finally pulled in from Crump's Landing with his fresh division, as rumors began to spread that the corpse brought out of the Hornet's Nest was not a Colonel "Jackson," but none other than the supreme commander, Albert Sidney Johnston himself, and as the tempestuous General Buell ferried his massive 20,000-man Army of the Ohio across the Tennessee River—an exasperated Nathan Bedford Forrest began to stalk the shadows in desperation.

Events that night would prove his worst fears correct. As the exhausted Confederate Army slept or scrounged among the captured opulent Union camps, and as its stupefied command retired for the evening, Forrest began to reconnoiter the Union lines. What he discovered was frightening. His patrols, many disguised in blue Union overcoats, in early evening brought back disturbing news. The Army of the Ohio was not miles away—as faulty Confederate intelligence had claimed during the morning. In fact, it was now crossing the Tennessee and pouring thousands of men into the Union camp at Pittsburg Landing!

Whole fresh regiments were streaming into Grant's demoralized and beaten army while the confident though exhausted Southerners slept. General Prentiss, captured with the collapse of the Hornet's Nest, was prescient, not boasting, when he had matter-of-factly related to his captors that the Union Army would return in renewed fury on early Monday morning. The South unfortunately was now fighting a rare man in Ulysses S. Grant. Far from being stunned by the near collapse of his army, the Union commander was not licking his considerable wounds, but eager to launch an offensive before sunrise of the second day of battle.

Forrest, however, found no one to share his amazing intelligence coup. His immediate superior, Brigade Gen. James R. Chalmers, was of no help. While sympathetic, Chalmers possessed insufficient rank to call out the troops. He had no idea where Generals Hardee, Bragg, and Beauregard were anyway. Forrest remarked to Chalmers, "You are the first general I have found who knows where his men are!" The barely literate Colonel Forrest's warning went unheeded:

> I have been way down along the river-bank, close to the enemy. I could see the lights on the steamboats and hear distinctively the orders given in the disembarkation of the troops. They are receiving reinforcements by the thousands, and if this army does not move and attack them between now and daylight, and before other reinforcements arrive, it will be whipped like hell before ten o'clock tomorrow.

Chalmers later reported that when Forrest at last hunted down the Confederate leadership and presented the same disturbing news to Generals Breckinridge and Hardee, "the unlettered colonel was told to go back to his regiment." In any case, it was now too late—nearly 3 A.M., with a renewed Union attack less than three hours away. The supposedly crushed Grant, not the victorious Beauregard, was eager to renew hostilities. Forrest's second legendary feat at Shiloh—roaming the battlefield into the early morning Cassandra-like in making desperate pleas to rouse the Confederates to preempt the Union counterattack—like his earlier charge into the Hornet's Nest, would later raise the obscure colonel to heroic status within the army. Yet both experiences also soured him on the competence and bravery of the far better bred and educated Southern high command.

The next morning, events transpired precisely as Forrest had feared. Grant's surviving army was joined by Buell and Wallace. A combined force of well over 40,000 Union soldiers—well over half of them fresh—now poured into the Confederate lines, steadily driving them back beyond the original demarcation lines of the prior morning. All ground won on Sunday was lost in Monday's first hours. A dispirited Forrest spent the morning rounding up stragglers, protecting infantry from flank attacks, and occasionally dismounting to join in sporadic Confederate counterattacks. But by noon, less than 15,000 remaining able-bodied Confederates were now on the verge of being demolished by the Union juggernaut.

Wisely, Beauregard at last ordered a general retreat, as artillery and cavalry—Forrest's regiment especially was preeminent—disguised the withdrawal with vigorous skirmishing. By Monday afternoon, what was left of the Southern army was at last safely detached and on its way back to Corinth, Mississippi. It took hours for the bewildered advancing Union army to grasp that its tenacious enemy was in fact retreating rather than readying for yet another murderous counterassault. By Monday evening, both sides were disengaged. The battle of Shiloh was over.

Or almost over. When Grant at last realized that his enemy was shattered and retreating, on Tuesday morning he ordered the redoubtable Sherman to pursue the demoralized Southerners. About four miles distant from his original headquarters at Shiloh Church, Sherman at last came upon the Confederate rear guard at a former logging camp called Fallen Timbers. Here Forrest seems to have left the world of Confederate gallantry and entered the realm of heroic myth where gods traverse the battlefield slaying with impunity mere mortals. We have a fairly accurate account of what happened next, inasmuch as both Union and Confederate witnesses—among them William Tecumseh Sherman—agree on most of the events.

Sherman caught up with the rear guard of the Confederate Army sometime on the morning of Tuesday, April 8. The terrain—muddy and covered with rotten timber—favored Sherman's infantrymen. They vastly outnumbered Forrest's skeleton rearguard force of some 150 cavalrymen aided by a motley assortment of 200 rangers from various scattered companies. Inexplicably, Forrest ordered his ragtag band to charge directly against the advancing Union infantry, who now numbered over 400 and were supported by another 200 cavalry—and in turn bolstered by an entire brigade in reserve.

Sherman in his memoirs matter-of-factly chronicled the sudden collapse of his men:

> The enemy's cavalry came down boldly at a charge, led by General Forrest in person, breaking through our line of skirmishers; when the regiment of infantry, without cause, broke, threw away their

muskets, and fled. The ground was admirably adapted for a defense of infantry against cavalry, being miry and covered with fallen timber. . . .

In a private letter to his brother John, he was more direct:

The Regiment did break, move to the rear and gather behind the flanks of a Brigade I held in reserve. We afterwards gathered up the muskets on the ground. I only found 3 dead secessionists on the ground, killed by the skirmishers in advance. The Regiment itself killed none.

Despite the uneven ground, the sheer fury of Forrest's first charge scattered both the Union infantry regiment and its supporting cavalry. But then Forrest refused to halt and rode into Sherman's entire reserve brigade. Suddenly he found himself quite alone, far in front of his retreating rangers—and now surrounded by hundreds of Union riflemen. "Shoot him! Stick him! Knock him off his horse," they yelled as dozens rushed Forrest. He fired off his pistol and wheeled around—only to be showered with a hail of bullets that rent his coat and slammed into his horse. Then one soldier ran up and shot his rifle point-blank into Forrest's hip, the bullet driving up through his lower back to lodge next to the spine. His right leg went immediately numb and useless. Forrest was about to be dragged off his mortally wounded mount, no doubt to be summarily executed by hordes of furious bluecoats.

With a severe spinal wound, his right leg unusable, bullets whizzing through his coat and peppering his exhausted horse, and thrashing about in a sea of bluecoats, Forrest, according to some witnesses, "reached down, caught up a rather small Federal soldier, swung him around and held him to the rear of his saddle as a shield until he was well out of danger, and then gladly dropped his prisoner, who doubtless saved his life." It is difficult to understand how an exhausted man of forty, bleeding with a near-fatal spinal wound, without the use of one leg, might lift up a man of at least some 130 pounds (with one hand as he gripped the reins with the other?), and throw him onto his mount—the soldier himself then apparently offering no resistance, neither shooting nor knocking his wounded captor off his mount.

Yet if the story seems supernatural, even more inexplicable is how Forrest made it out of the Union swarm in the first place. How a large target of a man over six feet could escape a hail of hundreds of bullets and ride back through a mob of enemies is equally perplexing—and suggests that Forrest used some type of cover, whether human or otherwise, that might account for his miraculous survival. In any case, Sherman ceased pursuit as his humiliated skirmishers regrouped. An exhausted and bleeding Forrest made it back to Corinth that evening, where he was treated and given a sixty-day furlough, his horse at last dropping dead when its rider reached safety.

During the next few weeks, the Southern public, initially buoyed by preliminary reports of a great "victory" on Shiloh's first day, sorted through the conflicting accounts of the battle's aftermath. The death of Albert Sidney Johnston, the horrendous casualties, and the presence of a huge and victorious Union Army deep in Tennessee and now moving south, all eroded any lingering faith in its generals. Yet a lowly colonel—who had plunged into the Hornet's Nest, where the Confederates obtained their greatest victory, who in the early hours of the fateful Monday morning had vainly tried to organize a final assault on Pittsburg Landing, and who had single-handedly stopped Sherman's pursuit—proved blameless and soon by word of mouth was becoming the South's new hero of the hour. Two prominent Confederates emerged from Shiloh with their reputations enhanced. One was the dead Albert Sidney Johnston; the other soon-to-be-general Nathan Bedford Forrest.

So a recuperating Forrest—the last man to be wounded at the battle of Shiloh—was summarily promoted to brigadier general and put in charge of a much larger cavalry command in central Tennessee. And if Shiloh brought Forrest to the attention of the Southern public and its top military and political leadership, it also changed the new general's entire attitude to the conduct of war. Gone was any modicum of respect he harbored for professional military men like Bragg, Hardee, or Beauregard, who had so bungled operations at Shiloh. From now on he would trust his own instincts, operate independently whenever possible, and avoid or ignore his educated superiors as he saw fit. Such intransigent independence ensured havoc for all Union forces in Tennessee for the next three years, but also guaranteed that Forrest would never, like Lee, Bragg, or Hood, exercise command of entire Confed-

These various types of American craft landing, unloading tons of supplies on Beach Yellow 3 at the mouth of the Misha River, were part of the largest invasion armada of the Pacific war in terms of firepower, total manpower involved, and tonnage unloaded. Indeed, the Okinawa landings may have been the most ambitious amphibian assault in the history of warfare.

By May, constant rain and bombardment had turned the landscape of Okinawa into a sea of mud, preventing the Americans from fully utilizing their marked advantage in mechanized vehicles and heavy armor. Here, crewmen of a tank partially submerged in some five feet of water are forced to bail before being towed to safety.

Bombing and artillery bombardment turned the Japanese defenses seemingly into a pile of rubble; in fact, most Japanese were safe and well concealed beneath extensive natural caves and man-made fortifications carved into the coral and rock. Above, American Marines of the 6th Marine Division crawl foot by foot to blast out defenders with explosives and close-range artillery barrages.

The most challenging problem confronting Americans was the vast network of caves on Okinawa—connected by tunnels running some sixty miles in extent beneath the coral. The openings to the caves were usually on the high ground, sometimes nearly invisible, and immune from both bombs and artillery. Here, an American Marine looks out from a captured Japanese outpost.

The author's namesake pictured here on Guadalcanal six months before he was killed on the evening of May 19, 1945, on the assault on Sugar Loaf Hill. On his right hand is seen the ring that was returned by his fellow Marine, Louis Ittman—fifty-seven years after he perished.

American carriers, with their wooden decks and need to stay offshore for weeks at a time, were extremely vulnerable to suicide bombers. Although no single carrier was sunk, hundreds of American sailors were incinerated at sea; nearly five thousand seamen in all were lost. Here, the flagship of the American fleet, the USS *Bunker Hill*, is hit and left burning after an attack on May 11, 1945.

Peter Madigan, on news that Victor Hanson had been killed on the evening of May 18, 1945, in anger left his foxhole and rushed the Japanese positions. He was immediately killed. Left to right standing: Alfred P. Papa, Victor Hanson, Howard J. Lewis, Burritt H. Hinman. Left to right front row: John Richard Griffith, Peter Madigan, Mauris Harry, Bill Twigger.

Somewhere along this pathway known as the Sunken Road, the Union army under General Prentiss made a last stand that stopped the Confederates at the Hornet's Nest for critical hours, giving time for Grant to reconstitute Northern lines to the rear. Not far away, Albert Sidney Johnston was killed trying to root out the Union soldiers from these woods.

Forty-year-old Col. Nathan Bedford Forrest was relatively unknown before Shiloh. After the battle, recovering from severe wounds, promoted to general, and basking in the glory of his Shiloh exploits, Forrest went on to become the most gifted, feared, and hated officer the Confederacy produced.

Johnston's broad shoulders, prominent jaw, and keen eyes enhanced his reputation as the embodiment of Southern manhood, courage, and determination. His undeniable physical presence, along with his death on the front line, explains much of the Johnston mystique—inasmuch as he won almost no victories for the Southern cause.

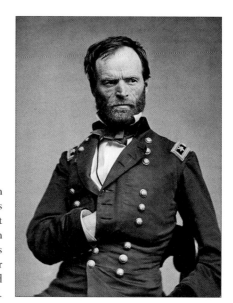

This photograph of Sherman in 1864 reveals both his seriousness and occasionally grim visage that had such a profound effect on friends and enemies alike. Note his rumpled clothes and unkempt hair that made him so familiar and beloved by his men in the field.

Only thiry-four years old, dashing and occasionally arrogant, Lew Wallace saw his career ruined on the first evening of the battle—quite unfairly, as postbellum analysis of Shiloh proved. His later literary efforts, including the bestseller *Ben-Hur*, were part of a desperate effort to reclaim his once sterling reputation lost in spring 1862. This marble sculpture of Indiana's proud hero is still on display in Statuary Hall in the U.S. Capitol—the only novelist to be so honored among the one hundred luminaries chosen from the fifty states.

Lew Wallace's novel became the greatest Broadway success in American history, touring the nation for twenty-one years. By 1920 it had been produced on over 6,000 occasions before a cumulative audience estimated at 20 million people.

An incised black limestone grave stele of the fallen warrior Saugenes reflects the last moments of the Boeotian contingent. Note the broken spear in the foreground and the feast of heroes in the afterlife portrayed in the heavens above the warrior. The artist of this impressive stele was probably the famous Aristeides of Thebes.

The modern seaside village of Delisi is built upon the site of the battlefield of 424 B.C. Attica can be seen in the distance over the mountains—in the general direction of the madcap Athenian retreat.

A balding, middle-aged Socrates helped save his friends through his courageous resistance during the retreat. This marble copy of a bronze original by Lysippus (c. 330 B.C.) emphasizes the ruggedness of the no-nonsense philosopher.

Plato was only four or five when the battle of Delium took place, but many of the stories that he heard from Socrates made their way into his later *Dialogues*. Roman marble bust (first century A.D., copy of a Greek original).

From the spoils of the battle the Boeotians hired the leading sculptors of Greece to craft commemorations for their dead. The artist has omitted Mnason's body armor to enhance his heroic and youthful physique; the Mnason grave relief, along with the Saugenes stele, may well be part of an entire set sculpted by Aristeides.

The courage of Alcibiades during the nightmarish run from Delium was proverbial and helped cement his reputation as a vigorous, heroic youth in Plato's *Dialogues*. This eighteenth-century Italian pastel emphasizes the ambiguous relationship between the older, more serious Socrates and his proud and sometimes dangerous student.

erate armies—with fortuitous results for Union generals like Grant, Sherman, and Thomas.

Still, the fame from Shiloh gave Forrest increased rank and public prestige. In the three years following the battle, the once-obscure colonel became the South's great hope for the preservation of Tennessee. There through a three-year resistance to Union incursions, he grew to be the most renowned cavalry commander in American history. By July, little more than two months after being wounded at Shiloh, Forrest had captured a much larger Union garrison at Murfreesboro, Tennessee, and established his terrifying practice of treating all captured black Union soldiers as chattel and returning them to the South as slaves. Rumors—and they would only increase in the next three years—abounded that he had also shot under murky circumstances one and perhaps two black captives. Then throughout most of December 1862, Forrest raided western Tennessee, attacking Union base camps and railroads and generally creating chaos by disrupting supplies destined for Grant's Vicksburg campaign. As the regular Confederate Army retreated farther south, most haphazard resistance was left to Forrest, who was determined to make the Federal occupation of his home state so costly that a Union withdrawal into Kentucky would seem preferable to a costly occupation of Tennessee.

After a brief setback at Dover, Tennessee, in early 1863, Forrest participated in a string of successes at Thompson's Station, Brentwood, and Franklin, capped off by the successful pursuit and capture of the Union cavalry expedition of Col. Abel Streight into northern Alabama. In all these engagements, Forrest's trademark way of war was becoming famous to the Southern public: near-complete autonomy of operations, constant aggression despite inferiority in numbers and matériel, reliance on ruse and speed, savage fighting characterized by occasional charges of brutality and gratuitous killing, relentless pursuit of the defeated to ensure their complete destruction—all peppered with swaggering political proclamations threatening vicious treatment of captured blacks, Southern Unionists, and white officers of black regiments. In addition, rumors abounded of Forrest's pride in individual combat; by war's end he bragged that he had killed twenty-nine men in battle, and had lost thirty mounts. Wilder stories spread about occasional beatings and even shootings of his own disobedient soldiers and deserters.

By fall 1863, Forrest's rangers played a key role at the Southern victory of Chickamauga, a battle where the combined casualties exceeded even those of Shiloh. As Forrest's reputation grew, he felt no compunction about engaging in verbal assaults with Generals Wheeler, Van Dorn, and Bragg over their failure to press home initial Confederate advantages. Most infamous was his face-to-face denunciation of Braxton Bragg, which ended with threats of physical violence:

> I have stood your meanness as long as I intend to. You have played the part of a damned scoundrel, and are a coward, and if you were any part of a man I would slap your jaws and force you to resent it. You may as well not issue any orders for me, for I will not obey them, and I will hold you personally responsible for any further indignities you endeavor to inflict upon me. You have threatened to arrest me for not obeying your orders promptly. I dare you to do it, and I say to you that if you ever again try to interfere with me or cross my path it will be at the peril of your life.

After his flare-up with Bragg, Forrest was transferred to southern Tennessee and northern Mississippi, where his success only continued. He pulled off another successful surprise raid in western Tennessee, and then forced Gen. William Sooy Smith's Union raiders to leave Mississippi and retire northward. In spring 1864, Forrest attacked the Union garrison on the Mississippi at Fort Pillow. Here transpired the most controversial event in his entire military career. After storming the fort on April 12, 1864, he purportedly either ordered or allowed his men to butcher black Union soldiers and their white officers; whatever the truth of such allegations, it was indisputable that of the garrison's nearly 605 defenders, nearly half were killed during the final assault, many of them trying to surrender or flee. In Northern eyes he would now become forever "Forrest of Fort Pillow."

But despite the uproar over the killing of prisoners, Forrest's greatest military triumph was yet to come two months later at the battle of Brice's Cross Roads. There Forrest outmaneuvered a much larger Union force sent to expel him from Tennessee and for all practical purposes destroyed it in the space of a single day. In pitched battle and lengthy pursuit, Forrest crushed the expedition of Gen. Samuel D. Sturgis, and with its demise the Union hope of ending Forrest's effort to disrupt the supply lines of Sherman's march toward Atlanta. Sherman himself was appalled:

> I cannot understand how he could defeat Sturgis with 8,000 men. . . . Forrest is the very devil, and I think he has got some of our troops under cower. . . . I have two officers at Memphis that will fight all the time—Smith and Mower. . . . I will order them to make up a force and go out and follow Forrest to the death if it costs 10,000 lives and breaks the Treasury. There will never be peace in Tennessee till Forrest is dead.

Even as Forrest prepared to encounter another huge punitive force of Union cavalry in Tennessee, the fame of his incredible victory at Brice's Cross Roads resulted in entreaties from Southerners throughout Georgia to save them from Sherman's march south by attacking his rear and disrupting his supply lines. Only Lee and Stonewall Jackson had achieved a similar level of renown and trust among the Southern public. Yet Forrest was never sent to Atlanta. Indeed, he could scarcely manage to stay alive, as he was surrounded by superior Union strength at Harrisburg, Mississippi, in July 1864. Given his infamy up north, he naturally attracted a series of would-be avengers. Forrest would spend the rest of the war pursued throughout Tennessee and northern Alabama and Mississippi by a host of numerically superior and better supplied Union armies until being assigned to the doomed army of John Bell Hood, and then finally ending up boxed in by the vastly superior mounted forces of the extremely capable Union general, James Harrison Wilson.

At war's end, contrary to suggestions from the deteriorating Confederate government and the fears of Sherman, Thomas, and other Union generals, Forrest disbanded his command a few weeks after Appomattox and chose to return home rather than conduct guerrilla warfare or settle outside the newly reconstituted United States. "Men, you may all do as you please, but I'm a-going home." He then ended his speech to his troops in early May 1865 with, "Any man who is in favor of a further prosecution of this war is a fit subject for a lunatic asylum, and ought to be sent there immediately."

When the conflict closed, Forrest may well have been the most infamous and hated Southerner in America. President Andrew Johnson's increasing efforts by 1866 to kill radical Reconstruction and reinstate state governments that had not ratified the Fourteenth Amendment only acerbated sectarian divisions. Northerners saw ex-Confederates like Forrest thriving rather than suffering from their treasonous defeat. Forrest himself confessed his ignominy to President Johnson in connection with his pardon request of November 1866, "I am also aware that I am at this moment regarded in large communities, at the North, with abhorrence, as a detestable monster, ruthless and swift to take life, and guilty of unpardonable crimes in connection with the capture of Fort Pillow on the 12th of April 1864."

Indeed, threats in the press abounded to try him on charges of murder at Fort Pillow. Flamboyant Northern veterans like Sherman's cavalry commander, Judson Kilpatrick, boasted that they would kill him on sight. Radical Republicans opposed the very idea of Forrest ever receiving a general pardon. He was formally charged with treason and forced to post a ten-thousand-dollar bond for his 1864 raid on Memphis. When a general amnesty was finally granted to Forrest in 1868 by the lame-duck President Johnson, the ensuing fury was still intense. "A foul fiend in human shape," one irate Union veteran wrote in demanding not pardon but punishment for Forrest, which "his atrocious crimes so richly deserve."

In contrast, Northern politicians felt that most Confederate ex-generals like Lee—as much a proponent of slavery as Forrest—had personally killed no Union soldiers, were of the genteel aristocracy, kept to circumspect pronouncements, and adopted conventional methods of war making, and so deserved a measure of Northern forgiveness if not sympathy. Sherman, who had first met Forrest at Fallen Timbers and developed great respect for him as a skilled marauder, had once written to Gen. George Thomas near the close of the war that "I would like to have Forrest hunted down and killed, but doubt if we can do that yet."

Forrest, then, was a different case altogether, a fanatic as admired for his rabid skill as a raider as he was hated for his alleged murder of prisoners. And he was an easy target for the Northern press. He could hardly read or write; his speech was often crude. And his demeanor reflected the ruggedness of his prewar status as a cocky slave trader who had struck it rich in the traffic of human chattel. Worse still, there were the rumors that he had bragged of killing Union soldiers in personal combat—what kind of general engaged in hand-to-hand fighting, much less kept such statistics of his victims? And he had shot civilians both before and after the war in a series of duels and heated arguments.

Again, unlike Lee, who laid down his arms in a formal ceremony at Appomattox, Forrest had weeks later simply quit on his own accord, reinforcing the idea that he had never been defeated in the field by his Northern adversaries, but on his own accord had wisely seen the futility in fighting on alone after the Southern command had capitulated. And while his final address was measured and realistic, just a few months earlier Forrest had issued a fiery written proclamation promising no peace ever with the Yankees and a fight to the death if the war continued.

It was entirely fitting, then, that later rumors abounded that after Robert E. Lee was first offered leadership of the Klan—which he refused on grounds of health (but not of disapproval)—he purportedly recommended Forrest as his second choice: "There is no man in the South who can handle so large a body of men so successfully. Will you pay my respects to General Forrest and tell him I hope he will accept." While those sympathetic to Lee dispute his remarks, his own private letters and testimony before Congress in 1866 reflect support for many of the positions later adopted by the Klan.

The degree to which Forrest was hated in the North gave him commensurate prestige in the humbled South of the late 1860s; enmity, not praise, from the Northern press was proof enough that popular ex-Confederate leaders had not joined their former enemy for personal gain. Moreover, as the fury over Reconstruction grew in the postwar decade, it became nearly impossible to fulfill the original humanitarian promises of the Union victory—especially under the administration of the unelected and Southern President Andrew Johnson, the ex-governor of Tennessee. The pledge to black Americans of absolute equality with their white counterparts in the South was problematic without the constant presence of Union troops of enforcement stationed throughout the old Confederacy. Yet such an open-ended commitment to change the hearts and minds of the white South would prove too much for a war-weary Northern public, which had already spent millions of dollars and hundreds of thousands of lives in ending slavery.

The dismissive view of many Northerners toward blacks was not all that

different from their former Southern enemies anyway (why else not urge aggrieved ex-slaves to migrate to New England, where they could be afforded
integration, economic security, and political protection?). And Southerners
were quick to point out the hypocrisy and sanctimony of Reconstructionists
who were not so utopian in their own home states. The rise of shrill radical
Republicans of the Northeast who would give the vote to blacks but not to
prominent white ex-Confederates, and the accompanying calls for the sus-
pension of habeas corpus in putting down night raiding and terrorism, also
bothered many Midwesterners. Besides, the destruction of Southern infrastructure during the war and the ensuing growing poverty were felt by many
north of the Mason-Dixon to be punishment enough for the former Secessionists. And the Union Army's terrible past experience with Confederate
cavalrymen like Forrest's raiders in Tennessee suggested to many seasoned
officers of occupation that it was preposterous that thousands of static gar-
risons of Northern soldiers in the South could stamp out nocturnal bands of
skilled horsemen.

Among an impoverished and disconsolate people, it was the unrepentant
Forrest, not its mostly ineffectual aristocratic planter and discredited political
class, who best symbolized unapologetic pride in defeat. The self-made man
who rose out of poverty only to lose his fortune through unstinting service to
the Confederacy became the popular ideal of Southern sacrifice and recalci-
trance. It mattered little that Forrest would mellow considerably or that his
tenure as the Klan's head would be short and finally at odds with his membership. In fact, his previous years as a slave trader seemed after the war to
have made him more, not less, sympathetic to blacks. Despite his occasional
fervent rhetoric, he sought out Union investors and partners and suggested
that freedmen enter the mainstream of public life. His funeral was attended
by hundreds of ex-slaves. Finally, either out of worry over his tenuous business ties with Northern capitalists or in real concern over the spate of killings,
Forrest disassociated himself from the Klan in January 1869 and as grand wizard purportedly ordered its official end as a national organization. Always the
realist, Forrest saw that the Republican victory in the national election of
1868 would strengthen radical Reconstruction in Tennessee, whose government now was mustering a militia to stamp out the Klan.

Most of Forrest's moderation came later; any earlier indications of a softening of his fury were lost in the immediate chaos of the postwar months, as Southerners were bewildered by former servants assuming superior positions in government and opportunistic scalawags and carpetbaggers purportedly buying up Southern property and assuming public office. The radical Republican reaction to Andrew Johnson's efforts at reinstating popular governments of Southern conservatives only acerbated the already tense situation, as calls went out to treat recalcitrant ex-Confederate states as mere territories under martial law.

Out of that conundrum grew the Ku Klux Klan. It apparently first appeared in Pulaski, Tennessee, sometime in spring 1866 and spread rapidly to other states between 1866 and 1867. True, in its original organization the Klan was not as radically racist as its second incarnation in the 1920s, with its far larger membership and more inclusive targets of hatred—Jews, Catholics, and foreigners. Ostensibly, the initial Klan arose as something of a lark, a secret society among displaced and irate veterans who were baffled by the disenfranchisement of prominent Southerners and the emerging political power of loyalist whites and freed blacks. Indeed, in its first manifestation it may even have enrolled a few conservative blacks who distrusted Northern radicalism. Forrest in later congressional testimony claimed that the Klan "was intended entirely as a protection to the people, to enforce the laws, and protect the people against outrages."

Still, inherent in its creation was the broad theme of returning the Negro to inferior status vis-à-vis the white man by destroying white-black unity leagues and black schools and private businesses—the logical precursors to the later intimidation of beating and lynching black political figures and sympathetic whites. At first the macabre secret rites, white sheets, and night riding were designed to instill terror more than to commit murder: the ghosts of the Confederate dead took over the night to do what they could not in broad daylight. But within a few months after its founding, the Klan became both more respectable and powerful—and increasingly was directly linked with the Democratic Party, which likewise championed a return of near-servile status to emancipated blacks. What distinguished the Klan from myriads of similar ad hoc secret societies and Southern white groups—the Confederate Relief and Historical Association, the Order of Pale Faces, and the Order of the White Camellia—were its mystic pretensions and professed fraternity of the defeated that helped it to cross state lines, form some type of general cohesiveness, and achieve a modicum of respectability and good-will even as it ratcheted up the level of brutality and intimidation against targeted individuals.

Klan messages were often a mix of professed concern for the white poor and calls for retribution against the forces of Reconstruction. During a visit of Forrest to Georgia in March 1868, the *Atlanta Intelligence* published a proclamation emanating from the "headquarters of the mystic order of the Ku Klux Klan." After bragging that it had done "justice to the afflicted and oppressed!" and had sought "to defend the orphan and protect the weak!" the published notice went on to proclaim that a sentence of death had been passed against "a traitor," and a "cowardly slayer of the innocent." Apparently in secret session, the Ku Klux Klan's leadership ordered the murder of an anonymous prominent Southerner who was to be "offered up as a sacrifice upon the altar of the innocent and lost." Shortly afterward, George W. Ashburn, a Columbus, Georgia, Republican leader, was killed by a mob of thirty-five disguised men. Rumors that Forrest was grand wizard of the Klan, evidence that the death sentence came from the organization's "headquarters," and the fact of the general's presence in Georgia at the time of the proclamation all suggest that he either ordered or knew in advance of the hit.

The circumstances of Forrest's exact role in the Ku Klux Klan are mysterious to this day—given the key role of secrecy among the klaverns, and the general's own worry that his public involvement might harm his efforts to forge partnerships with Northern businessmen or jeopardize his recent pardon. If in its infancy the Klan was still mostly a local Tennessee crackpot organization of white supremacists and misguided ex-Confederate zealots, it looked toward expansion through enlistment of a national figure who would galvanize support and increase membership—especially in light of the threat of newly enfranchised black voting in the election of 1867.

So, early in the spring of 1867 the nominal heads of the newly formed Klan, under the auspices of Forrest's former subordinate, Capt. John W. Morton, approached Forrest. Under somewhat disputed circumstances, he quickly emerged as the group's first grand wizard—a role that he would later deny in official congressional testimony. The bitter postbellum fights in Tennessee between ex-Confederates and Union loyalists, and Forrest's own famous career during the past four years in expelling Northern forces from the state, made the Tennessee native the natural choice for leadership of an in-home organization.

The Klan's birth was also overseen by an array of Confederate ex-veterans. And under Forrest, the Civil War hero, the Klan never lost its close connection with its military origins—the white sheets and night rides were originally intended to scare blacks into thinking the feared but long dead cavalrymen of the South had been called back to arms. Just as Forrest and other defeated Confederate generals believed in the fable of the Lost Cause—that chance, fate, or the singularity of Northern evil had quashed the South, not Northern power and skill—so the Klan tapped the same roots of Southern mysticism. The Klan was to be portrayed in the future in films like *Birth of a Nation* and *Gone With the Wind* not as the terrorist organization that it was, but, as Forrest hoped, a fraternal bulwark against dangerous Negroes and traitorous whites who preyed on innocent Southern women and destitute veterans.

Forrest, who was seeking to resurrect his fortune by forging railroad and insurance ventures with Yankee investors, was always cagey in admitting his presidency—even as he used his frequent travels on business to unify and expand the Klan organization beyond his home state. At forty-six he was famous, well-connected, eager to regain his prewar fortune and recapture the excitement of his Tennessee war years—and convinced that black enfranchisement would ruin the South. "Forrest commanded more brave men in the invisible army," a Klansman now bragged, "than he did while in the Confederate army." He at least admitted to a congressional committee in 1871 that he was receiving 50 to 100 letters a day from Southerners urging some type of reaction against Northern efforts to elevate the Negro to political equality with whites—inadvertent proof that he was generally recognized as a figure to whom the more desperate might turn. Given his later denials and the absence of written records, it is difficult to assess precisely Forrest's pivotal role in terms of active recruitment—though his itinerant career from 1867 to 1870 no doubt was useful for Klan activity. Usually his visits to various Southern cities on "insurance business" coincided with an upsurge in local Klan visibility and activity.

When reports grew that the Klan was turning more murderous, and as its more respectable supporters began to get cold feet after a series of harsh Federal countermeasures were promised, Forrest took pains both to "reform" the Klan—and finally distance himself from its more odious work. Yet his later renouncement of the Klan and his ostensible efforts to disband its local affiliates do not mask the reality that the general's name and support had done much to ensure its initial spread and leave his own ardent stamp on Klan activity. Indeed, in a controversial interview published on September 1, 1868, Forrest bragged to the *Cincinnati Commercial* that the Klan already had enrolled 40,000 members in Tennessee and about 550,000 throughout the old Confederacy. He went on to describe in intimate detail the general organization of the Klan and to assure the reporter that he could raise an army of 40,000 Klansmen "in five days" should trouble arise:

> I have no powder to burn killing Negroes. I intend to kill the radicals. I have told them this and more. There is not a radical leader in this town [Memphis] but is a marked man; and if trouble should break out, not one of them would be left alive. I have told them that they were trying to create a disturbance and then slip out and leave the consequences to fall upon the Negro; but they can't do it. Their houses are picketed, and when the fight comes not one of them would ever get out of this town alive. We don't intend they shall ever get out of the country.

Although he claimed in a letter to the *Commercial* and in later congressional testimony that he had been misquoted and in fact had never been a Klan member, many of his public pronouncements confirm the content of the interview and reflect his fervid views about the proper role of the Klan in the reconstructed South. Earlier he had addressed a crowd in Brownsville, Tennessee, in the same apocalyptic terms:

> I can assure you, fellow citizens, that I, for one, do not want any more war. I have seen it in all its phases, and believe me when I say, that I don't want to see any more bloodshed, nor do I want to see any Negroes armed to shoot down white men. If they bring this war upon us, there is one thing I will tell you—that I shall not shoot any

Negroes so long as I can see a white Radical to shoot, for it is the Radicals who will be to blame for bringing on this war.

Forrest then went on:

But if they send the black men to hunt those Confederate soldiers whom they call kuklux, then I say to you, "Go out and shoot the radicals." If they do want to inaugurate civil war, the sooner it comes the better, that we may know what to do.

Even after his official order to disband the formal Klan, Forrest still made it known that he approved of the general policy of terrorizing any who attempted to implement the aims of Reconstruction. In early 1870, a year after Forrest's purported disassociation from the Klan, Republican probate judge William T. Blackford was attacked in his home in Greensboro, Alabama. Over sixty Klansmen surrounded his house. Blackford in desperation immediately asked Forrest for clemency and protection—again evidence of the generally held belief that Forrest still controlled such night riders. After initially saving his life, Forrest nevertheless advised the judge to leave the South, remarking in explanation of his sudden departure that "he had given bad advice to the Negroes, and kept them in confusion, and off the plantations." Indeed, well after the official "end" of the Klan, Congress passed in 1870–71 a series of anti–Ku Klux Klan acts that equated the Klan with treason and allowed the President to ignore habeas corpus to hunt down suspected members. Congress clearly was reacting to the terrorist activity that continued or even accelerated well after Forrest's much publicized termination of the klaverns.

What, then, made the Klan so much more resilient and dynamic than numerous other hate organizations in American history? The answer lies not in its ideology per se, which was shared by many other racist groups. Rather, the Klan spread so rapidly due to its grassroots appeal to working middle- and lower-class whites, who saw its message as populist and reactive rather than merely hateful and xenophobic. The planning of assassinations, lynchings, and torture of targeted individuals also created a general climate of terror that no one was safe from the "invisible" empire. Klansmen postured as protectors of the working poor, defenders who feared the elevation of the blacks as threats both to their jobs and to their sense of privilege. Forrest told congressmen in 1871 that the Klan had arisen for just such a noble purpose. "My understanding is that those men who were in the organization were young men mostly; men who had been in the southern army, and men who could be relied upon in case of difficulty—of an attack from the Negroes— who could be relied upon to defend the women and children of the country."

Forrest further took pains to paint the rise of the Klan as a necessary unifying bulwark for the defenseless:

> There was a great deal of insecurity felt by the southern people. There were a great many northern men coming down here, forming leagues all over the country. The Negroes were holding night meetings; were going about; were becoming very insolent and the southern people all over the state were very much alarmed. I think many of the organizations did not have any name; parties organized themselves so as to be ready in case they were attacked. Ladies were ravished by some of the Negroes, who were tried and put in the penitentiary, but were turned out in a few days afterward. There was a great deal of insecurity in the country, and I think this organization was got up to protect the weak, with no political intention at all.

In Forrest's mind—and this would become a hallmark of Klan ideology—the "Negroes," not whites, were the aggressors. His organization was not offensive but simply defensive, formed to safeguard downtrodden poor Southerners from hostile blacks and their Union allies. Forrest himself had been born into poverty and had a natural affinity for the white poor, prompting Gen. Viscount Wolseley to suggest that his bleak upbringing—"what Napoleon termed the best of military schools, that of poverty"—was critical to his later military success. Forrest, the antiaristocrat and underappreciated general, understood perfectly the nature of the class resentment in Southern culture that became more manifest in the closing years of the Civil War—a seething of the nonslaveholding poor who had died on behalf of the rich plantation class and their wishes to protect Negro slavery.

In the immediate postwar years and before he entered into a series of entrepreneurial partnerships, Forrest helped draw on this rising Southern hatred toward Northern "radicals," who were trying to take the last vestige of pride—superiority over the Negro—away from the white Southern lower classes. "During the war our servants remained with us and behaved very well," Forrest admitted to the congressional inquiry, "but when the war was over our servants began to mix with the Republicans, and they broke off from the Southern people, and were sulky and insolent." That the Klan ostensibly became an organization of the masses, who in the short-term were not worried about endangering the influx of Northern cash or necessarily the efforts of the Confederate officer corps to regain their citizenship, was in part due to its first president, whose renegade past and unorthodox career gained him rapport across class lines.

Forrest himself was far more than an illiterate former slave trader. Beside his brilliant military record he was a cagey student of politics. His speeches and dictated letters in the decade after the Civil War reveal a constant theme of aggrieved whites, who alone were following the original intent of the Constitution against revolutionary efforts of radical New England Republicans to change the very nature of the federal government. In his way of thinking, he was not violating the laws of the United States inasmuch as the Northern-dominated Congress had consistently adopted legislation that was at odds with the spirit of the Founding Fathers. His folksy mixture of half-educated populism, grievances against Northern banks and insurance companies and their carpetbagger and scalawag hirelings, and threats to kill and return to the battlefield if need be, helped give the Klan its trademark character of unrepentant grievance for a forgotten constituency.

Under Forrest the Klan settled in on a pattern of predictable behavior: nighttime attacks on blacks coupled with daytime disavowals of violence. In his infamous interview with the *Cincinnati Commercial*, Forrest was canny in emphasizing the Klan's benevolent image. "I am not an enemy to the Negro. We want him here among us; he is the only laboring class we have; and more than that, I would sooner trust him than the white scalawag or carpetbagger." Again, the irony is that Forrest's own efforts at organizing resistance to Reconstruction were undermining his private plans to enlist Northern money in his own various farming and rail projects. When he realized that his public pronouncements to garner help from the North were at odds with his secretive life in the Klan, he seems to have attempted either to hide or end his active prominent role—perhaps a belated admission of his own culpability for a mass movement that had harmed the reputation of a struggling South.

No doubt the Klan or something like it would have emerged from the ashes of the Confederacy had Nathan Bedford Forrest either remained in obscurity as a lowly colonel on sentinel duty at the "damned" Lick Creek, or had a Union bullet at Fallen Timbers plowed a few more inches into the interior of his spinal column—or had the later renowned Forrest not agreed in 1867 to be the organization's first president. But without the prestige of Forrest as its initial national leader, the incipient Klan would have remained a different, far more fringe and ineffectual organization—something like the ephemeral Order of the White Camellia, without either the pretensions of political legitimacy or broad class appeal. The Klan, after all, also bragged among its members a handful of other ex-Confederate generals like Zebulon Vance, Wade Hampton, and John B. Gordon. But in most cases such boasts were either groundless or, if true, made no difference to the Klan's spread, given most ex-officers' lack of a popular following among middling Southerners or any rapport with the poor.

With Forrest it was a completely different case. He had gained a huge audience and possessed the temperament and skill to galvanize grassroots support. Lee was correct that no Southerner was better equipped to lead a large number of dedicated followers. His career as devilish marauder in the Civil War lent a natural aura to the Klan's trademark early practice of nocturnal rides of stealth and terror. Forrest himself may well have recoiled at the Klan's descent into murder and riot. And had he lived, he may well have been appalled at the later rebirth of the Klan as an exclusively racist organization—although his grandson became cyclops of the Atlanta Klavern Number One in 1921, an office gained largely through the prestige of his founding ancestor. But the very legacy of the Ku Klux Klan as America's premier hate group was in large part due to Nathan Bedford Forrest's own excessive temperament and unapologetic determination to return the South to its antebellum racial culture, to shoot down Northern radicals, and restart the Civil War if necessary in the process.

Forrest's career, like Sherman's, took off only *after* Shiloh and his remarkable charge into the Hornet's Nest, his late-night scouting of the Federal reinforcements, and his heroism in the final melee at Fallen Timbers.
Just weeks earlier his sound advice at Fort Donelson had been ignored, and
he was generally considered an iconoclastic nuisance to the Union Army
rather than a military genius to whom a significant theater of cavalry operations might be entrusted. Guard duty at Lick Creek was completely in line
with his previous commands. Only his precipitous charges at Shiloh freed
him from that obscurity and at last allowed his genius to emerge.

Just as Sherman was also attacked first in the battle and fought last, so
too Forrest seems to have never slept through the two days before being the
last man shot at Shiloh. Each was repeatedly nearly killed in his reckless efforts to ward off catastrophe and thereby emerge from either shame or obscurity. Such aggression at Shiloh had brought Forrest success while the
indecisiveness of Beauregard and the unimaginativeness of Bragg spelled defeat for his cause. From Shiloh, Forrest learned of the poverty of Southern
generalship and the wisdom of his own aggressive brand of war. The battle
made him famous, but famous in a particular manner as one at odds with
rather than as part of the Confederate command.

His independence and success at Shiloh gave Forrest the confidence to
act on his own and as he saw fit, and so turned him into a rebel within a rebel
movement. And when that rebel government collapsed and left disaster in its
wake, its most loyal and competent outsider rightly gained further credence
without culpability. No wonder Lee was reported to have turned down the
leadership of the controversial Klan and suggested Forrest instead; even if
the myth has no historical basis, it reflects general Southern perceptions that
a tired Lee was above such a controversial terrorist group, and that a precipitous and unabashed Forrest who had personally killed dozens of men was
not only not bothered by such an unorthodox organization, but also far better suited and eager to lead it out of local oblivion.

Forrest—slave trader, veteran of duels, overseer of executions, and killer
of twenty-nine bluecoats in battle—had once been praised by the Southern
military aristocracy for his undeniable service to the cause, but also been denied command commensurate with his unmatched military genius due to his
controversial background and near illiteracy (not to mention his dangerous

temper and reckless speech). So in the same fashion the Klan would serve the interest of an unrepentant South, which nevertheless publicly shied away from open association with the organization's repugnant methods of whippings, beatings, torture, lynchings, and murder.

There were many ripples from Forrest's heroism at Shiloh—both his subsequent short-term successes in prolonging the war in Tennessee and his lasting contributions to the idea of war as blitzkrieg ("firstest with the mostest"). It is no accident, for example, that Gen. George S. Patton, also a fan of the great marches of William Tecumseh Sherman, saw in Forrest brilliance unmatched by any other American general and may well have drawn inspiration from close study of his Tennessee campaigns. But rightly or wrongly, the legacy of Forrest has reverberated now for more than a century, most prominently through the rise of the Ku Klux Klan—a terrorist clique that rode at night with the same fervor and unapologetic violence as had once before its first grand wizard against Union intruders.

I end with an anecdote of a visit to Memphis in February 1999. On a cold February afternoon, I encountered not more than a half dozen visitors in the warmth of the Civil Rights Museum, now incorporating the hotel where Martin Luther King Jr. was assassinated. In contrast, outside in the wind and rain at the statue of Nathan Bedford Forrest in the city's central park I counted at least ten visitors, as well as flowers lying at its base. The public perhaps recognizes a ripple of Shiloh that military historians often overlook.

Postmortem

"The South never smiled again after Shiloh," wrote the New Orleans diarist George Washington Cable. However, in the battle's immediate aftermath it at least breathed a sigh of relief. General Halleck soon arrived to assume command from Grant of a huge force of invasion and then proceeded to fritter away any opportunity of destroying Beauregard's retreating army by a ponderous and dilatory march on a soon-to-be-evacuated Corinth, Mississippi. Still, if Shiloh did not lead immediately to a Southern collapse in the West, the undeniable Union victory left the Mississippi open. Soon a reassigned

Grant lost no time in assembling his Shiloh veterans for an assault on Vicksburg. Yet, despite the undeniable strategic significance of the Union victory, the enduring fascination with Shiloh lies elsewhere, in the human story of the soldiers who fought there.

The two-day battle destroyed two generals—Lew Wallace and Albert Sidney Johnston—and created the careers of two others, William Tecumseh Sherman and Nathan Bedford Forrest, with murderous consequences for their poor adversaries in the years to come. Many of the Civil War's military luminaries on both sides were also involved—Grant, Bragg, Beauregard, Halleck, and Buell. Two future presidents—Grant and Garfield—were veterans of the battle, along with a former vice president of the United States, John Breckinridge. The future navigator of the Colorado River, John Wesley Powell, lost an arm at Shiloh, and the Confederate Henry Morton Stanley, of later Stanley and Livingston fame, was captured there. Both felt that their later careers were formed in part by what they had seen and done at the battle. Was the human drama of Shiloh, then, in some ways different even from the larger and more momentous collision at Gettysburg, or the more murderous hours at Antietam or Cold Harbor?

Perhaps. While it was not the deadliest engagement of the national conflict, Shiloh was the first real carnage of the Civil War, a bloodbath in which there were nearly 24,000 combined Union and Confederate casualties. Of the some 110,000 who fought over the two days, nearly one in four men was missing, captured, wounded, or dead by Tuesday morning, April 8, 1862. In fact, there were more casualties in two days of fighting at Shiloh than in the combined total of *all* of America's wars up to that time—the Revolution, Indian conflicts, the War of 1812, the Mexican War, and the battles of 1861 and early 1862.

Due to the relatively small circumference of the battlefield, the inclement rain followed by unaccustomed heat, the two-day duration of the intense killing, and the inability of both sides to care for the wounded and dead, the battlefield was a macabre nightmare of stinking blood, flesh, and mud that left an indelible impression on all who fought there. And hundreds of reporters and sightseers sailed up in the battle's aftermath to survey the killing field. Adjacent to the Tennessee River and near to both Union and Confederate populations, Shiloh was an easy battle to reach for both sides;

in addition, the melodrama of the first day's Confederate advance followed by a stunning Union recovery made good copy and invited speculation on how the Confederates lost their first-day gains—and why Grant's victorious army was almost lost in the first few hours of the fighting.

The nation and the world were shocked by the butcher's bill, as newspapers and politicians rushed to assess blame, creating heroes and then demolishing them in a matter of days as contradictory reports from the confusing two-day slugfest trickled in for months afterward. Something or someone—Grant? Sherman? Wallace? Beauregard?—surely had to be responsible for the needless carnage, especially when the realization set in that after thousands of casualties, both sides claimed victory and neither army was really routed.

The sheer scale and unpredictability of the Western theater also made its first decisive battle utterly unique. Unlike the rather static front between Washington and Richmond, the West was a vast landscape where armies marched hundreds of miles to capture key cities like Nashville, Memphis, and New Orleans, seeking to turn entire border states such as Kentucky and Missouri into constant battlegrounds and wrestling over control of hundreds of miles of the Mississippi. A single set battle might open up or close down thousands of square miles of territory and thereby send whole states into the Union or Confederate camp—unlike the seesaw fighting in the quagmire of northern Virginia.

More important, Shiloh was the first full-scale battle in which rifled musket fire and canister shot on a large scale had ripped apart charges of heroic soldiers, shocking officers and enlisted men alike—and establishing the principle that the courage of running head-on against the enemy could be as suicidal as it was lunatic. Shiloh first took the glory out of battle. In forty-eight hours it dispensed with the idea that a single set engagement might settle the Civil War. Both sides learned that a day's killing might so disable an army that even the victors could not really dominate their adversaries given the huge parameters of theater war in the West. No wonder nightmares of the battle grew rather than diminished in the minds of veterans on both sides, despite the even greater killing to come.

The focus in the energy of the country had also shifted from east to west in the years before the war. It was no accident that presidents, novelists, and great generals to come were all assembled on the Tennessee River. Ohio, Michigan, Illinois, Indiana, Iowa, and the Western Confederacy of Texas, Tennessee, and the Mississippi River states were where the great transformations in American life were taking place, as the railroads, the nascent industry surrounding the Great Lakes, the frontier, and the Mississippi River all drew the most audacious and talented Americans of the mid-nineteenth century. So it was natural that among the tens of thousands of such men who met each other at Pittsburg Landing were dozens who would go on to change radically the course of American history—but only after they themselves were first changed by Shiloh.

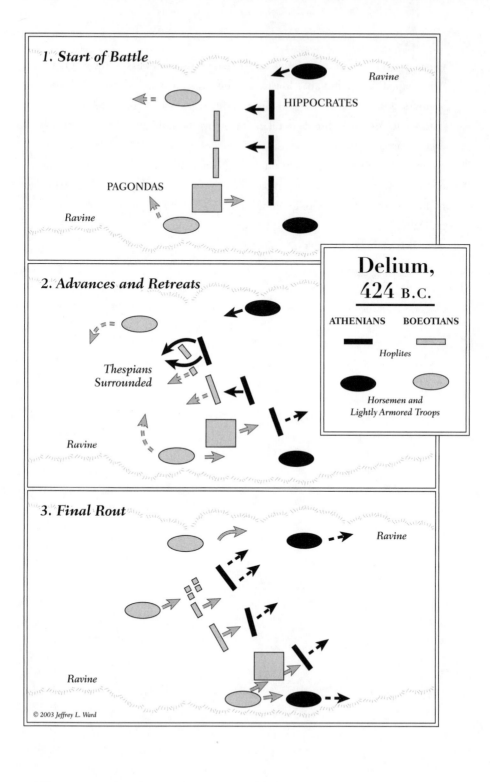

1. *Start of Battle*

Ravine

HIPPOCRATES

PAGONDAS

Ravine

2. *Advances and Retreats*

Thespians
Surrounded

Ravine

3. *Final Rout*

Ravine

Ravine

© 2003 Jeffrey L. Ward

**Delium,
424 B.C.**

ATHENIANS   BOEOTIANS

Hoplites

*Horsemen and
Lightly Armored Troops*

CHAPTER 3

The Culture of Delium,
November 424 B.C.

The Battle

Imagine a rolling plain of dry grain stubble, extending for not more than a mile before being cut off by ditches on both sides. Crowd fifty thousand men on it—some nearly naked, others weighed down with more then sixty pounds of arms and armor. Have them mass into two huge armies and then collide at a run with edged iron weapons—all striving to kill one another through their collective muscular strength at stabbing and pushing. Then end the entire sordid business in about an hour—with over two thousand corpses littering the ground in a trail of blood and entrails for a mile. Finally, simply forget about the afternoon's carnage and assume it never occurred at all.

The battle of Delium is just that—a gory nonevent. At best it is known only as one of many such hoplite bloodbaths of the past, in which thousands of Greek infantrymen lined up to spear the enemy, push the opposing phalanx off the field of battle, claim victory, and then return home. Most were obscure and sometimes stupid fights in far-off places of a distant age, of little interest or meaning in the grand sweep of history, rarely prominent even in the story of Greece, and entirely without any relevance for the lives of

Americans today. After all, not more than a few thousand out of some 300 million Americans know *what* or *where* Delium is.

Hoplite fights in ancient Greece are ostensibly no more or less worthy of remembrance than the thousands of horrific battles of the pre-Columbian Inca or Aztec empires, whose generals, soldiers, and dead are of no import to the cruel laws of history, lost entirely to subsequent generations when there is not a Herodotus or Bernal Díaz del Castillo to write what he saw or heard. Thus most of the large Greek battles such as Mantinea (418 B.C.), Nemea (394 B.C.), or Delium, while important in the shifting balance of power of the classical city-states, were often not landmark historical events. They were nothing like Salamis (480 B.C.) that saved Greece from the Persians and prompted a play from Aeschylus. The Athenian disaster at Sicily (415–13 B.C.) wrecked the Athenian empire and was fodder for Thucydides' observations of human folly. And Philip II's victory at Chaeronea (338 B.C.) ended the free and autonomous Greek city-state and led to the end of Demosthenes' career.

When the defeated Athenians trudged home, the neighboring state of Boeotia (pronounced "Beosha") was as before—oligarchic and still free from the Athenian empire. There was not even the drama of Spartan militarism pitted against the liberalism of Athens that illuminated other battles of the latter fifth century. The Peloponnesian War itself was not shortened by the Athenian debacle, or perhaps even lengthened because of the Theban triumph. An increasingly beleaguered Athens would continue to be plagued by enemies north and south, and a victorious Thebes would mount no grand invasion of Attica to follow up its victory at Delium below the walls of Athens. Perhaps only an Athenian victory might have had any significance in the war, knocking Boeotia out of the conflict—as the general Hippocrates promised his troops in the moments before the battle—and thereby lessening the odds of an eventual Spartan victory.

No great generals of antiquity—a Themistocles, Pericles, Epaminondas, or Alexander—fought at Delium. Hippocrates and Pagondas are scarcely known outside of Thucydides' brief mention of their respective commands for a day at the battle. Indeed, they vanish from his history as abruptly as they appear for their brief day. Even the tally of the dead was insignificant in

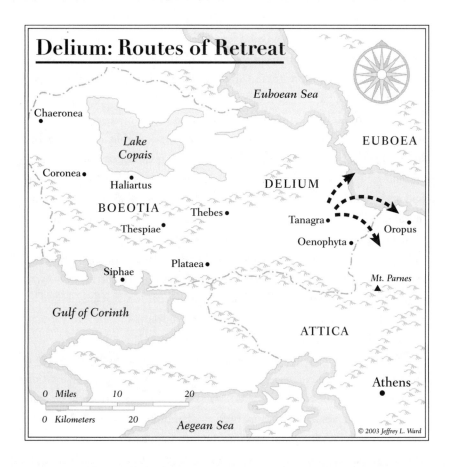

comparison, say, to the nearly forty thousand Athenian casualties a decade later at Sicily (415–13 B.C.).

Nor is Delium near either a great city or an important road. Unlike the sites of many key battles, it had no intrinsic strategic value—no geographical importance of any kind. It is not a key pass like Thermopylae, which was fought over for twenty-five hundred years from the Persian Wars to World War II. Delium was not the natural meeting ground of great cultures, like Adrianople at the nexus of major rivers and the site of fifteen major engagements since Roman times, a city that guarded access to the Black Sea, southern Europe, and the Mediterranean and often seen as the demarcation line between Europe and Asia, Christianity and Islam. The landscape of

Delium is not like the great battlefield of Chaeronea a few miles to the north, the critical bottleneck that opened onto the great plain of Boeotia and saw some of the greatest collisions of the classical, Roman, and medieval ages— and over the centuries with the likes of Philip II, Alexander the Great, Demosthenes, Sulla, and Mithradates on its soil.

There are no mute stone commemorations to the fight—no walls, castles, or even an occasional watchtower to be seen, no marble lion to mark the spot where the poor Thespians were slaughtered, no limestone plinth to memorialize the dusk run of the panicked Athenians. It is a hard battlefield to find today. Nature, the great leveler of the power of armies, played no macabre role at the battle: we are not horrified by the cruel seas of a Salamis (480 B.C.) that swallowed thousands of wrecked Persian seamen, or the horrible cold that froze entire armies at Stalingrad (1942–43). There was not even the horror of Okinawa's (1945) or Shiloh's mud (1862). Delium was mostly warm, flat, and mild. The suspense of this battle is not augmented by men falling into the sea as happened at Thermopylae (480 B.C.) or slipping off peaks tending Hannibal's elephants in the Alps (218 B.C.).

Yet what went on for about an hour or so in that nondescript plain changed the life of ancient Greece and the nature of European civilization itself—a Euripidean tragedy inspired, Socratic philosophy preserved and altered, an artistic renaissance launched, a community nearly erased, a monster at Athens spawned, and Western infantry tactics themselves created. The ripples of Delium have lapped even upon us, the unsuspecting, nearly twenty-five hundred years later—in ways that we can scarcely imagine.

The battle of Delium was the last gasp of a failed Athenian offensive into the neighboring state of Boeotia, the region surrounding the ancient city of Thebes. The fighting itself broke out near the sanctuary of Delium in 424 B.C., between the phalanxes of Athens and the Theban confederacy in a treeless, open plain, only a few thousand yards from the vaguely demarcated border between Attica and Boeotia. The ancient site is probably near the lovely modern hamlet of Dilesi, once rolling hills of grainfields by the Euboean Sea, but now a growing cluster of seaside vacation homes that serve as weekend retreats for harried Athenians.

There were always long-simmering disputes over the serpentine and mountainous boundary. This traditional Boeotian-Athenian enmity was fueled also by Thebes's past role during the Persian Wars. Nearly sixty years earlier she had led her Boeotian confederacy shoulder-to-shoulder with the Medes against her fellow Greeks. Indeed, at the Panhellenic victory over the Persians at the battle of Plataea (479 B.C.)—a few miles from Delium— the Athenians on the left wing of the Greek allied phalanx had plunged bitterly into the Theban turncoats and swept them in retreat along with their foreign overlords. In the bitter aftermath of the Theban humiliation during the Persian Wars (490–79 B.C.), raids and plundering expeditions by both neighbors continued throughout the fifth century B.C. as a series of stone towers and forts along their border was frequently captured, demolished, and rebuilt. Boeotia and Athens shared a history similar to France and Germany during much of the latter nineteenth and early twentieth centuries.

In the thirty years since the Persian Wars (479–47 B.C.), control of Boeotia had been decided on at least three occasions in its territory through dramatic pitched battles on the plains at Tanagra (457 B.C.), Oenophyta (457 B.C.), and Coronea (447 B.C.)—Athens first losing, then gaining, and finally losing for good its reign over her neighbor's land in the space of a few hours over the decade. Boeotians had grown quite accustomed to the efforts of Athenian imperialists to cross the borders in order to spread radical democracy among their own rural satellite villages.

But in 424 B.C. the battle was purportedly more than an outward fight over a few acres or even control over Boeotia itself. Rather, in the seventh year of her exhausting twenty-seven-year war with Sparta, now a major effort ensued by Athens to eliminate her "northern" front with Thebes so she might turn her attention southward exclusively to her Peloponnesian enemies. Only with a neutralized and largely democratic Boeotian confederacy would Spartan ravagers be prevented from marching on through Attica to rest in Boeotia. If the Athenians won a major battle inside Boeotia, raiding across the border would cease, and Athens might gain valuable Confederate troops from their newly pacified northern neighbors.

A few other factors fueled the Boeotian-Athenian hatred. Seven years earlier (431 B.C.), Thebes's unprovoked and unsuccessful nighttime attack on the nearby small village of Plataea, an Athenian protectorate, had marked the beginning of the Peloponnesian War. Add to these considerations that

Thebes and her Boeotian confederacy were governed by a moderate oligarchy and so were despised by the democrats at Athens. And in general Boeotians were habitually lampooned on the Athenian stage—backward rustics in comedy, and unbalanced inbred killers of Greek tragedy. Indeed, Boeotians shared a Panhellenic reputation as "pigs," rustic dullards who were both strong and stupid. For the Athenians the key to fighting these hardy farmers was to avoid a head-on collision of just the sort that took place at Delium. Later the historian Diodorus recorded that much of the Athenian defeat at Delium could be simply explained by "the superior bodily strength of Thebans."

How did the Athenians in late 424 B.C. end up at the obscure valley near Delium in an unwise hoplite fight against such formidable people? To invade Boeotia, the Athenians, in the spirit of the volatile war making of the Peloponnesian War, had devised an overly ambitious plan of combined naval and infantry maneuvers to deploy troops at the front and rear of the enemy—an impractical scheme, and one, like her other similar fiascoes to come at Amphipolis (422 B.C.) and Sicily (415–13 B.C.), doomed to failure given the poor logistics, communications, and general absence of secrecy among ancient militaries. The Athenian general Demosthenes had sailed three months earlier, intending to raise a democratic insurrection through the southern Boeotian countryside by an unexpected amphibious landing. Then, aided by partisans, he was in theory to move east toward Delium on the very day Hippocrates and his Athenian hoplites marched northward to the border. The outnumbered Boeotian army would scatter between the pincers and the surrounding countryside arise in open revolt. Or so it was thought.

Victory was possible only if the superior infantry forces of the Boeotians would face two simultaneously advancing Athenian armies. But unfortunately Demosthenes' naval assault to the west at the Boeotian town Siphae was timed too early. Once his plans were betrayed to the Boeotians, he was of little value in drawing off opposition from the Athenian land troops marching up from the south. Diodorus says that Demosthenes then sailed away "without accomplishing anything." In fact, he had ensured by his failure that a ragtag Athenian army of reservists would meet by themselves the finest infantrymen in Greece.

At first it seemed that there would be no fighting at all. On the news that

Demosthenes had failed, the rather motley army of mostly older Athenians and foreigners merely trudged to the border to occupy the sanctuary of Apollo at Delium. The worst they had done was to cut down surrounding vineyards and in general cannibalize nearby farmhouses for the flotsam and jetsam of the barricade. This Athenian occupation and dismantling of the temple at Delium, in addition to the fouling of sacred waters and grounds of the precinct, was a clear violation of the unwritten "laws of the Greeks," which even in times of war purportedly protected the Panhellenic sanctuaries. But like so many Greek protocols, religious forbearance was continually eroding in the escalating barbarity of the Peloponnesian War. By war's end the killing of prisoners, the massacre of civilians, and the defilement of sanctuaries were commonplace on both sides.

Consequently, in lieu of his intended but failed grandiose invasion of Boeotia, the Athenian general Hippocrates scaled down his plans considerably. In the end, after a two-day march out of Athens, he left only a small garrison at Delium. There is an aura of the carnival about Hippocrates' thirty-five-mile march out to Delium, reminiscent of the Union spectacle at First Bull Run. The Athenian *levée en masse* was an odd, unorganized, and motley group—frontline infantry bolstered by resident aliens, the poor, and the elderly. Later accounts suggest that there may have been well more than 20,000 Athenians at Delium, although Thucydides recorded that only 7,000 were hoplite infantrymen. The past idea that the hoplite phalanx of the Greek city-states reflected the exclusive agrarian makeup of the citizenry was no longer true at Athens. Her navy, empire, foreign trade, and radical democracy ensured that native-born farmers of Attica were not a majority of the citizens, much less entrusted with the exclusive defense of the polis. Add to that seven years of war, five enemy invasions of Attica, and the great plague of 431–26 B.C. (nothing, says Thucydides, so weakened the power of Athens), and it is remarkable that Hippocrates could field this second force at all.

With their own naval counterparts incommunicado and now sailing home, the overblown plans of the Athenians under Hippocrates immediately fizzled. Reduced to a little ravaging of the countryside, Hippocrates left a contingent at the now-garrisoned Delium and sheepishly took his throng a few thousand yards back toward Attica. In fact, when the main Theban army finally caught up to him, some of the Athenians were already nearly safe in their native Attica and about ready to disband. Under the normal protocols of Greek warfare, the crisis was now apparently over. The battle should not have been fought in the obscure valley near the sanctuary.

Most of the eleven *boeotarchs*—elected Boeotian generals of the state confederacy—had seen no reason to fight. These leaders, faithful to past conservative tradition, likewise urged demobilization of the army and a prompt return to their nearby villages. But a single *boeotarch* resisted—the Theban Pagondas, son of one Aeolidas, a gifted commander in his sixties and no doubt a veteran of the Theban triumph twenty-three years earlier at Coronea (447 B.C.). Through sheer force of personality and fiery speeches to the assembled rank and file, he convinced his colleagues to recommit the entire army and pursue the Athenians. Quite remarkably they were won over and agreed immediately to break camp and march after the Athenians.

Who was this strange man who alone had ensured that the battle at Delium was fought? We know almost nothing of him, except his mention as a well-bred youth in an ode of praise to his family by the Boeotian lyric poet Pindar (born 518 B.C.). Perhaps his noble birth and experience in the liberation of Boeotia one-quarter century earlier had given him the clout necessary to galvanize his reluctant colleagues. Later we shall see that his blueprint for the Theban attack at Delium was a landmark breakthrough in the science of tactics, suggesting a prior military precocity that remains shrouded to history. In any case, Pagondas's ardor and military ingenuity are good reminders that history is not merely the faceless story of larger economic and social currents at work that alone determine man's fate. Gifted individuals do count and by their very brazenness prove we are not pawns of forces beyond our control. In some sense the entire battle of Delium was fought because of a single old man's anger—and won because of his tactical acumen.

Such unusual initiative, nevertheless, posed psychological problems for defensive-minded troops of classical Greek armies. When pressed, hoplites battled superbly to protect their own land, but less so when attacking those of others. Sensitive to this reality that his men were no longer to defend Boeotia but were now on the offensive against an army soon to be on the opposite side of the border, Pagondas sought to reassure his men as the autumn afternoon waned. Since his agrarians had now left their defensive posture, Pagondas addressed bluntly the problem of morale:

> Boeotians! The notion that we should not give battle to the Atheni-
> ans, unless we catch them right in Boeotia, is one that none of your
> generals should have entertained. It was to ravage Boeotia that the
> Athenians crossed our frontier and built a fort in our territory.
> Therefore they are enemies of ours. . . . Between neighbors in gen-
> eral, freedom means simply the will to hold one's own. And with
> men such as these Athenians on our border, who are trying to en-
> slave near and far alike, how can we not fight it out to the bitter
> end?

In perhaps the first recorded defense of the strategy of preemption—of attacking an enemy that posed a long-term rather than immediate threat— Pagondas also set down the general principles of forward defense that have been enshrined in Western military thought from Vegetius to President Kennedy's speech urging a blockade of Cuba and the Bush administration's argument to strike at Iraq in early 2003. "Furthermore," Pagondas went on, "those who in confidence of their strength have a habit of attacking their neighbors, as the Athenians are now doing, are emboldened to march out against an adversary who is keeping quiet and will only defend itself inside its own land; but they are less ready to take him on when he is willing to fight outside his borders, and if opportunity arises, to strike the first blow."

Thucydides, who later may have heard parts of Pagondas's speech from Boeotian veterans of the battle, was keenly aware of the advantage in con- vincing offensive troops that they were in fact on the defensive. He records a startlingly parallel prebattle harangue by the Athenian general Hippocrates, who attempted to convince the Athenians that they too were fighting on the border not so much to annex Boeotia as to defend Athens from the yearly in- cursions of Boeotian horsemen. So in the minutes before the battle com- menced, both sides claimed that they were fighting reluctantly on the border for the sake of their home ground.

Pagondas concealed his Confederate forces behind a small hill, arrang- ing the phalanx by Confederate villages. His own Thebans, of course, were on the honored right wing of the allied Boeotian battle line. After a second harangue, the Boeotians suddenly ran pell-mell from the slopes. They caught most of the Athenians off guard. Those surprised were still listening to the speech of Hippocrates. The entire battlefield at Delium of gently curving hills could momentarily hide troops in valleys and depressions. That may well explain why the Athenians had little idea that the enemy was near, much less had occupied a superior position. On both sides of the plain, large gullies prevented the cavalry and the substantial auxiliary forces on the extreme flanks of both armies from even meeting.

Caught unaware, the Athenians had few choices. It was either lumber uphill into the Theban mass or retreat—or, if to stay put, to be bowled over. After hearing the fiery speech of Hippocrates, the Athenians chose to charge ahead. Hippocrates may also have thought that the confined battlefield offered some advantages in limiting the use of the enemy's feared horsemen, and he probably had no idea of the greater depth of the Theban right wing that was soon to smash his weak left. Thucydides' description of the actual fighting is brief—less than three hundred words to be supplemented by a mere one hundred words from our only other extant source, the historian Diodorus of the Roman era. Despite the uphill run, the Athenian right wing nevertheless quickly cut down the Boeotian Confederates opposite. Here all along the Boeotian phalanx on the left, the allies fell back in face of the Athenian upward assault.

The unfortunate villagers of Thespiae on the extreme left of the Boeotian phalanx soon were at the point of annihilation by the Athenians under Hippocrates. The allied contingents at their side had wisely, but less courageously, backed off from the charging Athenians. This abandonment sealed the fate of the Thespians, ensuring now that they would be cut off, detached from the main phalanx, encircled, and then butchered in toto.

Only confusion saved the Boeotian army as a whole, as the victorious Athenians mistakenly began attacking themselves—like some enormous renegade missile about to return course to obliterate its launch crew. In their bloodlust of butchering the enemy Thespians, the elated Athenians at the cutting edge of the phalanx now bizarrely began to shuffle in the wrong direction and collide with their own advancing troops from the rear. Before these enraged spearmen of the phalanx could be pulled apart, dozens must have been impaled by their own brothers, fathers, and friends. "Some of the Athenians," Thucydides dryly notes of this misadventure, "becoming confused because of the encirclement mistook and killed one another."

Such tragic mishaps are, of course, common in the modern mechanized warfare of explosives, internal combustion engines, and automatic weapons. Killing is accomplished anonymously across great distances, accomplished almost by mere thought and intent without the need of either physical proximity or muscular strength. A mere flick of the trigger finger can kill from afar unseen thousands where once "the work of war," to use Homer's words, was drudgery requiring hours to butcher a few hundred foes face-to-face. During the Cobra offensive of July 1944, shortly after the Normandy landings, American B-17s inadvertently bombed and killed in seconds over 135 Americans, in addition to wounding more than 500. Stonewall Jackson himself was fatally wounded by his own men in the aftermath of the Confederate victory at Chancellorsville (1863). Shiloh (1862) saw dozens of instances where Southerners fired upon each other in the dense thickets. Such examples are understandable and could be repeated thousands of times in the centuries—most recently during the war in Iraq in spring 2003—since the spread of gunpowder weapons in the fifteenth century. But how was accidental killing possible in the preindustrial world of classical antiquity, when men battled not with triggers and buttons, but during the day, face-to-face, and with handheld edged weapons? Cannot a man easily identify his foe a few inches away before he plunges a spear into his groin?

Not always. The apparent cause of the Athenians' calamitous blunder was the erosion of almost all sense perception during the melee of battle that allowed blood-drunk hoplites in column to stab blindly at anything at their front. When the fighting broke out, it was nearly dusk on the Boeotian border. Athenian hoplites, like all Greek infantrymen, wore ponderous helmets. At least some had on the old-fashioned Corinthian type with mere slits in the bronze plate for the eyes—and no cutouts at all for the ears. Thousands of heavily armed men on both sides of the battle line were also kicking up the early autumn dust of the rolling plains around Delium, no differently from the blinding clouds that follow a herd of hoofed animals on the run. Within minutes after the initial charge, no one—Athenian or Boeotian—could see much of anything at all. Thucydides remarked that under the best of conditions most hoplites had no idea of the fighting anywhere but in their own immediate vicinity. The tragedian Euripides a few months after the fighting at Delium has his character Theseus also lament of Greek infantry battle, "When a man stands face to face with the enemy, he is scarcely able to see what he needs to see." No one saw much of anything at Delium.

Nor could the combatants hear. The cacophony of thousands of wood shields banging against iron spear points, metal weapons in turn hitting bronze armor, wood spear shafts rattling on wood shields, mixed with the war cries of killers and their victims sobbing in extremis only added to the disorientation of the helmeted and heavily armed infantrymen. Euripides called all that "the great clouds of dust that reach the heavens"—heavy armament, the shock of massed columns colliding with like formations, and the sheer frenzy of killing. All explain why at the moment of greatest success the Athenian right wing began to encircle their Boeotian enemies, then gradually completed their turn back into their own advancing ranks.

Near these doomed Thespians, the other more self-interested Boeotian allies of the left and center had no easy retreat from the Athenians. They too were confused and in disorder prior to the Athenian uphill charge: some trying to flee, others attempting to fight and hang on. We should imagine that nearly all the five hundred Boeotian dead infantrymen of the battle were the surrounded Thespians or the trampled and smashed corpses of their disoriented and stampeding neighbors. Diodorus says at this point the Athenian right wing "slew great numbers" of the enemy.

What of Pagondas and his selected phalanx of Thebans a thousand yards away on the right wing? "Gradually at first," Thucydides says, they pushed the Athenian left downhill, clearing the battlefield through the advantage of favorable terrain and superior muscle. Their success was also due to the superior physical strength of the Theban hoplites. Only when the Thespian slaughter on his own left horn threatened to pour Athenian hoplites to the rear did Pagondas dispatch a reserve of cavalry to the left to come up over the hill to the rear of the victorious Athenians.

For thinking men at the moment of their victory, the mere appearance of two companies of horsemen need not have caused much alarm—radical as was the use of both reserves and integrated cavalry forces at this time. Armor-clad spearmen in column could always withstand wealthy aristocrats perched on ponies without stirrups. But to the victorious and exhausted Athenians, the idea that cavalry would play a decisive role in phalanx battle was startling—even more so the notion that such fresh troops on the horizon were still uncommitted and appearing seemingly out of nowhere over the hill. Busy spearing Thespians, flush with the revelation that the battle was won, the Athenians suddenly conjured up an entirely new army—and thus no rest for their labors, however heretofore successful. And so they simply disintegrated.

At this juncture, Pagondas on the Theban right took his cue, pressed on, and completed the destruction of the Athenian line before him. Soon the entire Athenian army was "in panic"—its once victorious and savage right wing now nonexistent, the left wearied, beaten down, and fragmented by the pressure of the accumulated shields of Pagondas's mass. All took off at a run to the rear for nearby Mount Parnes, the fortified sanctuary at Delium proper, the safety of Athenian ships, or the woods in the Oropus along the border in Attica. Some opportunistic Locrian horsemen arrived for the spoils and now joined the Boeotian predators in an open-ended killing spree.

Somewhere between 40,000 and 50,000 warriors fought at Delium, making it the largest battle of the so-called Archidamian War (431–421 B.C.), which marked the first decade of fighting of the twenty-seven-year Peloponnesian War between Athens and Sparta. For all its obscurity, Delium was one of the larger hoplite clashes in classical Greek history—and the first large one between Greek states for which we have an adequate historical account. Besides the 7,000 hoplites in each army, thousands more lightly armed troops and ad hoc skirmishers were present on the Athenian side and probably far more numerous than those present among the Boeotians (10,000+?). In any case, we know from our ancient sources that about 500 Theban hoplites together with 1,000 Athenian heavy infantrymen and an unknown but "great" number of lightly armed Athenians perished.

The pursuit of the Athenians from the battlefield must have gone on for much of the early evening until darkness and rough terrain put an end to the slaughter. Customarily after Greek hoplite battles, the victors immediately erected a trophy from the spoils of the battlefield—baggage and equipment abandoned by the defeated in addition to arms and armor stripped from the dead. Then, with acknowledgment of defeat, both sides exchanged the corpses for proper burial. The dispute was thus considered settled through occupation of the battlefield by the victors and the withdrawal of the defeated.

But at Delium the Boeotians soon learned that at least a few of the terrified Athenian fugitives had retreated to the garrison at Delium. Not only did the defeated occupy Boeotian ground, but they were ensconced in a precinct sacred to Apollo. Faced with this anomaly in traditional hoplite battle—the conquered were not entirely willing to sulk home in acknowledgment of their loss—the Boeotians themselves decided to hold the Athenian dead "hostage" until the sanctuary at Delium was completely cleared of its garrison.

After seventeen days in the open air most of the corpses were a putrid mess. In Euripides' tragedy *The Suppliants*, which was inspired by Delium, the recovered bodies from Thebes were described as "bitter to behold." Thucydides was struck by such blasphemy shown on both sides—a good example of the larger theme in his history that war broke down traditional custom and soon created a new barbarity in Hellenic relations—and thus gave a moving description of the formal Athenian reply to the Boeotian demand to exit the sanctuary:

> The Boeotians, in holding hostage the corpses in return for the holy places, were showing a far greater degree of impiety than those who were not willing to hand over the sanctuaries to get back that which they had a proper right to recover. And they [the Athenians] further made it clear to the Boeotians they must allow them to take up their own dead, not "on the condition that they leave the land of Boeotia" (for they were no longer in the Boeotian territory, but rather occupying land that they had won by the spear), but rather "in accordance with the ancestral protocols of making a truce."

The deadlock lasted seventeen days, until the Boeotians brought in more reinforcements from their allies and formally besieged the trapped Athenian refugees in Delium. They crafted an enormous flamethrower of sorts—a hollowed-out beam through which they blasted a pressurized concoction of sulfur, coal, and pitch to send out a jellied flame into the Athenian breastworks. Quickly the garrison went up in flames. The terrified Athenians boarded ships to evacuate the sanctuary, leaving behind another two hundred incinerated Athenians.

The sordid aftermath of an accidental battle was at last over.

Euripides and the Rotting Dead

Given soldiers' long established tendency to desecrate the enemy dead— from Xerxes' mutilation of Spartans at Thermopylae (480 B.C.) to the Japanese and less frequent American disembowelment of fallen soldiers on Okinawa—the Boeotians' failure to hand over immediately hundreds of Athenians who perished at Delium ranks rather low in history's scale of atrocity. Thousands of Aztecs, for example, were simply dumped in Lake Texcoco by Cortés's victorious conquistadors to decompose—while the Aztecs themselves often butchered the Castilians in gruesome rites of human sacrifice, eating parts of the corpses and then flaying the skins of what was left of the unfortunate Spanish remains. After the siege of Cyprus in the months before the battle of Lepanto, the Ottomans skinned and stuffed some of the captured Venetians. Fragments of thousands of arms, legs, and torsos were unearthed from the pulverized earth of Verdun for decades, as carnage from the anonymous howitzer shells of the First World War trumped the sacrilege toward the battle dead inflicted by history's worst killers.

Yet under the accepted conditions of Greek infantry warfare, the failure of the Boeotians to hand over the corpses immediately after the battle was considered an outrage for the times. The Athenians thought it a crime against the very *nomima*—or unwritten "laws" of the Greeks—that guaranteed that the dead were to be returned for an honorable burial upon the conclusion of battle. "The proper observance holds together all human communities," Euripides wrote of the Greek practice of returning the battle dead for burial.

Other factors contributed to the sense of outrage over the Boeotians' defilement. The Athenian soldiers had fallen on the borders of Attica itself— neither at sea nor in some distant land. The violation of kin rotting within a day's march of the Athenian acropolis further inflamed the citizenry back home. Moreover, the dead were not simply desecrated and then abandoned. Rather, they were held hostage as pawns to broker an Athenian exit from the garrison of Delium itself.

Over a year after the battle, probably during the spring Athenian festival in honor of the god Dionysus in either 423 or 422 B.C., the poet Euripides reopened onstage the painful and humiliating wound of the aftermath to Delium. While there is always controversy and uncertainty over the degree of allusion within Greek tragedy to contemporary political events, most critics agree that Euripides' *Suppliants* was offered to the Athenian citizenry as an occasion to assuage the recent trauma of Delium. *The Suppliants* is one of Euripides' nineteen extant plays—he purportedly wrote over ninety—and its presentation is explicable only within the larger context of the shame of Delium months earlier, and the stunning "violation of what all Greece holds to be lawful."

By the early fifth century B.C., the best of Greek tragedy had become central to the civic life of classical Athens. The city's most accomplished playwrights each spring presented dramas as part of the festival of the City Dionysia, the annual honorific pageant to the god Dionysus. The rules of dramatic presentation grew more or less to be standardized: each finalist in the competition presented at public expense three dramas and a fourth semi-comic "satyr-play." A panel of ten judges awarded prizes for excellence among the three finalist playwrights. The plays themselves lasted not much over an hour. They usually ranged from between a thousand and seventeen hundred lines—all chanted and sung in various rhythmic meters, making the productions somewhat akin to modern opera. Dialogue was interspliced with four or more choral odes set to music. No more than three actors were present at one time on the stage. All actors were male. And the train of nonspeaking actors and large choruses amid elaborate sets made a profound visual impression on the audience in the open-air amphitheater below the acropolis.

The theme and scope of Athenian tragedies were equally stereotyped: the playwright typically resurrected a standard heroic myth known to all the audience—the Trojan War saga, the house of Oedipus, or perhaps the grim stories surrounding the great heroes such as Theseus, Jason, Perseus, or Heracles. The script stayed fairly true to the well-known legends. The dramatists did not radically alter the received outlines of the myth: Jason and Medea could not be reconciled, Antigone would not be saved, nor Oedipus spared his eyes. But the actual dialogue, characterization, and action of the tragedies gave the playwright ample leeway to comment on issues and controversies of the fifth century germane to the contemporary world of the Athenian audience—thinly disguised, of course, beneath a mythic veneer.

New awareness over the role of stalwart women in Athenian society of the mid-fifth century, for example, might prompt Sophocles to rework the Antigone myth to create a strong female who was the moral superior of every male in her midst. The passing of an old generation of Athenian antidemocratic and heroic figures finds resonance in the uncompromising stance of Sophocles' Ajax or Philoctetes. Euripides laments the ongoing repercussions of the Peloponnesian War upon civilians by recreating the suffering of the innocent mothers and sisters of fallen Trojans; his *Trojan Women* was staged in 415 B.C., a few months after the final Athenian slaughter and enslavement of the neutral Melians.

In any case, in 422 B.C., Euripides chose to rework the mythical attack by seven heroes on ancient Thebes to present commentary on the recent disaster at Delium, the nature of Athenian society, and the unique differences between Athens and her Peloponnesian War antagonists. In *The Suppliants*—named for the chorus of mothers of the dead Argives who seek the return of the corpses of their sons—both of Athens's contemporary adversaries are castigated in no uncertain terms: Thebans are odious folk who "are violent and deprive the dead of their due burial," while "Sparta is savage and duplicitous in its character."

Euripides' audience knew intimately the general outline of the traditional myth of the Seven against Thebes. The exiled son of the blinded and discredited Oedipus, Polynices, gathers six champions from Argos to help reclaim the kingdom of Thebes from his brother Eteocles. The seven attackers march northward only to be soundly defeated while scaling the walls of Thebes. The sibling rivals Polynices and Eteocles kill each other in battle; King Creon, the new regent, then decrees that Polynices and his dead companions from Argos are to be denied proper burial—postmortem punishment for the insurrectionists' introduction of civil strife into Thebes.

Aeschylus and Sophocles also had resurrected the same general myth for their own various purposes of civic enlightenment. The *Antigone* of

Sophocles, for example, instead focused on the sister of the two slain brothers, Antigone, and her valiant attempt to bury Polynices—presenting the imperial Athenians with the growing dilemma between what is moral (the time-honored custom of burying the dead) and what is legal (Creon's edict to ensure postmortem punishment to the invaders). Aeschylus's even earlier *Seven Against Thebes* emphasizes the inevitable course of events that follows hubris, folly, and sin, as the failed attack on Thebes is proper punishment for the tragic flaws of the seven invaders while the crime of the victors of exposing the dead in turn will prompt a second—and successful—return by the children of the slain.

Yet for Euripides the old myth conjured up the new dual themes of the antidemocratic nature of Thebes and the burying of the dead—specifically the opportunity to offer a timely commentary on the recent disastrous battle with the Boeotians in 424 B.C. and the reassurance to the audience that they nevertheless had enjoyed a long-held moral superiority over the Thebans: although they had recently won a battle, the Boeotians remained the historic moral inferiors of the Athenians.

In his play, the Seven attack Thebes for the cause of justice in precisely the same manner as had Athenian democrats in 424 B.C. The Argive mothers of the dead (the "suppliants" who make up the eponymous chorus of the play) travel along with their king Adrastus to Attica to beg King Theseus of Athens to help in forcing the Thebans to return the bodies of their fallen: "The mothers wish to bury in the earth the corpses of those destroyed by the spear," Aethra, mother of Theseus, reminds her son. After some wrangling and being pressured by his mother, Theseus consents to the Argives' request. "Save the corpses, take pity of my misfortunes, and on the mothers whose children have been slain," Adrastus, king of Argos, begs Theseus.

In the first half of the play Euripides takes pains to emphasize that unlike the Thebans, the Athenian Theseus operates in a democratic society ("a city based on an equal vote"). Therefore, before mustering the army he must seek the ratification of the Assembly. In an exchange with a Theban herald, Theseus reminds the audience that the rule of law and equality are innate to the Athenian character—and Athens's sense of justice should properly extend across the borders of Attica. His motherland is thus bound to intervene in the affairs of other Greek cities to ensure justice for the oppressed: Athens will suffer much in the process but therein win great "good fortune." Euripides presents the audience with the proposition that Athenians went into Boeotia—both in the mythical past and the horrific present—as benign rather than grasping imperialists, and to bring the civilizing aura of good government to the backward and uncivilized Boeotians.

"The city," Theseus further boasts of Athens to the Boeotian herald, "is not governed by a single man, but is free. And the people themselves rule, and the offices are held by annual turns. Nor does the citizenry assign the highest honors to the rich, but the poor also have an equal share." The theatergoers—many of them no doubt surviving veterans of the disastrous Delium campaign—are not so subtly reminded that a little over a year prior they, along with their fathers, brothers, and sons, were in Boeotia fighting oligarchy and attempting to extend democracy to the peasants of Boeotia.

In a final long messenger's speech (most all action in Greek drama occurs offstage and is reported by heralds and messengers), we learn that Theseus and his Athenian hoplites are successful in defeating Creon and the Thebans. They recover the Argive bodies and in general demonstrate the morality and strength of democratic Athens. In his battle report the Athenian messenger also recounts how Theseus routed Creon's forces in a manner that makes the mythical Athenian victory almost follow the course of the contemporary defeat at Delium. Thus recently vanquished Athenians in the audience are reminded by Euripides that their mythical ancestors fought identically as they did and for a similarly noble cause.

The messenger in addition relates that Theseus and the elite held the place of honor on the right wing in the fanciful battle just as the general Hippocrates and his cohorts had led the Athenian right at Delium. The Athenian left—as also was true at Delium—was overwhelmed by the weight of King Creon and the Theban right. Euripides says of the mythical fight that since both right wings of the respective adversaries were victorious it was "a struggle evenly balanced." As the audience knew, so for a time had been the recent fighting at Delium.

At this point in the play the description of the battle must undergo the expected reversal from recent history: the audience is to be reminded *not* of Athens' recent inglorious defeat, but rather of its ancestral victory. Euripides thus has Theseus and his Athenians on the right—*not* the Thebans, as actually happened at Delium—send a relief squad to their beleaguered left wing: "making their way over to the struggling wing of the army." Thereupon King Theseus routs the Theban right, the entire Theban army then collapses, and the Athenians chase the defeated right into the city of Thebes itself—in precisely the manner that Pagondas at Delium had sent a relief squadron over to panic the victorious Athenian right wing, to shatter the morale of the entire army, and then to cause a general rout all the way back into Attica.

In the mythical world of *The Suppliants*, Euripides has nearly replicated the Theban tactics, but now transposed Athenians for Thebans—and thus before the defeated Athenians in the audience he has reinvented a magnificent victory! We moderns find such contorted reinterpretation of recent history bizarre if not farcical, but nevertheless we should remember that it is not a practice exclusive to the ancients. The Soviets broadcast films of the defeat of the Teutonic knights to remind their people of their recent victory over the Nazis, just as Hitler promised a final German victory in the manner of Frederick the Great's dramatic and unexpected resurgence against his numerically superior enemies. Ostensibly a mythical tragedy, *The Suppliants* ends positively for the Athenians in a way the tragedy of Delium of course did not.

The Suppliants concludes with a prophecy of the goddess Athena that the sons of the Seven, the so-called *Epigonoi*, will return to Thebes to avenge their fathers' deaths, sack the city, and thereby obtain everlasting immortality. Euripides' forecast is clear: just as the Argives at first failed to take Thebes and then were avenged by their victorious sons, so too the Athenians will raise another generation to wreak havoc on Thebes for their treatment of their dead elders.

The Suppliants can be seen partly as catharsis and partly as morale-building for the Athenians, mired in the eighth year of what would prove to be a twenty-seven-year war and recently reeling over the tragic destruction of their army a few miles from the theater itself. Unfortunately, unlike their mythical ancestors, no Athenian army arose to exact revenge for the desecrated dead.

To Euripides, both in the past and during the Peloponnesian War, Thebans had predictably shown a propensity to transgress the laws of the Greeks and dishonor the battle dead. Thucydides says that the Athenians who trekked across the border were the older men of the citizenry, a sort of home guard who had not quite expected to encounter the crack infantry of Thebes. Euripides perhaps had that tragic notion of an ad hoc muster in mind when he makes the Theban herald remark of democratic armies: "Whenever the issue of war comes before a vote of the people, no one reckons on his own death; that misfortune, he thinks, will come to others than himself. If death stood before his eyes as he cast his vote, Greece would not be self-destructing from a madness for the spear."

While *The Suppliants* is not considered to rank among Euripides' tragic masterpieces such as *Hippolytus, Bacchae, Medea,* or *Trojan Women*, it nevertheless contains some of the most striking paeans to Athens and the ideal of democracy in extant Greek literature. In that sense, *The Suppliants* remains a fountainhead of expression for the core values of Western culture. Moreover, rarely do Greek authors so cogently explain why the middle class—mostly the group of Athenian infantrymen who marched out to Thebes—is the glue that holds together any consensual society. "There are," Theseus proclaims, "three classes of citizens. The rich are of no use and always lusting after more gain; the poor who lack a livelihood are dangerous folk, who invest too much in envy, trying to goad the rich, as they are hoodwinked by the tongues of wicked leaders. But of these three classes those in the middle save states, since they preserve the order which the city has established." And the mythical Theseus (at a dramatic date centuries before democracy) brags further of contemporary democratic institutions at Athens: "Freedom is simply this: Who has a good proposal and wishes to bring it before the citizenry? He who does so, enjoys repute, while he who does not merely keeps silent. What can be more just for a city than this?"

What prompted this rare tribute to democracy and middle-class egalitarian culture in large part was the now forgotten battle and macabre fate of hundreds of Athenian citizens on a November afternoon along the Attic border. Quite simply, we owe the very existence of Euripides' *Suppliants* to the memory of the dead of Delium, and the sense of moral outrage over the transgression of the protocols of civilization itself. The Athenians, the historian Aelian tells us, as self-appointed custodians par excellence of Hellenic civilization, uniquely observed a law that required anyone coming upon an unburied corpse to bury it—and they seemed especially sensitive to any charge that the battle dead were left unattended.

Some eighteen years after Delium, in the aftermath of the last and greatest Athenian sea victory of the Peloponnesian War at Arginusae (406 B.C.), the democracy itself executed several of its own victorious commanders on grounds that they had been derelict in recovering the bodies of their own Athenian dead. On the eve of that battle at Arginusae, a soon-to-be-executed general had experienced a dream in which he and his companions in command were in the theater at Athens watching competitors put on Euripides' *Suppliants*—a clear warning to him of things to come the next morning when the victorious commanders were nevertheless condemned for not burying the dead. As Theseus sums up the morality of proper burial and custom, "Let the dead be covered by the earth, and let each thing return to that place from whence it came into the light of day, the spirit of a man to the upper air, his body back into the earth. For we do not possess our bodies altogether as our own: we live our lives in them and then the earth, our nourisher, must take them back."

I leave it to literary critics to judge the lasting importance of Euripides' *Suppliants* in comparison to both the playwright's body of work and the history of European drama in general. Yet the ripples of Delium perhaps did more than just prompt this single Greek tragedy. As the first bloody hoplite battle of the Peloponnesian War, and one fought in the environs of Athens itself, Delium helped shape Euripides' developing disgust over the war—and his growing propensity to use his drama to critique contemporary culture even in Athens's darkest hours. In that sense the rotting dead were not forgotten, but were catalysts that helped the playwright define a peculiarly Western tradition of writers, artists, and intellectuals, freely saying what they pleased about the conduct of atrocity in their midsts.

Thespian Tragedies

Not all the mourning was on the Athenian side. Across the battlefield, Delium would prove to be equally dreadful for hundreds of Boeotians from the hamlet of Thespiae, who would nearly be exterminated before the day was out. Thucydides believed five hundred Boeotian hoplites fell in all, but most of these were yeomen from the small town of Thespiae. It was their fate to be assigned on the weak Boeotian left wing opposite the crack Athenian troops. As we shall see, their deployment by the Thebans before battle was not accidental and their destruction thus came as no surprise.

Ancient Greek hoplite infantry battle is usually interpreted as a decisive collision of roughly equally sized armies, fights that the historian Herodotus once characterized as "most irrational," yet to be waged on the "fairest and most level plain." But in the age before the great Macedonian mercenary armies of Alexander, the Successors, and the legions of Rome, in nearly every major classical battle both sides were almost always composed of coalition forces. These were temporary alliances of small city-states whose militias occupied various places along their respective battle lines—mutually visible fronts that were usually not more than a mile or two long. Often they were only a few hundred yards apart. Literally dozens of small communities might send most of their manhood to line up to form one horn of a phalanx, and themselves be joined by additional allied contingents. Even apparently homogeneous armies were rife with tribal and class rivalries. While every ancient infantry force was eager to arrange its particular corps to find effective matches against an enemy for the good of the army at large, in the classical Greek practice of mustering militias from rival villages, the order of battle took on much greater political and cultural significance.

In theory the right wing of a Greek army was the place of honor. It was usually occupied either by those troops with the greatest military prestige or (in the case of armies on the defense) by local militias whose native ground was the scene of the engagement and warranted them preference. There were a variety of reasons why stronger forces were stationed on the right. But a primary consideration was tactical—to guard against the inevitable rightward drift of hoplites seeking protection in their comrades' circular shields for their own bare right spear-side. The furthermost file on the right of the phalanx—which had no shield protection for their vulnerable flanks—exacerbated the drift, seeking their own cover either in cavalry or rough terrain to their right. As entire companies shuffled crablike to their right to cover their right shoulders, armies such as the Spartans' might through careful drill develop this natural hoplite drift into a deliberate outflanking movement from the right side.

Consequently, less adept troops were usually stationed on the left wing, and perhaps the weakest of all corps in the center of the line—effectively reducing a hoplite battle like Delium to a contest where an army sought to win on the right before its own inferior left and center collapsed. Of course, the best fighters welcomed posting on the right where they could lead the charge. But they also realized that they would be butchering the poorest contingents of the enemy. Delium, then, was a classic instance where the crack troops of the Boeotian confederacy—the Thebans on the right—attempted to rout the weaker contingents of the Athenian army across the battlefield before their own suspect troops—the Thespians—collapsed and let the enemy into their rear.

The overall interest of an allied army was not always the paramount consideration of ancient generals. After all, the strong contingents on both sides of the battlefield customarily had a much greater chance of surviving the battle than did their own respective weaker left wings. There was constant tension—both ethnic and political—within a coalition when respective allied states were allotted their particular assignments, deployments that quite literally might mean survival or annihilation. Because of the close physical proximity of ancient armies before battle, and the usual decision to fight during the day and in summer, infantrymen always could view quite clearly the nature of the troops arrayed against them. Even in the confused opening charges at Delium, the Athenians were aware that the weakest Boeotians were on the enemy left wing—because they too had likewise placed their own suspect files in precisely the same place on their own line.

Once the fighting began, Greek hoplite battle was never a simple and simultaneous collision between two uniform armies. Instead it was a series of flash points as the two battle lines in places often collided haphazardly and sometimes not at all—given disparities in numbers, uneven terrain, and sheer confusion. As a result, casualties were usually not shared proportionally among allied participants. A century in the life of the small Boeotian community of Thespiae was quite literally determined by what befell its adult male citizens in no more than a collective few hours of fighting at Delium.

Nothing much remains of Boeotian Thespiae today. However, any modern visitor who surveys the rich Thespian countryside and the numerous small valleys of the immediate environs, the relative proximity to the Gulf of Corinth, and the access both to Attica and the Peloponnese via routes over the mountains of Pateras and Cithaeron can understand why Thespiae grew to be the second largest and most important polis in Boeotia—and thus a constant irritant to the aspirations of its larger and more powerful neighbor, Thebes. This rivalry between the two Boeotian city-states explains much of the tragic Thespian experience in hoplite battle for nearly two centuries. No wonder that in November 424 B.C., the Thespians drew the unenviable assignment of facing the elite right wing of the Athenians under Hippocrates.

We first hear of the ill-fated Thespian army over a half century before the battle of Delium, during the Persian Wars, when a contingent of seven hundred hoplites marched north with the Spartan king Leonidas to bar the Persian advance at Thermopylae. When the pass was turned, the Thespians along with some Thebans chose to stay with King Leonidas and his 300 Spartans. We should assume that they were annihilated to the man. Of the fourteen hundred Greeks who stayed behind with Leonidas, the Thespian dead represented 50 percent of the total allied casualties! This is a remarkable proportion when we remember that they composed only about 10 percent of the original Greek force of seven thousand hoplites. Posterity remembers the Three Hundred Spartans; few recall that over twice that number of Thespians died on the same day. Far fairer it would be for us moderns to associate the last stand at Thermopylae first with the "Seven Hundred."

Thespiae's larger contribution and smaller resources make its sacrifice for Greece even more remarkable than that of Sparta. We all remember the poet Simonides' famous ode to the Spartan dead under Leonidas ("Go tell the Spartan that here we lie obedient to their commands"; yet few of us recall the epitaph for the Thespian dead composed by the poet Philiades: "The men who once dwelled beneath the crags of Mt. Helicon, the broad land of Thespiae now boasts of their courage").

In the aftermath of the defeat, Sparta itself was safe from Persian attack. Thespiae, however, was in the immediate path of the invaders. Sparta lost at Thermopylae a little under 4 percent of its landowning citizen body; Thespiae probably most of its own. The victorious Persians, then, in the days after the pass at Thermopylae was breached, marched south and with Theban guidance demolished Thespiae. The surviving dependent population fled south to the Peloponnese. Thus, Thespiae as a material community of several generations ceased to exist once its army of hoplites was annihilated in a few hours to the north at Thermopylae.

Events the year after Thermopylae at the great infantry battle at Plataea (479 B.C.) confirm the unfortunate consequences of the Thespians' decision to stand fast the year before—and reveal how a single afternoon can doom an entire people. Herodotus says that the Athenian hero Themistocles made his child's tutor, Sicinnus, a citizen of Thespiae. Ostensibly he wished to help rebuild their community after the loss of the seven hundred at Thermopylae and the diaspora to the Peloponnese. Nevertheless, the exiled community sent its remaining scattered manhood—eighteen hundred strong—to join the Greeks at Plataea.

Interestingly enough, Herodotus remarks that the Thespians came without hoplite armor, confirming the notion that their city's hoplite yeomen and their arms and armor had been lost the year before at Thermopylae. A rough estimate would suggest that out of between two and three thousand adult males in Thespiae, a third (i.e., seven hundred) qualified for hoplite infantry service, and these had *all* perished at Thermopylae. The decision on day three at Thermopylae to stay with the Spartans resulted in the obliteration of the city, the death of most property-owning adult males, and the temporary evacuation of the surviving population to the Peloponnese.

Sometime in the two decades between 470 and 450 B.C., Thespiae would have rebuilt its walls and with new citizen musters reconstituted its citizenship to levels approaching its prior status before Thermopylae. But we do not hear of its army again until the battle of Delium in 424 B.C. There Thucydides says the Thespian left wing was encircled by the Athenians and "those Thespians who perished were cut down as they fought hand-to-hand."

The Thespian hoplites at Delium were additionally vulnerable on their flanks as a result of the massing of the Theban right wing to the unusual depth of twenty-five shields. More fighters taken out of the initial ranks and stacked to the rear shortened the overall battle line, making it vulnerable on the flanks. Was there a general Theban consensus that if there were to be casualties at Delium, better that they be from Thespiae? The left wing of the

Boeotian army—Thespians, and men from the villages of Tanagra and Or-chomenos—was not a natural geographical cluster that might explain these regiments' close proximity to one another on the battlefield. All three city-states, however, at times had shown open hostility to Thebes and even en-tertained pro-Athenian sympathies, perhaps explaining their deployment together against the enemy's better units: they would either kill Athenians or be killed. Either way Thebes benefited.

Thucydides does not give us a precise breakdown of the aggregate Con-federate dead—only that five hundred Boeotians fell, of whom the vast ma-jority must have been Thespians and perhaps also men from the town of Tanagra. Modern scholars, reviewing the epigraphical and archaeological ev-idence of casualty records on stone and burials from the battle, surmise that at least three hundred Thespians were killed at Delium, perhaps again from a militia present that day numbering six to seven hundred—or about two-thirds of the hoplite census of roughly one thousand landowning Thespians.

Somewhere near 50 percent of the Thespians present at the battle were killed in an hour or so of fighting—a third of *all* the small farmers at Thes-piae were now dead! Of the roughly seven thousand Boeotians present at the battle, perhaps 60 percent of the fatalities were from a group that made up 10 percent of the army. So roughly three generations after Thermopylae, Thespian hoplites had once again suffered a holocaust. Once more there were to be immediate consequences of an hour at Delium to the city, as the result of those losses would prove traumatic to Thespiae, both politically and spiritually.

Of the few archaeological remains we have from Thespiae the most prominent are the fragments of a public casualty list on stone most likely from Delium and partial remains of an elaborate common grave of the bat-tle dead, who were apparently honored in the city center by the dedication of a proud stone lion. We have the names of dozens of those killed at Delium, but not a shred of information about their lives. Who was Sami-chos? Did Polytimidas farm? Did the death of Philteros leave his family des-titute? Was Suateles a poet? Damophilos a musician? Or Aristokrates a builder? And what was Antigenidas thinking when he was surrounded and killed on the left wing, perhaps speared by Socrates or ridden down by Al-cibiades? And were Antanoidas, Anphicrates, and Euchoridas friends? Relatives? Neighbors? Perhaps fathers and sons? If not, why for posterity are they listed together on the inventory of the dead?

Thucydides reports that a few months after the battle, in the summer of 423, "The Thebans destroyed the walls of the Thespians, on the allegation of pro-Athenian sympathies. They had always wished to do this, but now they found an easy opportunity since the flower of the Thespians had been annihilated in the battle against the Athenians." Thespiae thus sacrificed its manhood at Delium, forgotten men like Pythias, Diakritos, and Chabas, to protect Boeotia from Athens—only thereby ensuring its own subsequent destruction by Boeotians from Thebes. Nine years later the Thebans helped put down an uprising of Thespian democratic sympathizers—not difficult since the city's fortifications had long since been dismantled in the ripples that followed the disaster at Delium.

Presumably in the three decades after Delium and ninety years after Thermopylae, a new generation of Thespians for a *third* time had brought infantry strength back up to normal levels of seven hundred to a thousand hoplite infantrymen. Whether the walls of Thespiae had been rebuilt after the destruction of 423, we do not know, but it is unlikely given the traumatic losses at Delium. Yet, tragedy struck Thespiae at the battle of Nemea in 394 B.C. during the war of allied Greek states against Sparta.

At Nemea the entire Boeotian confederation was placed on the favored right wing while the Athenian allies took up the far more dangerous left horn opposite the crack Spartans. The historian Xenophon provides us with little detail about the action, noting only that all the Boeotians were successful against their Peloponnesian enemies—except the Thespians. Unfortunately they were stationed opposite the doughty Peloponnesian Achaians from the town of Pellene. Xenophon states that while other Peloponnesians fled and were pursued by Boeotians, the hoplites from Pellene and Thespiae "kept fighting and were falling in their places"—an unusually vivid observation in an otherwise succinct narrative, suggesting a general slaughter at this point of the battle line on both sides.

What were the consequences of yet another catastrophic loss of landowning hoplites at the battle of Nemea? For the next twenty-three years until the fight at Leuctra (371 B.C.), an impotent Thespiae was at odds with the Boeotians in general and Thebes in particular, offering assistance to either Athens or Sparta, depending on the two states' respective hostility to Thebes at any given time. Thespiae may have still remained unfortified after Delium, and apparently lacked the strength to rebuild her walls until 378—and then only with aid from the Spartans.

Tragic consequences that follow hoplite battles were not always the results of large numbers killed in action. The Thespians learned that in 371 at the battle of Leuctra, when Epaminondas expelled their hoplites from the Boeotian army that was to face off against the Spartans—another indication that the presence and deployment of Thespian troops on the Confederate battle line was always rife with political implications. Not allowed to fight and without walls, Thespiae's only hope was a Theban defeat. But when the general Epaminondas instead achieved a stunning victory, the Thebans moved quickly to finish their earlier attack on Thespiae. Sometime after Leuctra her buildings that remained were razed for at least a third time and her population expelled from Boeotia altogether. Given a century and more of continual destruction in the aftermath of hoplite battles, it is no wonder that the present-day traces of classical Thespiae are essentially nonexistent.

The history of the Greek city-state cannot be understood apart from the histories of pitched battles. The fate of entire communities literally depended on where, how, and against whom their landowning hoplite soldiers were deployed in particular engagements. In some sense the entire history of the people of Thespiae is the story of little more than three or four tragic hours of fighting. The community that had nearly been wiped out by Thermopylae was lost at Delium—a disaster that itself led to yet another half century of additional misery. What were the ripples that followed the fallen Thespians whose names we now read on broken stones? From what little we know, their untimely destruction led to the complete end of all that they held dear—in a tragic chain of misery that ended at last when the ill-fated hamlet of Thespiae was no more.

The Faces of Delium

As at Shiloh, battle not merely changes whole communities or the cultural life of thousands, but just as often is the story of people. Rarely, however, do we receive much information about individual infantrymen of the ancient world. Usually the classical historians Herodotus, Thucydides, and Xenophon list by name only the respective generals, or on a few rare occasions cite for commendation especially brave warriors. Herodotus, for example, claimed that he had memorized the names of all 192 Athenians who fell at Marathon—although he provides no such list in his history. Casualty records on stone—we have a lengthy Boeotian public document of the Delium dead—give us little more than names.

Yet at Delium, the only pitched battle of the Peloponnesian War fought in close proximity to Athens, we have information about at least five notable Athenians and a few Boeotians. Close examination of these Athenian veterans—some in their forties, fifties, and sixties—reveals that they were among the elite of ancient Greece, interrelated to one another in a variety of intriguing ways, and were responsible in large part for the peculiar events at battle. In turn, they went on to shape thousands more through their own experience on that ghastly day.

Unfortunately for some quarter million residents of the Athenian state, there was a young twenty-six-year-old aristocrat present among the small contingent of Athenian horsemen at Delium. Worse still, for his generation, he fought extremely well at this, his first and most savage pitched infantry battle. Alcibiades not only survived the harrowing retreat in the fighting's aftermath, but he established a reputation for bravery as an Athenian cavalryman who protected the philosopher Socrates and other desperate infantrymen as they sought salvation from a host of marauding pursuers. The acclaim and spiritual capital won at Delium thrust the young firebrand—purportedly the most handsome man in wartime Athens, if not the most outrageous with his exaggerated lisp and fancy clothes—into the forefront of Athenian politics for a generation to come, with unfortunate results for thousands of Athenians not yet born.

Alcibiades was orphaned at the age of three. His father, the aristocrat Cleinias, had been killed at the battle of Coronea (447 B.C.)—an earlier Athenian failure to annex Boeotia some twenty-three years prior to, and not far from, Delium. With his younger brother, the junior Cleinias, Alcibiades grew up under the guardianship of the famous Athenian statesman Pericles and his brother Ariphron. Soon he also came under the tutelage of the middle-aged philosopher Socrates. Scurrilous ancient tales abound about his reckless youth—extended runaways to join older male lovers, charges of incestuous relationships with his mother and sister (an impossible story, not because Alcibiades was incapable of such outrage, but because he seems not to have had a sister), illegitimate children, and gratuitous brawling. Indeed, Socrates—to his later detriment—was blamed for the notorious career of Alcibiades, despite the admission of the latter that he had spent his youth fleeing from the moral strictures of his mentor.

Alcibiades probably saw his first military service a few years before Delium at eighteen, during an Athenian expedition to the northern Greek city of Potidaea on the eve of the Peloponnesian War. The Athenians conducted a brutal two-year siege of the port, causing widespread starvation and outbreaks of cannibalism among the entrapped townsfolk. During the ordeal, Alcibiades was caught isolated and wounded. He survived only due to his companionship with Socrates, who stayed by his side, preserving both his life and armor. In Plato's *Symposium*, the obstreperous Alcibiades in a mood of drunken candor blurts out that although he was later given a citation for valor at Potidaea, it was really Socrates who deserved the award.

In a military context, Alcibiades next appears at Delium, eight years after Potidaea. There, as a cavalryman, he attempted to fight a rearguard action against Boeotian and Locrian patrols. Immediate reports of the young Alcibiades' stalwart action served as a catalyst to his budding political career. Within months of the battle the pampered aristocrat had nevertheless positioned himself as a radical opponent to the traditional conservative leader Nicias and his colleague Laches—another veteran of Delium—who were attempting to find a peaceful solution to the war. Despite Alcibiades' vehement opposition, the two older establishment figures would soon engineer a truce with Sparta in 421 B.C., resulting in the so-called Peace of Nicias. The murderously internecine Peloponnesian War looked like it was at last over.

But by 420 B.C., a mere four years after Delium and a year after hostilities had ceased, Alcibiades had schemed to enact a treaty with democratic Argos, Sparta's chief antagonist in the Peloponnese. He then convinced the Athenians to threaten the general peace with Sparta: with his new mandate and popularity, Alcibiades succeeded in barring Sparta from the Olympic Games of 420, established points of resistance throughout the Peloponnese, and finally created a coalition of Peloponnesian states to fight Sparta at the climactic battle of Mantinea (418)—a brutal slugfest that saw the Spartans instead triumph over Athens's newfound allies.

No Athenian had done more to ensure that the Peloponnesian War would continue than Alcibiades, who undermined the Peace of Nicias and made Sparta stronger in the process. More astounding was his ability to galvanize popular support against Athenian conservatives. Given his own aristocratic birth, privileged upbringing, and elite tastes in clothes, horses, and entertainment, in some ways Alcibiades made an unlikely demagogue.

Once the peace ended for good, Athens returned to its traditional policy of multifaceted campaigns of aggression throughout the Aegean. Most notorious was the siege of the neutral island of Melos in 416 B.C. Once the city fell, the Athenians enslaved the women and children and executed the entire adult male population. The famous "Melian Dialogue" ending the fifth book of Thucydides' history provides a chilling account of arrogant Athenian envoys dismissing the Melian entreaties for neutrality. Power, not justice, the Athenian invaders lecture, is always the final arbiter of state relations; self-interest, not morality, is what guides and must guide the behavior of states. Appeals to mercy or hope for reprieve are misguided, not rooted in either logic or a realistic understanding of human behavior. The Melians must either capitulate or be destroyed, inasmuch as they are the weaker power, the Athenians the imperial hegemon. We are not sure of Alcibiades' precise role in the executions that followed the Melians' capitulation, but the biographer Plutarch relates that he had a large hand in the barbaric sentencing of the island's captured citizenry. Popular myth further related that he fathered a child by one of the enslaved women of the island.

In contrast, there is no doubt about Alcibiades' large responsibility for the disastrous Athenian expedition to Sicily that sailed from Athens a few months after the slaughter on Melos. Thucydides recounted in detail the great debate in the Athenian Assembly over the undertaking, highlighting Alcibiades' rhetorical success in convincing the citizenry to send a vast armada to Sicily 800 miles distant—even as an undefeated Sparta and Boeotia threatened the very Athenian hinterland. Worse yet, on the eve of the fleet's sailing, herms throughout the city—sacred phallic fertility statues to the god Hermes placed in front of Athenian temples and private homes—were found mutilated. Rumors spread about the outrage: the defacement meant either that omens were now unfavorable to the embarkation or, more cynically, that radical subversives were trying to undermine the democracy itself. Added to that sacrilege, additional stories circulated that the sacred rites of the Eleusinian mysteries had been profaned by mock celebrations in private homes—the equivalent of prominent American politicians caught lampooning the Last Supper or comically reenacting in drag the Crucifixion. In both instances of profanation, Alcibiades was alleged to have been a prominent ringleader. Although he had long departed with the fleet to Sicily when the formal inquiry concluded, Alcibiades' enemies quickly made plans for his recall, trial on charges of sacrilege, and hoped-for execution.

The comic poet Aristophanes once remarked of Alcibiades that "it is not wise to raise up a lion within the state—but once someone has reared him, one better pay attention to his moods." The voters of Athens failed miserably on both those counts. After entrusting the monumental campaign against Sicily to Alcibiades' singular genius—he officially held command with his co-generals Nicias and Lamachus—the Athenians now ordered his recall just as they were beginning to move against Sicily's pro-Spartan capital of Syracuse. After turning their lion loose on their enemies, the Athenians abruptly sought to cage him as he neared his prey. When state officials arrived at Sicily for his arrest on charges of profanation, Alcibiades escaped to Italy and shortly thereafter made his way over to the Peloponnese. There he provided the Spartan command with information about the entire Athenian theater of operations as well as more astute advice on how to wear down his own native city. The next two years resulted in the destruction of both the initial Athenian army in Sicily and an equally large relief force, resulting in a total of nearly forty thousand Athenians and their allies who never returned home. Athens was now nearly without sailors or ships.

By 413 B.C. the entire Sicilian expeditionary force was lost and the catastrophe rightly perceived as largely a direct result of Alcibiades' prescient advice to Sparta to send help to Sicily without delay. Nothing is more dramatic than Thucydides' account of the failure of the Athenian siege: a Spartan armada under the General Gylippus arrives in the nick of time at the Great Harbor at Syracuse to save the Sicilian capital from the besiegers. But the damage to his native country was not yet completed. During his two-year sojourn in Sparta (415–13 B.C.), Alcibiades not only advised the Spartan counterattack on Sicily but also helped devise the permanent occupation and fortification of Decelea—an outpost inside Attica not more than fifteen miles from the walls of Athens itself!

The result was that while Athens was bleeding in Sicily and losing most of her fleet and last reserves, a Spartan garrison was organizing systematic attacks on the Athenian countryside with relative impunity, driving away stock and slaves, attacking farms, and keeping many Athenians inside the city proper. Still not satisfied and ever eager to cement his position in the volatile world of Spartan high politics, Alcibiades now traveled to western Asia Minor in an effort to encourage the eastern Aegean subjects of the maritime Athenian empire to revolt, through a combination of Spartan political support and Persian money.

If earlier the chameleon Alcibiades had reinvented himself as a dour Spartan—no doubt discarding the customary lavish clothes, coifed hair, and ostentatious lisp—now in the court of the Persian satrap of western Asia Minor, Tissaphernes, Alcibiades had the easier task of playing the role of the pampered and effete Eastern court noble. Just as the Spartans had welcomed their Athenian convert to the brutal Laconian military life, so now Tissaphernes lavished praise on his newfound naturalized Persian grandee. Plutarch remarks of his protean persona:

> In Sparta he adopted gymnastic training, the simple life, and a dour disposition; in Ionia he pursued luxury and pleasure; at Thrace he was a great drinker; in Thessaly he was absorbed with horses; and at the court of Tissaphernes, the Persian satrap, his own pomp and profligacy outdid even Persian extravagance.

Yet a mere three years after his escape from an Athenian capital sentence, Alcibiades was close to being put to death again, this time by his new benefactors as well—allegations of seducing and impregnating a Spartan king's wife did his cause no good. Facing both Athenian and Spartan death sentences, Alcibiades for at least two years (413–11 B.C.) continued his brilliant intrigue with the Persian lord Tissaphernes. Why not play Sparta off against Athens, Alcibiades argued to the Persian court, giving money to both sides to ensure that the Peloponnesian War continued in stalemate? Three decades of war could only help Persia in its larger aim of wrecking Greece.

Eventually the Persians also grew tired of Alcibiades' conniving. The only avenue of escape was a recall back to Athens. Political upheaval in 411 B.C. gave Alcibiades another opening. Athenian rightists had staged a coup and for a few months managed to instill an oligarchy in efforts to seek some end to the political infighting and redress the disastrous conduct of the war—perhaps with a rapprochement to Sparta. Although those rightists were his old political enemies, Alcibiades now embarked on a brilliant policy of triangulation to find his way back to Athens.

To the Persians, he argued the wisdom of supporting Athens: only that way could the growing power of Sparta be stemmed. A friendly Athenian navy would leave the coast of Asia Minor alone; two balanced adversaries would damage each other in ways Persia could not. To the Athenian oligarchs who were tenuously holding power, Alcibiades reminded them that—with the proper intermediary—Persia was likely to look favorably on their more narrow government; he also offered implicit support for their efforts at checking the mob; the volatile Assembly, after all, had demanded his own death sentence four years earlier. And finally, to the democratic resistance he offered inspired military leadership and a renewed crusade to lead a reconstituted fleet against the Spartans. All the while he stayed away from Athens, constantly monitoring the ebb and flow of the relative balance of power between Persians, Spartans, Athenian oligarchs, and democrats as he intrigued with Athenian seamen on the nearby island of Samos and avoided making explicit shows of support for any side.

The strategy worked brilliantly—and solely for his own narrow personal interests. Within a few months the oligarchy collapsed and Alcibiades was recalled (although he dared not yet visit Athens). As a stalwart of the reenergized democracy, he led the Athenian fleet in a sustained and largely successful naval campaign in the Hellespont—a theater conflict that resulted in the short-term resurgence of Athenian maritime supremacy and the near destruction of the Spartan fleet. At last by 407 B.C., Alcibiades sailed into the Piraeus and was greeted by popular acclaim and the return of his confiscated property. Enemy of domestic reactionaries, foe to the hated Spartans, and guardian of Hellenic freedom from the threats of Persia, the reinvented Alcibiades now rallied the democracy to renew the war effort. He was only forty-three and at the pinnacle of Athenian politics—all thanks to his brilliant start at Delium seventeen years earlier.

But given the volatility of the Assembly, the mercurial character of Alcibiades, and years' worth of accumulated enemies, his renewed ascendance was but the calm before the storm. After an Athenian naval defeat at Notium (406 B.C.), Alcibiades' naval campaign faltered and he was relieved of command. Surmising that dismissal, as in the past, would lead to indictment, and indictment to a sentence of death, he fled to one of his safe estates in Thrace. There he did his best in reduced circumstances to plot yet another return to Athens while he intrigued with the local Persian satrap, Pharnabazus. But with the defeat of Athens in 404 B.C., Alcibiades had played his last card.

A second and far more violent right-wing cabal now overthrew Athenian democracy in April 404 B.C. Its leaders quickly made it known that they would tolerate no return of the perennial Athenian firebrand Alcibiades and so agitated for his death. There were receptive ears abroad. The architect of the Spartan victory and protector of the Athenian revolutionaries, the admiral Lysander, welcomed the opportunity to settle Sparta's own grievances against the traitor Alcibiades. Meanwhile, dynastic succession threatened the Persian Empire as the satraps Pharnabazus and Tissaphernes watched carefully the growing rivalry between Artaxerxes and his usurper brother Cyrus for the Achaemenid throne—an increasingly dangerous landscape for the old intriguer and outsider Alcibiades, now ensconced on Persian-occupied soil. With enemies like these, Alcibiades was hunted down in Phrygia and executed at the age of forty-five, his political ambitions in ruins—along with the Athenian empire he had sought both to expand and destroy.

Despite Alcibiades' undeniable military acumen, political skills, and the perfidy of his enemies, his political record was one of abject catastrophe for Athens. His legacy was far more than the cynical manipulation of the Assembly, his self-serving embrace of allies and foes, and his criminal indifference to the role of Athenian religious symbolism and traditional values. He was also responsible for fundamental damage to Greece as a whole that went well beyond the loss of Athens's empire. Alcibiades' efforts at conspiracy in the Peloponnese—when they failed—helped undermine the Peace of Nicias and ensured that a remission from the killing and a brokered peace would evolve into another decade and a half of even more brutal internecine Hellenic war. In the increasing savagery of that conflict, a democratic Athens butchered innocents as did no other Greek oligarchy—and Alcibiades seems to have been the proponent of just such an ironhanded policy, as the murder of the Melians perhaps attests. He was architect of the Sicilian expedition, a harebrained Athenian scheme to conquer Syracuse, the largest democracy in Greece, that nevertheless might have worked had its instigator not betrayed its plans and galvanized Spartan intervention. The cost of tolerating an Alcibiades was the destruction of Athenian naval resources, the revolt of imperial allies, and the annihilation of a generation of Athenians.

The creation of the Spartan fleet with its critical subsidies of Persian money was in part a result of Alcibiades' conniving between 415 and 411 B.C. The ruination of the promise of classical Greece at the end of the fifth century was not Alcibiades' legacy alone, but no other Greek did so much to kill other Greeks and promote war for war's sake, unconcerned with morality, ideology, or nationality. Pericles, Cleon, Brasidas, Lysander, and most other prominent proponents for war in both Athens and Sparta were at least nationalists—if not believers in the respective causes of radical democracy or narrow oligarchy. Alcibiades embraced no belief other than himself.

Had Alcibiades died at Delium, the Peace of Nicias might have survived—or at least the Athenians would not have entered upon the disastrous policy of provoking the Spartans without sending commensurate forces abroad to back up their brinkmanship. The destructive last two decades of the Peloponnesian War might have been averted. Had other firebrands subverted the truce, and war renewed, Athens nevertheless probably would not have gone to Sicily. From Thucydides' account of the debate over the expedition, Alcibiades' brilliant rhetoric almost single-handedly sways the volatile Assembly to reject the prudent advice of Nicias to stay home. In consequence, thousands of Sicilians, Melians, and Athenians might well have lived had Alcibiades perished at twenty-six rather than at forty-five years of age.

Tragically, he not only survived Delium, but thrived precisely because of the unique circumstances of that disastrous day in Athenian history. It was not merely his bravery in the retreat, but the peculiar nature of the battle itself that served as his catalyst. In a society where tradition and family meant everything, the sight of the mounted twenty-six-year-old orphan fighting inveterate enemies who had killed his father on the same soil of Boeotia stirred his compatriots. More important still, Alcibiades fought not in isolation, but alongside an entire cadre of luminaries of Athenian society, many of whom, unlike the young upstart, either ran or perished at Delium. Alcibiades' brave day at Delium in sight of Socrates and his friends would prove to be a time bomb for Athens.

The Athenian army was commanded on the right wing by another young aristocrat in his early thirties, Hippocrates, son of Ariphron, who had just reached requisite age to be elected to the board of generals two years earlier. Thucydides records his speech to the army in the moments before it was surprised by Pagondas and his Thebans.

> If we conquer, the Peloponnesians will never again invade your native soil with the help of the Boeotian horsemen. In just a single battle, you will win not only this ground here, but also ensure the freedom of your own. So charge out against them in a manner worthy both of your city—the most preeminent in Greece which as your fatherland each of you adore—and of your fathers who once vanquished these same men at the battle of Oenophyta under Myronides and so became the lords of Boeotia.

The rhetoric, if it was really Hippocrates' and not the historian's own, shows flashes of brilliance and a determination to lead his ragtag army head-on against the best infantry in the Greek world. What little we know of Hippocrates suggests that he was an avid supporter of an aggressive Athenian pursuit of the war and a coplanner of the invasion of Boeotia. Hippocrates was also the nephew of Pericles, the distinguished imperialist who had led Athens into the Peloponnesian conflict before dying from the plague in the second year of the war.

In most Greek battles, generals were posted on the right wing, occupied the front line, led the charge, and perished in defeat. Frequently their sudden deaths in the melee served to hasten the collapse of the phalanx itself. For Athens, the ruin of its right wing at Delium had irrevocable effects on the ultimate course of the battle. We do not know whether Hippocrates' death preceded or followed the ruination of his elite right—Pausanias in his *Description of Greece* relates that he was killed rather early on in the fighting. But had he survived and perhaps held together his already victorious hoplites, the Athenians may well have won the battle outright, and then either annexed parts of Boeotia or at least forced a Boeotian withdrawal from the war—a coup that may well have brought the Spartans to negotiations at the end of 424 B.C.

From all accounts, despite his youth Hippocrates was a capable and energetic leader at the forefront of those Athenians determined to press home the war. Earlier in the conflict he had proposed Athenian citizenship for the survivors of the small Boeotian town of Plataea that had been overrun by Theban oligarchs and their Spartan supporters. And weeks before Delium, Hippocrates had attempted to stir up insurrection in nearby Megara and bring this critically important city near the Isthmus over to the Athenians. Moreover, the battle at Delium was part of a strategically ambitious theater campaign that failed largely due to the incompetence of his fellow general Demosthenes. Hippocrates' entire tenure as general is evidence of relentless support for radical imperial democracy in the tradition of his uncle Pericles, advocacy of continued aggression toward Sparta, and keen interest in conquering or neutralizing neighboring Boeotia.

But even more intriguing, Hippocrates' father was Ariphron, making him the nephew of Pericles—and the *stepbrother* of the adopted Alcibiades, who was six years his junior. We know little else about the personal life of Hippocrates other than he orphaned three children with his death at Delium. Yet his brief career suggests that his stepbrother Alcibiades was influential in his bold decision to invade Boeotia, and no doubt was stationed among the mounted Athenian elite that guarded the right wing. Hippocrates' death, coupled with the bravery of his adopted sibling, had the effect of enhancing Alcibiades and removing a talented rival from among the radically democratic leadership. For Hippocrates and Alcibiades, Delium was the key moment in two stepbrothers' promising careers, one aborted by death, the other launched in defeat. For Athens it would have been far better had their fates been reversed.

Other notable Athenians at Delium were also connected to Alcibiades through mutual acquaintances. Plato, the best remembered pupil of Socrates, nearly a half century after the battle wrote his *Laches* nominally on the subject of courage. The dialogue takes place between the Athenians Socrates, Laches, and Nicias. Purportedly set sometime around 420 B.C., four years after the Athenian defeat, the discussion draws on the battle in a variety of interesting ways. Laches was a prominent democratic statesman and general who is often mentioned as a leader in most of the Athenian campaigns and political initiatives during the first decade of the Peloponnesian War. In the *Laches*, the speakers have just watched young men training in armor. The question then arises as to the best type of education necessary for young Athenian infantrymen—should they learn set military moves and skills or simply rely on traditional bravery to win battles?

Nicias—the conservative general whom Alcibiades outmaneuvered to win approval of the Sicilian expedition—argues for specialized training. In doing so he seems to recall the situation at Delium:

> The greatest advantage [of being trained in using weapons] arises when the ranks of the phalanx become broken, and the need arises for one-on-one fighting, either in pursuit attacking someone who is fighting back, or in flight defending against the attacker. Whoever possessed such skill, would not suffer anything in single engagements, nor even if attacked by a host of enemies; he could prevail in any situation.

Well over four decades after the battle, Plato here explicitly uses Socrates' skill in escaping the Boeotians as proof that young men of his own age must learn how to use their weapons through set moves. Only that way can infantrymen of fourth-century Athens avoid just such a debacle as the defeat of a generation past. Delium serves the philosopher's larger goal of stressing that education and training are not antithetical to innate ability, but rather, if properly pursued, refine and improve upon nature. Laches is made the foil to Socrates in his own eponymous dialogue. He confesses that the middle-aged philosopher "made his way with me in the retreat from Delium, and I can tell you that if the other Athenians had been willing to be like him, our city would be standing tall and would not have suffered such a terrible fall." Later in the dialogue Laches reiterates that Socrates was alongside him during the rout and proved unshakable in the ensuing calamity.

Plato was only five when Delium was fought. Yet he must have grown up with general stories of the Athenian disgrace and Socrates' own extraordinary courage in particular—so that the battle once again found itself immortalized in classical Athenian literature. A final footnote to the career of Laches: although he had been instrumental in brokering the peace with Sparta in 421 B.C., he also led the Athenian contingent at the battle of Mantinea in 418 B.C.—a result of the anti-Spartan confederation engineered by Alcibiades. The latter, who helped force the battle, was not present at the actual fighting. Laches, however, was. And six years after Delium, he seems to have experienced once more a similar failure of courage. Although cogeneral of the Athenian contingent at Mantinea, he joined in the panicked flight of his men from the pursuing Spartans. This time, however, there was no Socrates at his side. He, along with some two hundred Athenian hoplites, was killed. Plato must have had these two incidents in mind when he wrote *Laches* decades later: a shaky Laches saved at Delium by his proximity to the redoubtable Socrates, only to be later killed at Mantinea when he once more lost his nerve.

What explains this strange interest of Plato in Delium, a battle fought when he was a tiny boy? Besides the towering figure of Socrates, we also know that Plato's own stepfather Pyrilampes was part of the call-up of the home guard, fled the battlefield, was wounded and then captured—only later to be ransomed from the Boeotians. Pyrilampes was probably fifty-six at Delium. His age reminds us again that Hippocrates' home guard had drawn from the reserves of Athenian manpower and was full of hoplites well past their prime. Pyrilampes was a notorious Athenian bureaucrat, infamous for his lavish junkets to Persia to conduct state relations, and ridiculed as well for the prized peacocks he brought home from one such trip—and habitually showed off at public displays for years afterward. If Plato first met Socrates a decade and a half after Delium (somewhere around 410 B.C., when he was about twenty), he would have heard of the battle even earlier from his stepfather—and Pyrilampes' own retreat, capture, and ransom would contrast markedly with Socrates' successful fighting withdrawal. In fact, that very divergence in mettle between stepfather and mentor at Delium may have haunted Plato for the rest of his life.

In his utopia of the *Republic*, for example, a middle-aged Plato presents a variety of ideas about military service, along with advice to the state about how to improve the spirit of its soldiers. Fathers (does he have his stepfather Pyrilampes in mind?) are to take their sons out to the battlefield to make them watch the fighting, with the guarantee that the "older guides" can direct them away in safe retreat "if the need arises." But those who are caught alive (again, like his stepfather?) are *not* to be ransomed but left to the desires of the enemy: "Any one of them who leaves his assigned rank or tosses away his arms, or is guilty of any similar act is to be demoted to the farmer or craftsmen class."

Plato goes on to be quite clear about the fate of captives: "And anyone who is taken alive by the enemy, should we not give him over to his captors to deal with their 'catch' any way they please?" In contrast, the courageous— i.e., the Socratic—shall be given military prizes for their heroism, be greeted by all as heroes, even to the point of being publicly kissed by well-wishers. Had his general policies come true, Plato's own stepfather would have languished in a Boeotian jail or have been summarily executed after the battle.

Delium affected a handful of individuals in the most remarkable ways— Alcibiades emboldened, Hippocrates finished, Laches and Pyrilampes embarrassed. The Socratic and Periclean common connections between all four are uncanny and perhaps provide a small glimpse into a close-knit cadre of friends and associates, mostly very young and middle-aged, who marched and rode out together somewhere on the Athenian right wing, hardly expecting to collide without support against the finest infantry in Greece. While the later careers of these notables affected the course of Greek history itself, one man's experience at Delium—the common nexus to them all—changed the ages.

Socrates Slain?

Classical Greek thinkers saw no contradiction between a life of action and contemplation, even in the extreme polarities between military service and philosophy. Plato sighed that fighting "always exists by nature between every Greek city-state." In classical antiquity philosophers rarely argued for pacifism or conscientious objection to military service. The idea of a "just war" centered on only two criteria—neither involving the moral question of killing the enemy in battle. Fighting instead was to follow the laws of the Greeks pertaining to the treatment of prisoners, heralds, and civilian populations; and war should be in the true interest of the state.

Nor did the intellectual class find it either fashionable or compelling to castigate war itself. Instead they were more likely to find themselves with spear and shield than in a study condemning man's folly. A number of Greek writers, thinkers, and statesmen fought in the phalanx. The lyric poet Archilochus was killed in battle on the Aegean island of Thasos. The poets Tyrtaeus, Alcaeus, and Callinus, the playwrights Aeschylus and Sophocles, the democratic leader Pericles, the historian Thucydides, and the orator Demosthenes all took their slot in the files of the phalanx or on the banks of a trireme.

Plato himself may have served as a hoplite in the Corinthian War. At the siege of Samos (440 B.C.), Melissus, a Samian philosopher and student of Parmenides, led his ship into battle against Pericles' fleet. Sophocles was also at sea there, among the elected high command of Athenians who came to enslave the island. The philosopher and mathematician Archimedes died in the storming of Syracuse, in his final hours employing his novel military machines against the Roman besiegers.

Likewise Socrates, the father of Western ethical philosophy and veteran of the fighting in the campaign of Potidaea, found himself on the battlefield at Delium. He is not mentioned by either Thucydides or Diodorus in accounts of the battle, who must have either not known of his presence there or felt that his battle service was not unusual and thus not worthy of special mention, given that only elected officers on both sides are expressly noted. Instead, what we know of his ordeal derives from Plato and the Platonic tradition that turns up in later writers such as the biographer and essayist Plutarch. In these sources Socrates fought heroically and was nearly killed. While we have mention of his actual hand-to-hand fighting in the melee, his fame derives from his stubborn retreat and refusal to join the panicky frenzy that overtook most of the Athenian army.

After the appearance of the Theban cavalry reinforcements and the subsequent hysteria that infected the Athenian right wing, and the continual battering on the left by Pagondas's deep columns, most of the Athenian army took off at a run to the rear for safety in different directions. They headed in four directions—either to nearby Mount Parnes, to the fortified sanctuary at Delium proper, to the beach and the refuge of Athenian triremes, or to the woods in the Oropus along the border in Attica.

There were already over 10,000 lightly armed Boeotians present at the battle in addition to 1,000 cavalry and another 500 light-armed skirmishers. With the Locrian reinforcements and the victorious hoplites, there may well have been a swarm of nearly 20,000 or so enemy pursuers, many of them either mounted or agile, lightly equipped auxiliaries. The early evening chase turned into a massacre. The routed Athenians, without much cavalry support or auxiliary skirmishers, and struggling to fling away their heavy armor, were vastly outnumbered, slower, confused, and in many cases disoriented in the growing twilight. Theirs was a nightmare long remembered at Athens.

Socrates—he later thanked his "divine" voice for directing him out of danger—wisely avoided both the escape routes to Delium and the high ground of Parnes. And so he found safety in a third way through the forested borderland of the Oropus. Again, the disaster of this Athenian "home guard" must have quickly taken on mythic proportions and been recounted constantly throughout Athens: Hippocrates, nephew of Pericles, stepbrother of Alcibiades, and general of the army, killed; Alcibiades' bravery during the retreat soon to inaugurate his meteoric political career; Laches' dubious courage in the flight from Delium foreshadowing his demise at the subsequent battle of Mantinea (418 B.C.); and Plato's own stepfather and greatuncle, Pyrilampes, captured when Plato was but a mere boy.

In three later dialogues—*Laches, Symposium,* and *Apology*—Plato makes direct mention of Socrates' gallantry in the flight, how he backpedaled and made an orderly withdrawal toward the borderland of Oropus accompa-

nied by both Laches and Alcibiades. In the *Laches*, Socrates is made to lecture about the proper technique of attacking and fending off blows when in
isolated combat, with a clear allusion to his own nightmarish experience after Delium. Laches brags of Socrates that "if other Athenians had been willing to be like him, our city would be standing tall and would not then have
suffered such a terrible fall."

In Plato's *Apology*, the last speech of Socrates' life, the seventy-year-old
philosopher reminds his accusers, who sought to have him executed on spu-
rious charges, that long ago in three terrible battles he had kept rank and not
left his position. The man they charge as a corrupter of youth and blasphe-
mer of traditional religion was in fact a war hero. In Plato's *Symposium*, Alcibiades gives a detailed description of the acute danger Socrates found
himself in during the general rout after Delium:

> I happened to be riding; he was serving as a hoplite. As the army
> was scattered he was retreating with Laches when I happened on
> him. At first sight I told them to keep their courage up as I told
> them I would not abandon them. Then I had even a finer view of
> Socrates than at Potidaea. For my part I was less afraid since I was
> mounted. First off I noticed how much more in control of his
> senses he was than Laches, and how—to use your own phrase,
> Aristophanes—he made his way there just as he does here in
> Athens, "swaggering and glancing sideways." So he looked around
> calmly at both his friends and the enemy; he was clearly giving the
> message to anyone even at a distance that if anyone touched this
> man, he quickly would put up a stout defense. The result was that
> he and his partner got away safely. For it is true that attackers do not
> approach men of this caliber but instead go after those fleeing head-
> long.

Plutarch, centuries later in his life of Alcibiades, also recalls this widely
circulated story that Alcibiades rode past Socrates and his isolated contingent who were in dire straits. But in Plutarch's version Alcibiades' mounted
presence saves the life of Socrates as the enemy "was closing in and killing
many." In his *Moralia*, Plutarch adds an additional twist—that Socrates'

choice of escape alone saved him and his friends, as most other Athenians who headed over the mountains were ridden down and slain, while those who reached Delium were eventually besieged.

The disparate ancient evidence nevertheless points to two characteristics of Socrates' retreat: Delium was a horrific Athenian catastrophe where hundreds were mercilessly hunted down and killed right on the border of Attica, and where Socrates' courage and good sense brought him out alive when most around him were killed. Had the middle-aged philosopher been stabbed by an anonymous Locrian horseman, or if his small band had been overtaken by pursuing Theban infantry, or if he had chosen to flee toward either Delium or Mount Parnes, where most of his terrified comrades were killed, the *entire course of Western philosophical and political thought would have been radically altered.*

Would Socrates' ideas have survived without a young Plato to gather, write down, and interpret them? Plato, approximately forty years Socrates' junior, was a boy at the time of the battle of Delium. Had Socrates been killed, then the entire scope of Plato's dialogues would have been fundamentally changed. Even had a mature Plato written philosophical treatises, his dialogues—if there were to be any dialogues at all, since the original genre is patterned directly after Socrates' oral interrogations—would have largely been non-Socratic both in form and content. In his autobiographical *Seventh Letter*, Plato admits that he was naturally gravitating toward a life of politics until his association with Socrates. Perhaps his youthful disillusionment over the philosopher's execution prompted him to turn to philosophy and reject an active life in government.

Much of Plato's singular literary genius drew inspiration from the magnetic character of an elderly Socrates, who wandered the streets of Athens engaging the strong, smug, and secure in tough question-and-answer sessions. In the process he apparently made an impression on the adolescent Plato, who probably came under Socrates' tutelage sometime in his twenties—roughly in the last decade of the Peloponnesian War (e.g., 410–404 B.C.). The influence of the elder Socrates on the young student remained profound until the old man was executed when Plato was about thirty.

Socrates is the chief interlocutor in the majority of the Platonic dialogues and the hero of the masterpiece *Apology*, which chronicles his final

defense on charges of impiety and moral corruption before an Athenian jury.
Socrates' concern that philosophy should deal with ethics, not the mere natural inquiry or cosmology of earlier formal speculation, characterizes nearly
all of Plato's early work. The idea that from knowledge comes virtue, and that
ensuing morality can thus be taught through rational choices and the sup-
pression of desire, seems to be derived from the thought and actual practice
of the historical Socrates. And the notion of Socratic duality—men have
souls whose integrity they must not endanger by a surrender to the appetites;
the world we sense and live in is but a pale imitation of a divine and perfect
counterpart—forms the basis of Plato's later sophisticated investigation into
morality, language, the hereafter, politics, and the fine arts.

Plato's interest in philosophy—had he eventually developed such an interest from *other* contemporary thinkers—would have had little to do with
Socrates. And Socrates himself wrote nothing. He founded neither a school
nor an institutional framework to perpetuate his ideas. The philosopher received no money for his teaching. He had no literary executor. There was no
formal cadre of trained students who were obliged to keep alive his teaching.
In an imagined post-Delium world where Socrates never met Plato, would
we now know anything about the itinerant philosopher or his ideas? Did the
course of Western philosophy rest on how well Socrates avoided the jabbing
of spears at Delium?

Could there have been any other contemporary record of Socrates without Plato—had the forty-five-year-old philosopher never made it out of the
hills of Delium? Our other main source of Socrates' thought is preserved in
the works of the historian and essayist Xenophon, whose dialogues *Memora-
bilia, Apology, Symposium,* and *Oeconomicus* feature Socrates as the main
questioner on topics as varied as love, agriculture, war, politics, and his own
career as combatant against the Sophists. But like Plato, Xenophon also grew
up under the influence of Socrates, veteran of Delium. He was born sometime around 430 B.C. and was probably at most a year or two older than
Plato—despite later erroneous tales that Socrates had saved him at the
battle.

Consequently, had Socrates been killed by a Boeotian spear when Plato
and Xenophon were children, it seems impossible that *any* of their later work
would have centered around the lively presence of Socrates as interlocutor,

their tough questioner and role model who serves as the fountainhead of their own ideas. Socrates' influence rested on two general criteria: memorable question-and-answer sessions that took place during his late forties, fifties, and sixties, and the written memoirs and derivative philosophy of Plato and Xenophon. Both facts required that the philosopher survive the spears of Delium.

The famous orator and educator Isocrates also claimed to be a pupil of Socrates. He is mentioned favorably in Plato's *Phaedrus* as a star student of the old philosopher. But Isocrates was born in 436 B.C., twelve years before the battle of Delium, making him nearly a generation older than both Plato and Xenophon. Had Socrates been killed in 424 B.C., when Isocrates was twelve, the older philosopher would have had little if any indirect influence on the young orator, whose thought seems derivative from Socrates, especially the latter's disdain for radical democracy. It would have robbed Isocrates of any indirect knowledge of a quarter century of Socratic anecdotes and teaching. His ideas probably would have had little place in Isocrates' massive corpus of work.

Would we know anything of Socrates' thought without the testimony of Plato and Xenophon? The philosopher Aristotle, of course, refers to Socrates often. But much of what he criticizes is derived from Plato and Xenophon, inasmuch as he was born (387 B.C.) twelve years *after* Socrates was executed (399 B.C.). A slain Socrates at Delium would also have played almost *no* role at all in Aristotle's own thinking for a variety of reasons. First, there would have been no mention of Socrates in either Xenophon or Plato. Second, Socrates would have died not twelve, but instead thirty-seven years before Aristotle's own birth. Third, a dead Socrates would have been deprived of a final twenty-five years of life in which his own thinking reached maturity. These were precisely the years that gave his ideas a chance to filter through the oral tradition of discourse at private parties and personal recollection of the last quarter of the fifth century B.C. in Athens. Most likely, a dead Socrates at Delium would not have even appeared by name in Aristotle's entire corpus—much of which gains its power from its deliberate posture against the politics and theology of both Socrates and Plato.

Were there other writers and philosophers who might have captured for posterity Socrates' ideas *before* he marched out at Delium? Not many. As we have seen, Thucydides, the contemporary historian and chief source for the battle of Delium, does not mention Socrates in his history at all. We also have no public or private Athenian inscriptions that mention him by name.

Instead, only a few names of other philosophers survive in association with Socrates. They, like Xenophon and Plato, were self-proclaimed followers of the unique Socratic emphasis on philosophy as ethics and dedicated themselves to ensuring his memory as a great man who fought rather than joined the Sophists—those contemporary intellectuals who charged stiff fees for their lectures that championed moral relativism and situational ethics. The chances, however, that any of these writers would have developed a sizable Socratic corpus of work had the philosopher died in 424 B.C. are nil.

The rather obscure Antisthenes, for example, may have been the same age as Socrates—and even known him well *before* Delium. Fragments of Antisthenes' work survive. What little we know of Antisthenes suggests that he was especially interested in the Socratic method and lifestyle—or at least the need for the man of contemplation to set himself apart from society and the temptations of the flesh. But Antisthenes could hardly have kept alive the ideas of a middle-aged, rather than seventy-year-old, Socrates. For one thing, he seems to have written largely to combat Plato—and thereby may not have authored anything had Plato never met Socrates.

Plato names Antisthenes as being present at Socrates' last hours. Much of what little we know about his work seems prompted by Socrates' martyrdom and the fate of philosophical stalwarts who opposed mobs like the frenzied crowd of Athenian jurors. Had Socrates died at Delium, then, Antisthenes would not have found his striking model of principled resistance to the ignorant crowd.

Finally, we have only fragments of Antisthenes' work. Although he seems to have been known to Aristotle and a few others, the chances that his work in changed circumstances would have survived classical antiquity seem remote. It is absurd to think that had Socrates died at forty-five rather than seventy, we would know any more of him through Antisthenes than the tiny scraps of his work we now possess; indeed, it is more likely that we would know nothing of Antisthenes at all!

Another Socratic follower, Aeschines of Sphettos, wrote seven dialogues. The theme of his works was apparently a defense of Socrates' association with the dissolute Alcibiades. None of these dialogues survives except in a few fragments and quotations. But since Aeschines was roughly the same age as Plato and Xenophon, like the latter two, he met Socrates only *after* Delium—and thus obviously he would *not* have devoted his life to a philosopher who did not write and whom he did not meet. In short, without a direct Socratic connection, we have little reason to believe any of Aeschines' work would have survived had Socrates died in 424 B.C.

Were there any others who might have known Socrates before Delium? Phaedon of Elis is just a name. Mere scraps of quotations of his two dialogues are extant. A near contemporary of Plato and Xenophon, he too was a small boy at the time of Delium. Nothing remains either of the work of Aristippus or Cebes, who both purportedly wrote panegyrics of Socrates. Again we are left with the conclusion that most Socratic followers who were inspired to write about their mentor did so only after meeting him in the period *after* the battle of Delium—when they were of an age to wander along after the itinerant questioner.

Many of these adherents seem to have been prompted to write *after* Plato began his early dialogues surrounding Socrates' death, either to enhance or reject the Platonic testimony. Socrates' other admirers, whose works are essentially lost, appear to have been influenced especially by his last courageous stand against his accusers in 399 B.C., in addition to the striking contrast between the grandfatherly philosopher and their own youthful zeal and impressionability. But in any case, the work of these lesser Socratics was either scarcely known or not highly regarded.

We are left with an inescapable conclusion: almost everyone who wrote anything about Socrates and his thinking came to maturity *after* the battle of Delium. Socrates' influential students were nearly all acquaintances from his late forties, fifties, and sixties. Had he died at the battle in 424 B.C., the later Western tradition of philosophy would have known almost nothing firsthand about either Socrates' life or thought.

We do, however, have at least one contemporary source for the life of Socrates who knew him well *before* the battle of Delium, a critic who has left us a gripping portrait a mere year after the battle—the comic playwright Aristophanes. The picture of Socrates in his *Clouds* (423 B.C.) is not pretty.

His Socrates is a vicious caricature of a middle-aged huckster. Indeed, because of Aristophanes' influential status, and since he portrayed Socrates on the stage before thousands of Athenians, both Plato and Xenophon in part spent their entire lives trying to counteract that apparently commonly embraced Aristophanic portrait of Socrates as con man and Sophist. Aristophanes' depiction of Socrates reached far more Athenians—mostly the men in the street who made up the audience of Attic comedy—than did his portrait by either the more refined Xenophon or Plato.

Some scholars have suggested that Socrates' hagiography in the works of both Plato and Xenophon was partly meant as a response to the vehemence of Aristophanes' earlier slander. Other comic poets—Ameipsias and Eupolis especially, whose works are now lost but were widely popular during the 420s—also caricatured Socrates onstage. They reinforced the devastating portrayal by Aristophanes, whose lasting vilification so bothered Plato and Xenophon. Again, small numbers of elites read or attended private recitations of Plato and Xenophon. In contrast, *thousands* of working Athenians viewed the comedies of Aristophanes and his rival comic poets.

In Aristophanes' comedy *The Clouds*—often considered his masterpiece and produced on the stage in 423 B.C.—Socrates is the *worst* of the sophistic charlatans. He appears as a leader of that infamous collection of slick tricksters who made a living by filling the heads of an idle rich elite with word games and relativist morality—relativists who were in part responsible for the cultural decline of Athens and its purported increasing lethargy and decadence during the long war with Sparta. In the comedy, Socrates attempts to "make the weaker argument stronger." He is a windbag. His superficial cleverness with words is attractive to untrained minds like the play's main characters, Strepsiades and Pheidippides, father and son who are willing to pay for a foolish veneer of learning in hopes of hoodwinking other Athenians into giving them something for nothing. At the end of the play an irate Strepsiades, cured of Socratic double-talk, burns down Socrates' "thinking house"—and presumably incinerates Socrates with it!

So influential was Aristophanes' invective that in the last speech of his life, as reported in Plato's *Apology*, Socrates attempts to defend himself from the popular prejudice incurred from the attacks of the "comic poets." One tradition has it that he watched the comedy and purportedly stood up during a presentation of *The Clouds* to assure the audience he was not bothered by the caricature. Plutarch records that Socrates remarked that the attacks on him on the comic stage were no different from barbs at wine parties.

Without Plato's and Xenophon's earlier acquaintance with Socrates, neither writer would have had any zeal to counteract the more prevailing view of Aristophanes, who unlike themselves, at least had met and known Socrates for a good many years. Thus Socrates dead at forty-five would have survived in history as little different from the notorious but obscure Gorgias, Hippias, Protagoras, and other Sophists whose writings are for the most part lost, but whose reputations have generally been sullied by nearly all their contemporaries. Socrates would not have been the hero of Plato and Xenophon—impressionable youths who both idealistically worshiped the aged philosopher whom they watched at seventy be unjustly killed by an ignorant mob.

Instead, he would have remained the rascal of the cynical and jaded Aristophanes, joining the scoundrels Cleon and Alcibiades, whose reputations as knaves par excellence were cemented forever on the Athenian comic stage. Had Socrates died that afternoon in 424 B.C., whatever and whoever he was until the age of forty-five when he stalked the battlefield of Delium would mostly be unknown and of little interest to us outside the rather devilish creation of Aristophanes a year later.

Finally, it is impossible to gauge the development of Socrates' own thought at age forty-five, inasmuch as he wrote nothing. Nor does Plato's work give us any clue to any chronological evolution in Socratic reasoning. Nevertheless, there is some evidence that his development as a first-class thinker came during the last twenty-five years of his life. Only then did he attract the best minds of Athens to his side, such as Alcibiades, Agathon, Plato, Xenophon, and Isocrates—as well as the ire of Aristophanes. Other older and near-contemporaries of Socrates, for example, who appear in Plato's dialogues as his close friends are curiously often non-Athenian— Phaedo of Elis, Echecrates of Phlius, Simmias and Cebes of Thebes, Aristippus of Cyrene, Euclides and Terpsion of Megara. And these elderly men are often interested not so much in ethical questions, but rather in natural philosophy and cosmology—especially Orphic thought, the teaching of Pythagoras, the ontology of Parmenides, the natural inquiry of Empedocles, and the radical views of Anaxagoras. When and where did Socrates meet these other disciples, who seem somewhat different from his later and more famous Athenian adherents?

Perhaps before the outbreak of the Peloponnesian War (431 B.C.), Socrates was even better known outside of Athens as an itinerant natural philosopher in the earlier tradition of speculating about the nature of matter, the cosmos, and the soul. Only later, with the outbreak of the war and the difficulty of these former associates to travel freely and to live in Athens (Elis, Thebes, and Megara were all on occasion at war with Athens), an older and more Athens-bound Socrates turned his attention increasingly away from these earlier concerns of cosmology to personal ethics, rhetoric, and politics.

There were issues of vital interest as he watched his home city tear herself apart in open assembly during the war. When *The Clouds* was staged in 423 B.C., although Socrates was perceived as part and parcel of the new sophistic trend, he nevertheless is caricatured often for his obsessions with "the heavens" (*ta meteôra*) and "the things above earth," suggesting a long prior career that concerned itself with cosmology and astronomical speculation.

A new following among wealthy, young, and impressionable Athenians suggests a more mature Socrates in his forties and fifties—beginning around the time of the outbreak of the Peloponnesian War. During the war he traveled less and focused his philosophy on more germane concerns of everyday life. Thus, not only would we have known little about Socrates had he died in the darkness of Delium, but what little information that would have survived would suggest to posterity a picture of a rather obscure natural philosopher who only very recently had turned his attention to ethical inquiry inside Athens, and so caught the attention of Aristophanes and the comic poets. The original fault line of Western philosophy—pre-Socratic as cosmology and natural inquiry; Socratic as ethical and moral thought—would not have existed. And of course there would be no such term as "Socratic" at all.

Can we continue our counterfactual speculations about Plato's own career without the influence of Socrates? If we would now know very little of Socrates without Plato, what would we know of a non-Socratic Plato?—of a philosopher who never met Socrates? The purpose of Plato's most famous treatises—*Euthyphro, Apology, Crito*, and *Phaedo*, the tetrad that surrounds the trial and death of Socrates—would vanish with a Socrates dead in 424 rather than executed in 399. But even more important, at least a third of Plato's earliest work, the so-called early Socratic dialogues, would probably not have been written at all, or at least not written in their present form.

Scholars have spent the past century trying to arrange Plato's thirty-one dialogues into some sort of chronology by date of their composition—a difficult task given that Plato probably wrote over a forty- to fifty-year period and told us little about his own life as an author. But on stylistic grounds, philosophical content, and contemporary references to historical events, there is now a rough consensus of what represents his "early" work (*Apology, Crito, Laches, Lysis, Charmides, Euthyphro, Hippias Major and Minor, Protagoras, Gorgias*, and *Ion*) written in Plato's thirties and forties (i.e., 390s B.C.). They are rather distinct from the twelve subsequent "middle" dialogues (written in the 380s and 370s B.C.) and a final eight "late" works (composed in the 360s and 350s B.C.).

The first group of dialogues is usually considered to deal primarily with moral issues and the need to establish proper definitions of ethical problems—in contrast with Plato's middle and later interests that turn to metaphysics, ontology, and epistemology. In addition, Socrates is the primary figure of Plato's first eleven dialogues. But he seems to fade somewhat in importance in later texts. Indeed, in the *Laws*, considered one of Plato's last treatises, he does *not* appear as a questioner. Some scholars believe that Plato began his early dialogues while in his late twenties (e.g., 408–399 B.C.), at a time when Socrates was still alive.

In any case, at least eleven of his most important works were written within a decade and a half of Socrates' death, employed Socrates as chief questioner, and dealt with concerns made famous by Socrates during the last years of his life. Had Plato never met Socrates, then, these eleven dialogues either would *not* exist or would not exist in their present form.

Plato's middle and later dialogues, in contrast, when the memory of a Socrates was decades past, show renewed interest in the work of Parmenides, Protagoras, and Empedocles, drawing on their notions of causation, change, sensation, cosmology, and reincarnation. Like the younger

Socrates, Plato seems to regard these earlier thinkers—who, unlike Socrates, wrote substantial works—as the most influential philosophers of the Greek tradition. As Plato matured, as the memory of life and conversations with Socrates dimmed, and as the value of the written philosophical texts of others was more appreciated, Plato diverged from Socrates in important areas of philosophy and relied more and more on these earlier giants.

An irony thus arises. The philosophical interests of the elder Plato resemble somewhat the thought of the younger Socrates. This suggests that the last two decades of Socrates' life were an exceptional period in the history of Greek philosophical thought, devoted far more to the practical and ethical, and attuned to debunking the false knowledge prevalent in the streets of Athens during the stressful period of the Peloponnesian War. Had Socrates died at forty-five at Delium, at least a third of Plato's most interesting work would either be gone or not exist in its present form. His entire corpus might better resemble his middle and later dialogues—and thereby belong more to the mainstream of Hellenic cosmological and ontological speculation.

Finally, Plato himself seems to have sensed that Delium was a momentous event in Socrates' life, one that was related over and over to the younger student by a variety of associates. Not only is the battle mentioned three times in his work, but there are a number of veiled allusions that arise unexpectedly elsewhere as well. In the utopian *Laws* and *Republic*, the nightmare of Delium is never far away. Both the disgrace of the Athenian loss and the Theban sacrilege in the battle's aftermath offer implicit lessons for the military reformer. In the *Laws*, for example, Plato urges regular peacetime military drill, regardless of weather and lasting for an entire day (Delium atypically took place in the late afternoon in November). All residents—men, women, and children—are to join in, but in an ordered and disciplined manner (surely unlike the chaotic *levée en masse* at Delium).

Plato also makes it clear in his *Republic* that the dead shall not be stripped or desecrated. And he insists that the corpses of the defeated must be returned to their countrymen for a decent burial (in contrast to the notorious Theban behavior). Nor should the Greeks (as the Thebans did after Delium) display the weapons of the defeated in sanctuaries as dedicatory offerings but instead regard such desecration as "pollution." Many of Plato's discussions about war, then, as we have seen in veiled references to his step-father Pyrilampes, probably drew on the experience of the horrifying tales of the battle surrounding the elder Socrates and his friends.

One of the most moving texts in Western literature is Plato's *Apology*—the account of Socrates' final rebuttal before his peers in the Athenian jury (dramatic date 399 B.C.). The influence of Plato's version of the speech has been enormous in the past two and a half millennia. Two fundamental tra-ditions in the practice of Western philosophy followed from that majestic de-fense. First is the accepted notion that even a free society through its legal institutions can kill those who question its authority and values. Thus the role of the true philosopher is properly to be tragic. As a principled outsider he will inevitably meet with the revenge of the more unenlightened masses if he remains true to his ideas.

Second, democracy—not oligarchy or autocracy—killed Socrates. In large part because of its trial and execution of Socrates—so vividly portrayed through four moving dialogues of Plato—Athenian democracy suffered a ter-rible reputation among subsequent political thinkers, from Cicero and Machiavelli to almost every major philosopher until the late-eighteenth-century revolutionaries in France and America.

In addition, the early Christian apologists of late antiquity, many re-sponding to the renewed interest in Socrates among the Neoplatonists, found the parallel with the martyr Jesus especially unmistakable. Both men were teachers who wrote nothing but were quoted widely by a close cadre of disciples. Both were also dragged before the mob, publicly humiliated, and then executed by lesser men who made use of a frightened and paranoid es-tablishment. In the view of the early Christian apologists, Socrates' coura-geous end—and his advocacy of preferring to be hurt rather than to hurt others—was confirmation of his prescience: he surely had a blessed premo-nition of Jesus—and therefore, like Jesus, preached that we do not die with our bodies but rather have an eternal soul that lives on after our physical death. Socratic thought, via Plato, became critical to the early exegesis of the Christian Church.

Needless to say, there would have been no image of Socrates as pre-

Christian pagan martyr had he died at Delium. Rather than a tragic man of conscience, he would have been a nondescript Athenian patriot and sophistic thinker who fell during an Athenian rout. In that sense, Socrates perhaps would have been embraced by, rather than at odds with, Athenian democracy. Nor would we have quite the negative appraisal of Athenian democracy itself, had it honored Socrates as a fallen hero of 424 rather than executed him as the perceived subversive agitator and tutor to the right-wing revolutionaries of 404 B.C. who, for a time, overthrew the government.

Perhaps the chief significance of the entire battle is the philosopher's close escape from Theban pursuers. On that autumn late afternoon in 424 B.C., Western philosophy as we know it was nearly aborted in its infancy. Had Socrates been speared or ridden down by the enemy, today we would know almost nothing about him. The philosophical tradition would claim him only as an early and rather obscure cosmologist and natural philosopher in the tradition of Pythagoras, Parmenides, and Empedocles—or perhaps a budding Sophist. He wrote nothing. So his legacy was entirely dependent on the remembrances of others.

There would have been no Platonic or Xenophonic Socrates. Plato's own work—even if Plato would have gone on to write about philosophy without the tutelage and inspiration of Socrates—would be far different and probably exist as rather abstract utopian and technical theory with far less concern with everyday ethics or politics in general. A large percentage of Xenophon's treatises would never have been written. *The Clouds* of Aristophanes, produced a year after Delium, not the *Apology* of Plato, would be the sole source of Socrates the man, a character not much different from the other rogues that inhabit the Athenian comic stage. A dead Socrates at Delium might mean today there would not be a book in any library or bookstore on Socrates. Plato himself might be as little known to the general reader as a Zeno or Epicurus.

More important, Socrates' death at seventy—why and how he was killed—had fundamental repercussions in the Western liberal tradition. Had he fallen to a spear thrust in the twilight of Delium and not been dragged away to be executed on the verdict of a jeering and ignorant mob, the image of the philosopher would be entirely changed today, the heritage of Athenian democracy far brighter, and the obvious association between Socrates, martyr and founder of Western thought, and Jesus, who died on the cross to establish Western religion, not so apparent.

But Socrates did not die at Delium. He instead fought courageously. Bolstered by that record of bravery, he withstood the attacks of Aristophanes. His proven courage helped him weather the assaults of radical demogogues, as he went on to teach Plato and Xenophon—before as an old man earning a martyr's death at the hands of the very democracy he fought so hard to save a quarter century earlier on that terrible autumn afternoon.

Beauty from the Dead

Boeotia was a fertile region of nearly 1,000 square miles and home to about 250,000 residents, with a rich heritage that dated back to Mycenaean times. Yet it was a land mostly agricultural. There were neither great cosmopolitan cities, major seaports, rich gold and silver mines, nor tourist attractions, major Panhellenic festivals, or strategic trading centers. The intrigues of the ancient royal house of Thebes were grist for the mill of Athenian tragedy across the border, where playwrights felt at ease chronicling the tales of hereditary incest, fratricide, and parent-killing among their bitter enemies over the mountains.

So tragedy was mostly an Athenian, not a Boeotian, event. The same was true of Hellenic literature in general—Hesiod, Pindar, Corinna, and Plutarch are notable exceptions—that was usually associated with Athens, Sicily, Ionia, and Corinth rather than with the agrarian states of the northern interior.

The same generalization applies to Greek art and architecture. Although some remarkable treasures have been unearthed in Boeotia—decorative Mycenaean terra-cotta sarcophagi, Archaic miniature clay figurines of men and women at work, and marble statuary from the Hellenistic age—the best Greek vase painting, the most impressive temples, and the great bronze sculptures come from Athens, the Peloponnese, Ionia, Sicily, and southern Italy.

In the ancient world, mastery of art usually required large cities. Only there could commerce and money provide artists with either patronage or sales, in addition to the knowledge of novel rival work. In contrast, in a society of farmers it is difficult for both artists and their audience to find either time or money. The isolation of the farm offers seclusion rather than the fellowship of cities. For all the protestations of the artist that he is a creature of independence and solitude, his stock and trade are people—viewers of his paintings, buyers of his pots, rivals for his trade, teachers and students of his craft, coteries of genuine admirers and flatterers alike. The great Theban general, patriot, and democrat Epaminondas once boasted to his Athenian enemies that should they continue to pry into Boeotian affairs, he might well storm their acropolis and carry off the Propylaea, the monumental entranceway to the Periclean temples, only to rebuild it on the Theban Cadmea—a provocative boast of Theban military power, but also an admission that there was nothing in Boeotia at all like the majestic buildings of the Athenian acropolis.

Yet for a single day in November 424 B.C., a small plain near Delium was the greatest city in Boeotia, where some fifty thousand men crowded together in an area less than a mile wide, comprising a population twice the size of Thebes herself. The equipment of the respective combatants alone might have totaled eighteen tons of wood and metal. In the battle's aftermath from those warriors came much death and spoil, and from death and spoil tragedy and money—and so from tragedy and money at last art!

Greek armor was not cheap. The helmet, breastplate, and greaves were cast and worked from bronze, the sword, spear tip, and spear-butt forged from iron. The massive three-feet-in-diameter shield required careful fabrication of planks of cured oak along with a hammered and polished bronze veneer. Altogether the hoplite's ensemble might weigh from sixty to seventy pounds and cost 100 to 300 drachmas—the equivalent of three months' wages for a laborer.

Seven thousand Athenian hoplites fought at Delium. Although only a thousand were killed on the battlefield, the majority of the rest fled in panic and must have jettisoned most of their armor to escape their Boeotian and Locrian pursuers. Perhaps at least 5,000 panoplies were lost, somewhere around 500,000 drachmas' worth of bronze and iron—enough capital to put a thousand men to work every day for nearly a year and a half, or to pay the staging costs of two hundred lavish Greek tragedies. In addition, most Greeks took money for food and expenses with them to battle, so there may well have been even more loot among the detritus of Delium. What the ultimate tally of captured treasure was is not recorded, but it must have been a vast sum.

In any case, nearly four hundred years after the battle the historian Diodorus remarked of the radical effects that the windfall of captured booty had upon the city of Thebes, in a passage that emphasizes the often forgotten relationship between military lucre and the creation of art:

> From the proceeds of booty, the Thebans not only built the great stoa in their marketplace, but also adorned it with bronze statues. In addition, they also covered with bronze the temples and the colonnades of their marketplace by nailing up the armor from the spoils of the battle. And finally, they instituted the festival called the "Delia" from money they acquired from the spoils.

This money from the sale of the captured armor and any other loot found on the bodies also found its way into other avenues of artistic expression in Boeotia. Some of the most beautiful of all Boeotian art consists of larger-than-life painted and incised grave steles, with figures of the last moments of hoplites etched into black limestone. Interestingly enough, at least two of the inscribed names of the fallen heroes on these six extant sculptures—Saugenes and Koironos—also appear on a stone casualty list uncovered from the Boeotian town of Tanagra, in the neighborhood of Delium, where some of the steles themselves were unearthed. Since the left wing of the Boeotian battle line—made up of hoplites from the hamlets of Thespiae, Tanagra, and Orchomenos—suffered the majority of the casualties from the battle, it is likely that an entire series of grave sculptures was commissioned to commemorate the ghastly losses that these small communities suffered at Delium.

The annihilation of the left wing at Delium, and the enormous amount of booty captured from the battle, together account for the creation of these extraordinarily beautiful and moving sculptures. The trove perhaps suggests that some unknown gifted artist was hired by these otherwise rural and poor communities to craft a series of commemoratives on premium black lime-stone for their fallen townsmen. In fact, some scholars believe the painter and sculptor was the famous Pythagorean innovator Aristeides of Thebes.

In the Saugenes stele, the Tanagran warrior steps forward to fight with short sword and shield. His broken spear rests at his feet, along with several stones that have apparently been hurled at him. The ground is uneven and hilly—as we know was true of the Delium battlefield. The scene most likely accurately captures the desperate last moments of the Theban left, where the overwhelmed hoplites must have had their spears shattered and were forced to turn to their secondary swords. In an artistic sense, Saugenes him-self is not merely sculpted to a near-perfect human proportion, but the en-tire scene displays a mastery of perspective, as the artist is able to make the hoplite's shield appear concave rather than merely round, and to capture trees in the distance. On the right border of the stele an enemy spear point intrudes, aimed right at the face of Saugenes, leaving no doubt that we are witnessing the last seconds of the doomed defenseless warrior. At the top of the sculpture are scenes from a banquet scene—the first example of Greek funerary sculpture to equate death with dining—emphasizing the Pythago-rean idea that the departed are treated to perpetual feasting in the hereafter.

The steles represent the high point of classical Boeotian sculpture and match the excellence of any inscribed figures in Greece. What prompted Aristeides, if indeed he was the artist, so lavishly to sculpt these otherwise nondescript rural warriors must have been both the fame of their sacrifice—and the money—that accrued after sale of the Athenian loot. These black limestone incised warrior steles—their polychrome painted finishes have mostly faded—seem to appear out of nowhere, suggesting that Delium was an important day in the artistic history of this rural province. As in the case of the great paintings that followed the Christian celebration of the victory over the Ottomans at Lepanto (1571), a magnificent victory and the accom-panying spoils of battle can be the catalysts of artistic genius.

The Birth of Tactics

All societies war with each other. Since the birth of civilization in the Near East during the fourth millennium B.C., with the advent of large settled populations and agricultural surpluses, states steadily enhanced their ability to field vast armies that sought to annihilate their adversaries in set battles. The early Hittite and Egyptian clash at Kadesh in Syria (1283 B.C.), for example, purportedly involved thousands of mounted troops, infantry, and chariot forces. Civilized war could not only evolve on a monumental scale, but also become so frequent as to resemble an annual event. During the first centuries of the Greek city-state (700–500 B.C.), small rural communities frequently faced off against the militias of neighboring states in near ritualistic duels between phalanxes of heavily armed hoplite infantrymen.

Yet until the fifth century B.C., ancient armies usually collided together in rather simple fashion. Both forces lined up, charged on signal, and then jabbed and pushed until one side collapsed. Victory went to the army with the largest number of brave, well-armed combatants. While ruse and ambush were common among light-armed skirmishers and guerrilla fighters during raids, plundering expeditions, and nighttime attacks, sophisticated feints and deception on any large scale were rare in set infantry battles. Usually the major face-offs in the early Greek-speaking world followed mutually recognized conventions and were fought during the day and on level ground. In some ways, pitched battle was seen more as an intramural contest of nerve and muscle between like states than a military operation hinging on generalship, tactics, or training aimed at annihilating foreign enemies.

When did this ancient practice of uncomplicated head-on collisions change in Greece? Sometime in the 150 years between the repulse of the Persians and the onslaught of the Macedonians, the nature of infantry battle evolved into what we would recognize as the science of tactics. If the Athenians at the battle of Marathon (490 B.C.) in simple fashion weakened their center to lengthen and strengthen their wings, a century and a half later in the era of Philip II and his son Alexander the Great (360–23 B.C.), Macedonian armies routinely practiced feints, used reserves, and attacked in wedges and staggered lines.

Alexander typically concentrated his force upon a particular spot in the enemy line, and with combined heavy and light infantrymen in concert with cavalry and missile troops sought to shatter his way through as reserves poured in to exploit success. The size of an army suddenly was not so important if the initial battle could be confined to particular points and contingents and be led by highly trained professionals. At his tactical masterpieces of Issus (333 B.C.) and Gaugamela (331 B.C.) he was able to scatter forces five times larger than his own by brilliantly marshaling and coordinating the diverse elements of the royal Macedonian army. In other words, the discovery of Western tactics—the abstract knowledge of how to manipulate forces on the battlefield to overcome enemy numerical superiority, unfavorable terrain, or inadequate training and weaponry—is usually first attributed to Alexander and his father, Philip.

But if we define tactics more narrowly as the movement of forces on the battlefield itself, then where did the Macedonian kings learn of such innovations in phalanx fighting? Macedon, although it lay outside the world of the polis, was fascinated by things Greek and habitually imported Hellenic expertise of all sorts—from catapult builders and siege engineers to natural scientists, philosophers, and playwrights.

Consequently, most military historians identify Hellenic roots in the Macedonian military renaissance of the latter fourth century B.C. and thus connect Philip's new army to the exemplar of the great general Epaminondas the Theban, who led the democratic federation of Boeotia to a brief decade-long hegemony over the Greek city-states (371–62 B.C.). At his first and greatest battle at Leuctra (371 B.C.), Epaminondas had led an outnumbered Boeotian army to a crushing victory over the crack hoplites of Sparta. Key to his success there was the massing of troops on the left flank to a depth of fifty shields to blast apart the Spartan right wing opposite and to kill King Cleombrotus.

In some ancient accounts of Leuctra, there is also mention of cavalry and infantry coordination and an *en echelon* attack—in reality Epaminondas had no choice but to advance at an angle to reach the Spartan right that extended far beyond his flank. Since Philip II, architect of the deadly Macedonian army, was a hostage at Thebes in his teenage years (ca. 369–67 B.C.), historians suspect that the future king witnessed Epaminondas's new model army firsthand and returned to Macedon determined one day to emulate the Boeotian manner of attacking in depth with only a portion of the army on the left rather than right wing.

But who influenced Epaminondas in his decision to mass troops on a single wing? To find the origins of Western tactics prior to the fourth century B.C., we must return a half century to Delium—not earlier and not outside of Boeotia. Most traditional Greek phalanxes adopted a depth of eight shields. That number was eventually standardized as the apparent ideal ratio between length and depth. Massing deeper would take valuable infantrymen out of the killing zone (only the first three ranks of a phalanx could reach the enemy with their spears in the initial charge) and leave the entire battle line vulnerable to enemy outflanking movements. But columns less than eight shields were felt to lack the weight necessary both to absorb enemy blows and to break enemy formations, inasmuch as there would be neither enough pushing with shields from the rear nor replacement hoplites to take the place of the fallen.

The Macedonians—whose pikes extended to sixteen feet and more in length—increased the phalanx from a depth of eight men to sixteen, apparently in emulation of Epaminondas's success at Leuctra and the second battle of Mantinea (362 B.C.), where the Theban general had created a shock column of fifty shields. But even prior to Epaminondas, the Thebans at the battle at the Nemea River (394 B.C.) two decades earlier had arrayed themselves sixteen men deep. Apparently throughout the fourth century B.C., Greek generals—especially Thebans—came to understand that particular segments of their battle line could be strengthened to attack in depth and overwhelm specific areas of the enemy's army. The Thebans, whose hoplites were legendary for their superior body strength, gained a reputation for attacking in deep columns, confident that they could crush a particular point of the enemy line before their own thinned contingents were outflanked or enveloped.

Yet neither Epaminondas nor his immediate Theban predecessors of the early fourth century B.C. were the first to adopt such innovations. In fact, the first recorded instance in Greek history of an army charging in a depth greater than eight men was at Delium. There Pagondas's twenty-five shields on the Boeotian right bowled over and crushed the Athenian left wing.

Pagondas, in fact, seems not only to be the forefather of the Theban practice of massing in column, but in some sense the inventor of Western tactical thinking itself.

In most battles even during the early and mid-fifth century B.C. the outcome was determined solely by the troops who lined up opposite each other in the minutes before the first charge. And once these one-dimensional forces collided, most classical Greek generals—to our knowledge none were either mounted or to the rear—essentially lost control of events and joined in the melee themselves. Their displays of physical courage, not mental acuity, usually brought success in battle. Yet at Delium, Pagondas must have been somewhere other than in the immediate front ranks of the Theban right wing that was charging downhill against the Athenian left wing. Only by being posted outside the heat of the first-rank fighting could he have ordered two companies of horsemen to ride out of sight to the other side of the battle line, where they suddenly appeared over a hill to attack the victorious Athenian right. Thucydides relates that when these relief forces surfaced out of nowhere, the Athenians were so confused that they wrongly surmised that an entirely fresh army was on the horizon. Thus at the moment of their victory, the Athenian right simply panicked and fled from the appearance of a few hundred horsemen. Generalship—not physical strength or mere numbers—destroyed the Athenian right wing and brought the Boeotians victory.

Not only were these reserves a remarkable new development, but the use of horsemen in close action with infantry was also unusual and antedated Macedonian combined tactics by nearly a century. At most hoplite battles, hostilities began with skirmishing between horsemen in the no-man's-land between the two phalanxes. Occasionally, successful cavalry action might confuse and disrupt temporarily the subsequent infantry charge. But in most cases horsemen had no success against heavily armed spearmen. Skirmishing before and pursuing after battle, in addition to protecting the flanks of the phalanx, was the traditional—and limited—domain of small numbers of classical Greek cavalrymen, themselves mostly aristocratic prancers rather than professional chargers.

So Pagondas's decision to send mounted troops against an infantry wing marked a breakthrough in Hellenic tactical thinking, one that would reach its apex in the deadly charges of Alexander and his mounted companions who punched holes in the Persian royal army and were followed by columns of phalangites. Deepening a column was a dramatic way to tear gaps in the enemy line, but it was also a dangerous gambit—in that it inevitably robbed valuable troops from the front ranks elsewhere on the battle line, leaving the entire army vulnerable to enemy outflanking maneuvers. Reserves, preferably mounted, were the requisite complement to massed columns. Such mobile relief companies could be sent to any trouble spots where the enemy appeared to outflank a shorter line. Somehow the old Theban had thought all this out before his men ran to meet the Athenians in what the latter assumed would be a simple pitched battle. How odd that Boeotian rustics, not Athenian sophisticates, would prove to be the real innovators in the art of war.

If Delium marks the first occasion in the history of Western warfare where deepened columns and mounted reserves appear, there were also other innovations in this strange army of Pagondas. The historian Diodorus mentions the presence of select troops of foot soldiers who fought alongside mounted troops. He notes "out in front of the entire army fought a select group of 300 called 'the charioteers and foot soldiers'."

This same force of *parabatai* is also mentioned in Euripides' *Suppliants* in the tragedy's allegory of the battle. And after Delium, a Theban select body of 300 soldiers is always associated with the so-called Sacred Band of 150 pairs of lovers. They fought, Plutarch tells us, undefeated at the forefront of Theban battles until exterminated at Chaeronea (338 B.C.), where they were buried by Philip II under the proud stone lion that now watches over the modern highway. We do not know exactly the relationship between the original 300 "charioteers and foot soldiers" at Delium and the later famous "Sacred Band," but apparently the presence of a similarly sized number of professionals in 424 B.C. marked the beginning of a gradual specialization in infantry practice—a departure from the old idea that hoplite farmers marshaled as militiamen for only a few days of campaigning. In the latter fifth and fourth centuries, we hear of similar elite corps at Argos, Arcadia, and Elis who trained hard at public expense.

Finally, a few of the panicked Athenians fled not back home to Attica but to their small fortified garrison in the precinct of Apollo at Delium. These desperate Athenians were quickly besieged by the victorious Boeotians and their Locrian allies. But instead of the usual—and often unsuc-cessful—Greek practice of storming a fortified position through rams, tun-neling, aerial assault, or simple blockades to induce starvation, the Boeotians created a huge mobile flamethrower of sorts. Their contraption apparently resembled a queer wooden gun barrel on wheels with iron insides. On one end the attackers used bellows to force a searing blast of lighted coals, sul-fur, and pitch out of the muzzle into the Athenians' wooden barricade, quickly sending the entire wood palisade—and some of the defenders with it—up in flames.

Military historians usually associate the invention of artillery with Dionysius I's siege of Motya on Sicily in 399 B.C. During that assault, Syra-cusan engineers developed nontorsion "belly bows"—essentially large cross-bows that were cocked by a slide and stock to hurl iron bolts and spears. A half century later Philip of Macedon first employed true torsion catapults, whose springs of either bundled hair or sinew gave them the propulsive power to shoot with accuracy bolts and stones over three hundred yards dis-tant. Both developments were lamented in classical literature. Traditionalists felt that the new artillery brought a disturbing randomness to the battlefield: both bravehearts and cowards could now be killed from afar without dis-tinction by such infernal machines. Personal courage and muscular strength meant little against the spring-loaded bolts of heartless artillery.

Yet the flamethrower at Delium predated Philip's catapults by nearly a century and would much later be emulated by the infamous Greek fire that first emerged at Byzantium somewhere around A.D. 675. Although the exact ingredients and their ratios of mixture remain unknown to this day, the tor-rent of flame that was shot out of Byzantine galleys was apparently a potent fusion of naphtha, sulfur, petroleum, and quicklime that could not be extin-guished by water—a nearly unquenchable toxic spume that could incinerate enemy ships in seconds. While the delivery system for Greek fire was far more sophisticated than the fire gun at Delium, it operated on the same prin-ciple of using compressed air to ignite a flammable fuel at the end of the bar-rel, resulting in a stream of continuous flame spurting out toward the target. The dozens of Athenians who were incinerated in the sanctuary attest to the deadliness of Pagondas's strange new weapon.

How are we to explain these extraordinary military developments of the

Boeotians that first appear at Delium? What is unfathomable about the course of the battle is not Delium's military influence on subsequent commanders, which was both profound and revolutionary—but how such innovative tactical thinking arose from the mind of an obscure general in his sixties, at the head of an army of rustics, who alone wished his army of yeomen to fight at Delium *and* apparently possessed the military acumen to achieve victory.

The train of events that arose from Delium would have been impossible without the will of a lone Theban who single-handedly brought the Boeotian army to battle. And yet after Pagondas appears out of obscurity in Thucydides' history to win Delium, he is abruptly forgotten in the narrative when the battle concludes. Nevertheless, his ingenious deployments in the battle were not forgotten, but rather over time became enshrined as the cornerstones of classical tactics—massed columns, reserves, joint infantry and mounted attack, elite units, and sophisticated military technology.

Alexander the Great did not invent Western tactics nor did Epaminondas the Theban. Rather, both generals followed in a strange and now-forgotten tradition of Boeotian warfare that had its inaugural day at Delium. Rural Boeotia—of all places—was the embryo of Western military thought, home to the first battle in the history of European civilization in which there appeared a real science of sophisticated tactics.

What Was Delium?

Delium was an accident. The battle in an out-of-the-way place between two Greek city-states should never have taken place. Only the ardor of one old Theban aristocrat galvanized the Boeotian army and convinced it to pursue to the border a demoralized enemy that had largely abandoned its prior intention of fighting. Why, then, did such a seemingly unimportant clash in a backwater theater of the Peloponnesian War affect thousands more beyond the battlefield, both then and now?

Delium was not merely influential because of the sheer number of warriors assembled. Compared to other ancient engagements, its magnitude was still not that unusual. There may have been 250,000 seamen at Salamis. Between 60,000 and 80,000 Romans died in three hours at Cannae. In Alexander's great battles, sometimes over a quarter million men collided. Delium's 50,000 were far less than the over 100,000 Americans who charged each other over the two days at Shiloh.

Of course, the thousands who fought at Delium had families and friends, and so the killing, wounding, and trauma of that huge encounter changed hundreds of thousands of lives that are completely lost to the historical record—and in ways we can scarcely begin to imagine. The fate of Thespiae is but a glimpse of the subsequent decades of ruin for thousands of Boeotians that followed from that single afternoon's killing. We have the names of 164 dead Boeotians at Delium, but not a clue as to how their individual sacrifices changed the fate of either their families or communities.

As cruel as it is to confess, the historical significance of Delium is not in the numbers of the nameless ranks of the veterans and their kin. Nor are the battle's consequences found in the realm of grand strategy. Even if one can make the argument that the Peloponnesian War was a watershed event in the history of Western civilization, it is not altogether clear that the Athenian defeat at Delium really changed the course of that conflict.

But why again has Delium affected us to this day in fundamental ways insidious and scarcely appreciated? The answer, I think, lies in the peculiar nature of the respective city-states of Athens and the Boeotians at a particular moment in 424 B.C. Delium was the first great infantry battle—and defeat—of Athens during the Peloponnesian War, a traumatic setback for an imperial city in its greatest age and at its very border. The result was that there were thousands of classical Athenians of every age drawn up together, fighting in rank, killing, dying, and running away in sight of the Attic border. As cities and civilizations go, Athens in the 420s B.C. was an extraordinary culture, and many of its soldiers who fought were rather different from most warriors past and present.

Despite the horrific losses of the plague and the waste of the first seven years of the war, Greek tragedy was at its zenith in 424 B.C. True, in the urban area of Athens proper there were no more than one hundred thousand residents—one hundredth the size of greater New York or Los Angeles. In modern terms of material wealth, we would find the city abysmally poor. Yet the combination of radical democracy and imperial grandeur had energized the citizenry, creating a unique but fragile—and transitory—symbiosis between politics, commerce, and the life of the mind. In late-fifth-century Athens there were no real divides between public and private spheres, politics and intellectual inquiry, art and the science of architecture, much less between business and cultural pursuit. The talented were not engaged in the esoterica of financial speculation or the hunt for capital, at least not entirely. No Wall Street brokerage concerns, international law firms, Madison Avenue, or Hollywood wooed bright Athenians with promises of the good life. For a very brief period—six or seven decades at most—the very gifted of Athenian society found avenues for their talents in the most public and intellectual of ways.

Sophocles' great masterpiece *Oedipus Rex* was presented just a few years before the battle. The playwright himself earlier had served on the same board of generals as did the general Hippocrates. Many who fought the Boeotians in 424 had seen the *Oedipus* (which was set in Boeotia) and dozens like it in the theater of Dionysus less than thirty miles from Delium, on the slopes below the recently finished Parthenon. Sophocles' *Electra*, *Philoctetes*, and *Oedipus at Colonus* were to follow in the years after the battle. His younger contemporary Euripides—who like Sophocles probably saw military service—was in his late fifties by 424 B.C. Since the outbreak of the Peloponnesian War in 431 B.C., he had presented in succession *Medea*, the *Heracleidae, Hippolytus, Andromache*, and *Hecuba*. In the next two decades after the battle, besides *The Suppliants*, his masterpieces *Electra, Bacchae*, and *Iphigenia at Aulis* were to follow. When the Athenians marched into Boeotia, the brilliant comic poet Aristophanes was in his mid-thirties; his showpiece *The Clouds*, the savage attack on Socrates produced the year after Delium, was no fluke. Months before the battle he had put on *Knights*. And after Delium his greatest comedies were to come—*Wasps* (422 B.C.), *Birds* (414), *Lysistrata* (411), and *Frogs* (405).

Pericles, after guiding Athens for some thirty years of imperial expansion abroad and monumental public construction at home, had just died, and his succession was fought over by young firebrands like Cleon and Alcibiades. Socrates was at the height of his powers at Delium, but not alone in his philosophical brilliance. The famous Sophist Gorgias had made his way to

Athens for the first time in 427, and the excitement of his visit and its effect on rhetoric and the art of persuasion were just beginning to snowball when the Athenians marched out three years later. Protagoras was still alive in 424 and was joined by a host of other Sophists and philosophers who are usually associated with the first Western intellectual renaissance. Hippocrates, the founder of Western medicine, was a frequent visitor to late-fifth-century Athens. The creator of town planning, Hippodamus, was at the end of his career, while the orator Antiphon, fifty-six at the time of the battle, was delivering his famous courtroom speeches throughout the 420s, as he refined his antidemocratic views that would lay the foundation of the oligarchic revolution of 411.

The monumental gateway to the Acropolis, the Propylaea, had just opened in 424, a few years after the final dedication of the Parthenon—the crown jewel of the Periclean building program. The third great monument on the acropolis, the Erectheum, was begun just three years after Delium, and the fourth, the smaller temple to Athena Nike, was completed by 410. The architects of the Parthenon, Ictinus and Callicrates, at the time of Delium were at work on a host of other temples and buildings in the city. Phidias, Greece's greatest sculptor and creator of the famous monumental statues of gold and ivory of Athena and Zeus, housed respectively in the Parthenon at Athens and the great temple of Zeus at Olympia, had died the year before the battle. When the Athenians marched into Delium, Polygnotus, the founder of Western realist painting, was likewise at the end of his career.

The father of history, Herodotus, was revising his *Histories* in the early 420s and probably finished a polished version of his Persian War narratives a year or two before the battle. In fact, Herodotus may have died in or around the very time of the fighting at Delium. Thucydides, perhaps the greatest of Western historians, knew intimately veterans on both sides and wrote our only contemporary account of the fighting from his own research and interviews. He too was on the same Athenian board of generals as Hippocrates in 424 B.C. and no doubt knew the slain commander well. Indeed, had Thucydides not been sent to the north with the Athenian fleet, he may well have served alongside Socrates at Delium.

Shortly after the incineration of the Athenian garrison at Delium, Thucydides was charged with incompetence for his failure to relieve the northern port city of Amphipolis. He was disgraced and then exiled—by a vote of a hysterical citizenry, itself demoralized by the recent events of 424 that had seen its home army butchered a few miles from the assembly hall. The growing frenzy that was unleashed on Thucydides, the historian of Delium, had at least some of its genesis in the Athenian anger over the catastrophe of Delium—which may explain why he devotes a vivid description to a seemingly unimportant battle.

Taken in this cultural context, Delium was a wounding of the nerve system of Athens. Therefore, given the very nature of Athens at this time, it affected dozens of writers, philosophers, and statesmen whose legacies transcended the meager confines of their city, ensuring ripples of the battle well beyond either the strategic or political importance of the engagement itself. And because Athens was Greece's greatest city at its greatest age, and since Greece was the laboratory of Western culture itself, a battle so dramatic and fought so close to the city at this time was bound to have repercussions far beyond its mere tactical or strategic consequence.

Just the opposite was the situation in Thebes and its Boeotian confederation—or so it would seem at first glance. Art, literature, and culture were stagnant. We know of few statesmen of any merit; there was no lasting Boeotian imprint on the history of ideas. But that was not quite the whole truth. If Athens was exploding in a final burst of culture, Boeotia was simmering, stung by its disgraceful support of the Persians a half century earlier and years of Athenian interference and occupation. Yet among the rural cantons of this vast agrarian state was latent genius, waiting for some catalyst like the victory in 424 B.C. over an Athenian army of invasion.

Not all the Boeotian ripples of Delium were local and confined to the tragedy of small rural hamlets like Thespiae, the refurbishing of public buildings, or a small renaissance in sculpture. Well before Delium, Theban thinkers had apparently been experimenting with the science of tactics, or the idea that abstract laws of maneuver and articulation, not mere muscle and spirit, would determine who lived and died on the battlefield when armies collided. The victory of Delium unleashed that knowledge of reserves, cavalry coordination, deepened columns, elite forces, and tactical articulation which reverberated throughout the Greek world, finding its way into the mind of Epaminondas and eventually to Philip and Alexander—with untold consequences on millions to the east. If the Athenians at Delium were a people of the arts, then what killed them was an art, too, albeit one of a darker sort to be used for the destruction, not the creation, of culture.

The Imprint of Battle

If battles are the generators of history, are they all of roughly equal importance? If we can agree that they change events in a manner that the development of the comic book or gender issues within the cloister do not, what gives precedence of memory to particular engagements, allowing some to leave a larger imprint on history than others? Why is Delium more recognized than the battle of Nemea (394 B.C.), but less than Marathon (490 B.C.), Shiloh more so than Bentonville (1865) but not as much as Gettysburg (1863), or Okinawa more familiar than Peleliu (November 1944) and in turn not so well known as Guadalcanal (1942–43)?

In these three studies I sought to demonstrate how millions of unsuspecting people have been changed by events that are either forgotten or hardly known—and that there are battles important in insidious and often undetected ways, even if they are deemed not so critical by the arbitrary calculus of history. But what precisely is that logic of history? If all battles have important ripples, what determines which engagements deserve more official recognition both formally and in the popular imagination?

Various criteria come to mind; yet it is nearly impossible to sort out their comparative weight on any given occasion. We should, of course, note the more narrow interests of military historians that focus attention on set pieces like Leuctra, Adrianople, Austerlitz, Chancellorsville, and Inchon because they are stellar examples of tactical brilliance, and thus enshrined as case histories in which the mind of a single general can determine the fate of thousands. In most cases, however, the tactics of Epaminondas at Leuctra or the efficacy of longbows at Crécy are not as well known to the public, and so public recognition requires more from battles than the bloody art of killing—even if such esoterica of new maneuvers and weaponry can have effects upon millions not yet born.

Oddly, the number of combatants in and of itself is not always a reliable indicator of a battle's perceived historical import. The enormous American and Japanese forces on Okinawa (eventually to number together nearly a half million on land, on sea, and in the air) no doubt explain the ferocity and horrific losses that in turn changed the lives of hundreds of thousands of veterans as well as those of the relatives and friends of the fallen. Yet most Americans seem to know more about Guadalcanal or perhaps even Iwo Jima. As noted, more probably fought at Nemea than at Delium; the former may have been the largest hoplite battle between poleis in the history of the Greek city-state—an engagement that many classicists nevertheless recall nothing about. The Nationalist Chinese lost an army of nearly six hundred thousand at Suchow in late 1948—and few outside China know a thing about the battle. How many fought can help determine a battle's legacy, but there is also more to the historical equation than the mere number of combatants who file onto the field of battle.

Does the sheer number of dead, then, more likely guarantee remembrance? Usually, horrific casualties capture the attention of future generations—but tragically not always. Otherwise the siege of Leningrad would be far more noteworthy than Little Bighorn—900 days of constant killing and perhaps a million dead versus an hour or so in which 215 were annihilated. Yet the latter, not the former, is probably the most written-about battle in modern military history. There is a cruel arbitrariness to formal history that puts the fate of a few hundred over the tragedy of hundreds of thousands—in addition to the still greater number of those affected by such catastrophic losses. Clearly the dead alone do not determine whether a battle is well known or merely a footnote of history.

Location seems particularly important. Again, we know at least something about Delium because, like Marathon, it took place near Athens and was seared into the memory of prominent contemporary Athenians whose lives and works we still are familiar with today. Thucydides, after all, gave it three hundred lines. But Coronea, Oenophyta, Nemea? These are fights in the rural hinterlands, closer to Thebes or Corinth than to the grandiose city Pericles built, and so their thousands of dead have always rested in obscurity. Okinawa took on an importance greater than Tarawa or Burma not simply because of its butcher's bill, but in part perhaps because of its proximity to the Japanese homeland. Had the al-Qaeda terrorists of September 11 chosen to crash their hijacked jets into Fresno's only two existing "skyscrapers," there may well have been three thousand Americans dead while at work in their offices, but it is not so likely that the nation itself would have been so radically transformed. The reason is not just that the World Trade Center is a national icon and known internationally and our Security Bank Building is not.

Rather—*terribile dictu*—there were not Fresnans in New York's twin buildings, but instead far more influential men and women who write our books, edit our newspapers, bring us the evening news, run our companies, and monitor our financial health. These so-called movers and shakers saw firsthand, and in some cases were in, what would become an inferno of twenty acres in the very midst of the most powerful city in the history of civilization. Shiloh was located in between North and South, easily accessible by river transport, and a strategic nexus of the entire enormous Western theater in a manner that even the greater nightmare of Cold Harbor was not.

Timing is critical as well, both in the more immediate sense of a battle's effect on the tactical and strategic computation of an ongoing war, and on the pulse of a larger popular culture. Delium closed down an entire front; in the same manner Shiloh opened one up even larger. The much-heralded Chaeronea ended the free Greek city-state; the nearly forgotten second battle of Coronea a few miles away did not. In contrast, it is hard to determine precisely what the terrible shelling and bombing at Khe Sanh accomplished—other than perhaps blowing apart as many as fifty thousand North Vietnamese in a few weeks and serving as an exemplar of American courage, tenacity, and frightening lethality. Okinawa will be forever connected with the decision to drop the atomic bombs and the armistice that came only six weeks after the island was declared secure; and yet we know less than we should about its suicidal horror only because the end of Nazism and the close of the European theater were simultaneous events that drew American attention away from the Pacific. Chance has much to do with the hierarchy of formal historical commemoration.

But just as important as space and time in calculating the immediate military ripples of battle are the more long-term cultural and social currents that can arise. September 11 seemed to be a divide in a variety of contexts, coming immediately after the end of the Clinton administration and in the inaugural year of the Bush presidency—marking an end to a two-decade era of apparent restraint in the face of dozens of past terrorist attacks upon the United States. The loss of three thousand was almost immediately recognized by Americans as the straw that broke the camel's back—in the same way perhaps the invasion of Poland became the powder keg of World War II, while the earlier extinction of Czechoslovakia is nearly forgotten. The lost at Pearl Harbor seemed to have had more effect on the world than the many thousands butchered at the Rape of Nanking—the former brought to Americans their own dead and led them to war, the latter provided us abstract outrage at the fate of far distant others.

Cannae is also heralded in a way the immediately prior brutal fighting at Lake Trasimene and Trebia is not. Hannibal's masterpiece victory took place no closer to Rome and saw not too many more casualties than Trasimene. But Cannae came at the end of a string of Roman defeats and left Italy demoralized and bereft of frontline legionaries for almost six months—Rome itself being relatively vulnerable to immediate attack. Tet was a devastating military defeat for the communist forces in South Vietnam and one of the most lopsided victories in American military history. Yet it is remembered today with a strange mixture of humiliation, loss, and regret—inasmuch as the fighting in Saigon broke out just a few weeks after an American administration had promised that the war was near a close and the enemy exhausted. To many influential Americans—and especially Walter Cronkite—that the communists could lose forty thousand men in and around South Vietnam's major cities oddly seemed to reflect power rather than the promised desperation. Timing, the offspring of fate and chance, can be everything in determining an engagement's legacy.

There are, of course, the flukes of history that affect, perhaps unfairly and cruelly so, the degree of historical deference given to battles. Had Socrates not fought at Delium, we would have no mention of the fighting in any of Plato's dialogues. Little Bighorn is infamous because of the improbability of Native Americans killing all opposing federal troops who a decade earlier had fought so magnificently on both sides in the Civil War—and perhaps also because the annihilation of every single American soldier under Custer at that small hillock came amid chauvinistic celebrations of the centenary of the nation's birth. That being said, had colorful, handsome, boisterous, and unstable George Armstrong Custer been absent we would have known much less of a final encirclement forever immortalized as "Custer's Last Stand."

I know many literary critics who can recall that Cervantes fought at the Battle of Lepanto, or that Byron wrote a poem about Don Juan, but otherwise know nothing of the battle's gruesome details or larger historical context. They certainly care little about the near-contemporary siege of Malta or the horrific fighting on Cyprus weeks before Lepanto. Take Teddy Roosevelt away from San Juan Hill and the Spanish-American War is not much more seminal than an entire series of successful U.S. interventions at places now unknown and unremembered in Cuba and the Philippines.

Tactics, numbers, the dead, location, timing, political aftershocks, and luminaries all, then, affect the ripples of a given battle. But there is still this lingering question not of actual, but of perceived, import—one that goes directly to the heart of culture, the nature of history, and the dominance of Western civilization. Quite simply, we know about some battles and not others because veterans, eyewitnesses, or historians wrote about them—and often for reasons not entirely explicable by the criteria outlined above. We are still numbed by Hernán Cortés's final obliteration of Tenochtitlán, where maybe 200,000 Aztecs perished in the inferno; yet less than a half century earlier that same doomed people may well have sacrificially murdered nearly 90,000 of its neighbors at a daily rate that sometimes exceeded the killing tally of Auschwitz—a fact almost unknown today. But then there was no Bernal Díaz del Castillo or Bishop Sahagun around to record thousands walking up the great pyramid to their deaths—and neither printing presses, a book market, nor a literate reading public in Nahuatl-speaking Mexico.

Well before Little Bighorn there were tens of thousands of Native Americans who butchered each other yearly—but no yellow journalists, New York papers, or dime-store novelists to record the carnage for posterity.

The divide is not explicable simply in terms of literacy and illiteracy, or the presence of traditional history versus a less sure oral tradition. There is something about Western civilization itself, and particularly in recent years American culture—the power of market capitalism, the dynamism of individual freedom, and the zeal of unbridled inquiry—that combines to skew the remembrance of battles. In Russia, of course, Leningrad is more important than Little Bighorn, and our own myopia about the relative significance of the two battles is irrelevant to most Russians. Yet it remains true that more books—printed in English, available to millions in Europe and the United States, serialized in magazines and adapted to the big screen—deal with Custer than the hundreds of thousands who died among snow, rats, and typhoid to stop Nazism. Someone in Buenos Aires is more likely to know of Custer's blond locks than about the Russian or German generals at Leningrad.

So the ripples of battle in their formal sense are guided by the presence of historians, and that means originally Westerners, and more recently in large part Europeans and Americans. And such distortions do not always play out in bias toward Westerners, especially in the present age. In April 2002 the Israeli Defense Forces entered the West Bank community of Jenin to hunt out suspected suicide-murderers, whose comembers had blown up hundreds of Israeli civilians over the prior year. Although fewer than sixty Palestinians were killed in Jenin—the great majority of them combatants—the world media seized upon the street fighting, dubbing it "Jeningrad" as if they were somehow the moral equivalent of one million Germans and Russians lost at Stalingrad. Yet just days after the Israeli withdrawal from Jenin, Pakistan squared off against India. The stakes were surely far higher: One-fifth of the world's population was involved. Both sides were nuclear powers and issued threats to use their arsenals. In the prior year alone nearly four times more Indians and Pakistanis were killed than Palestinians and Israelis. By any calculation of numbers, the specter of the dead, the geopolitical consequences, or the long-term environmental health of the planet, the world should know all the major cities in Kashmir rather than a few street names in Jenin. And if the world sought to chronicle destruction and death in an Islamic city, then by any fair measure it should have turned its attention to Grozny, where an entire society of Muslim Chechnyans was quite literally obliterated by the Russian army.

The idiosyncrasies of historical remembrance of battle do not hinge alone on the presence of a Socrates or Teddy Roosevelt in the ranks. Sometimes there are wild cards of culture and politics as well. In this case and at this time, the fact that the Israelis fit the stereotype of affluent and proud Westerners abroad while the Palestinians were constructed as impoverished and oppressed colonial subjects brought to the equation the sympathies of influential Americans and Europeans in the media, universities, and government—the prominent and sometimes worrisome elites who determined to send their reporters, scholars, and diplomats to Jenin rather than to Islamabad or Grozny.

Like it or not, Westerners from Herodotus's time to the present age carry historical weight far out of proportion to their numbers, and so create waves where there should only be tiny ripples. In the decade of the 1990s alone there were literally millions of innocent Africans butchered in Rwanda, the Congo, Somalia, and Mozambique, more killed in a single month than all those lost on the West Bank or in Israel proper in the last half century—but for a variety of perverse reasons those dead carried little moral capital with the arbiters of the world's attention and memory.

Of course, history is only a capricious recorder of battles, the craft that elevates remembrance of a few thousands who battled at Thermopylae over the hundreds of thousands who perished in oblivion when Cambyses conquered Egypt. But there are also the parallel ripples—those that I tried to chronicle in this book—of private experiences and individuals who are lost to the historical record, but *not* lost to the great train of events that equally affects the human condition, whether that be the decision to drop the A-bomb, the lessons of battling suicides, the Lost Opportunity, *Ben-Hur*, Euripides' *Suppliants*, the complete annihilation of Thespiae—or the death of an obscure Swedish farm boy in 1945 on far distant Okinawa.

Quite apart from what most people remember or read, some forgotten battles will silently and without acknowledgment still continue to change the way they live and think. So we do not know what saint or monster, what devilish cult or humane religion, or what great poem or worthless doggerel will arise out of the holocaust of mass killing and fighting in Rwanda, but right now, unbeknown to the world, the swells from that horrendous hand-to-hand slaughter are billowing out, and on what shores they will finally lap we can hardly imagine. And we Americans in our professed greatest age of security and affluence are not immune from battle and its ripples.

The United States was roused from its siesta on September 11 to learn in dismay that millions abroad were *pleased* over its losses. Many of its supposed friends among "moderate" Arab regimes were silent. Some, in fact, either inadvertently or deliberately, may have been involved in aiding and abetting the terrorists themselves. Post-9/11 polls revealed that as many as 70 percent of those surveyed in most Arab countries shared a dislike of the United States. The bombing exposed a previously ignored but vast fault line between the Western and Islamic—and particularly Middle Eastern—worlds, all the more dramatic given near-instant satellite transmission of celebrating throngs in the streets of the West Bank, Pakistan, and Egypt. Terrorism on a grand scale in minutes strips away the pretensions of peace. It shows things the way they really have been among the masses rather than how events and ideologies were supposed to be presented by those elites in government, universities, and the media.

Millions of Americans had forgotten that the easy use of the Internet, participation in the World Cup, or showy foreign jets at major Western airports had little to do with the nature of civil society abroad. For all the veneer of Westernism in the Islamic world—cell phones, television sets, luxury hotels, and fast-food franchises—citizens of the United States were rudely reminded in the aftermath of 9/11 that there are few, if any, legitimate democracies in the Arab Middle East. Whether theocrats in Saudi Arabia, Iran, and Afghanistan, dictators in Libya, Syria, or Iraq, or milder autocrats in Egypt, Jordan, and Morocco, not one government is subject to audit, recall, or removal by its populace. Such an absence of consensual politics permeates all such unfree societies that are more likely to be without religious tolerance, free expression, truly secular institutions, sexual equity, and an unbridled media.

This sudden sobriety ushered in on September 11 also reminded us of the vast differences between freedom and tyranny in a supposedly uniform global culture at "the end of history." After the honking in the streets celebrating the American dead in some Muslim countries, few Americans perhaps saw Mr. Arafat as a responsible force for peace, the tribal yet ultramodern sheiks of Saudi Arabia as temperate friends—or even many of the NATO allies that voiced anger at America in the months after as real comrades in arms.

Neither diplomats nor strategists immediately could grasp that the world—as happened after Salamis on September 28, 480 B.C. or the Fall of Constantinople on May 29, 1453—had suddenly cracked apart and would not be put back together with quite the same pieces. Thus the 9/11 tragedy and its aftermath in Afghanistan and Iraq led to fundamental rethinking about NATO, the role of the United Nations, and American relationships with continental European countries. Europeans loudly pronounced a new anti-Americanism and talked of a separate "German way"; Americans silently seethed and were resigned to give them their wish. After September 11, Europeans vented against the American protectorate even as average citizens in Des Moines and Tulare quietly shrugged and likewise asked why the United States at great cost is defending a continent that has a larger population and economy than its own.

Culture, like politics, is not immune to these billowing waves of combat. And we can look to the past to see that cultural repercussions usually follow from battles. The catalysts for modernism were Verdun, the Somme, and the general carnage of the First World War trenches. Out of those infernos spread the belief that the old foundations of staid manners, traditional genres of art and literature, unquestioning patriotism—*dulce et decorum est pro patria mori*—and national politics had somehow led to Europe's millions being gassed and blown apart for years in the mud of the French countryside without either victory or defeat.

Perhaps the present brand of postmodernism was born primarily in France as well. After the humiliating drive of the Panzers through the Ardennes in May 1940, the collapse of Europe's largest army in six weeks, and the rescue by the Americans and British in August 1944, theories were easier to accept than facts. For a few elite but stunned postwar Frenchmen, fiction was more palatable than reality, text and discourse a refuge from a truth as unacceptable as it was bothersome.

The crater in New York at the very epicenter of American arts and let-ters perhaps will have a similarly profound though more likely *opposite* ef-fect—as we reply to a temporary loss with a more confident pursuit of victory rather than embarrassing denial. Without the World Trade Center on the New York skyline, it will be discomforting to suggest that events are mere historical fictions or constructions of power. Who now will insist that papier-mâché and urine jars best capture the human condition? Not that such art and literature born often out of sarcasm and nihilism will evaporate. Such sensationalism will not—at least for a time and among a few. But most people, desperate for transcendence and something real—and perhaps even exquisite—amid the recovery from catastrophe, will gradually be less inter-ested in the clever but empty games of relativists who spawn such faux-art a few blocks away from the detritus of the greatest foreign attack on American shores in our nation's history.

Carefully arranging together some concrete and steel, putting it on dis-play in a gallery, and then calling such impressionism "art" will not be as pop-ular as before. Millions, after all, have seen and then judged the jumbled mess on a far grander scale—mixed with flesh and bone no less—to be not sculpture, but a catastrophe and an abomination. *Where* terrorism and killing take place is often as important as how many fight and die and who wins.

The creed of contemporary multiculturalism sought to establish that all societies were roughly equal and that the "other" was but a crude Western fiction. But we were reminded that people like the Taliban who did not vote, treated women as chattel, and whipped and stoned to death dissenters of their primordial world *were* different folk from citizens of a democracy. A chief corollary to such cultural relativism was that Americans have wrongly embraced a belief in the innate humanity of the West largely out of ethno-centric ignorance. But surely the opposite has been proven true: the more Americans after September 11 learned about the world of the *madrassas*, the six or seven varieties of Islamic female coverings, the Dickensian Pakistani street, and murderous gangs in Somalia, Sudan, and Afghanistan, then the more, *not* less, they are appalled by societies that are so anti-Western.

Blasts in Manhattan followed by televised pictures of women in *burqas* having their brains blown out in an Afghan soccer stadium have a tendency to make people rethink what they had been told—and just maybe to realize what a rare and beautiful gift is the Western heritage of democracy and freedom. So it was also after Thermopylae and the invasion of Poland in 1939, and so it is after 9/11—a date that has blown apart history as we have known it over the last few decades.

Others among the influential for a moment after the retaliatory strikes of October 7, 2001, talked of moral equivalency—the conventional wisdom that American precision targeting of an enemy in time of war carried the same ethical burden as the terrorists' deliberate mass-murdering of civilians at peace. But billions worldwide knew that the selective wreckage of al-Qaeda safe houses in Kabul was not comparable to the smoldering crater that was once the World Trade Center. Why else were terrorists and the Taliban hiding in mosques and infirmaries to avoid American bombs while their own manuals instructed killers to commit mass murder in Jewish hospitals and temples? So the reality that average folk viewed on their televisions made them question the bottled piety of the last decades that they heard from a powerful and influential few. And in that moral calculus, September 11 shocked an affluent and at times self-satisfied American citizenry into confessing that it was no longer either too wealthy, too refined, or too sensitive to kill killers.

Knowledge of the past would have reminded us that battle does such things to a people. Socrates cannot be understood without appreciating that his thought came of age only during the murderous three decades of the Peloponnesian War. Battles, as Delium and Shiloh suggest, can create prominent men and can destroy them as well. The same is true of ideas. The pacifism of the post-Vietnam generation shamed Americans into thinking that all conflicts were bad. Relativism sometimes convinced them that they were not that much different from their enemies. Conflict resolution advised that there was rarely such a thing as a moral armed struggle of good against evil—to be scoffed at as "Manichaean"—and that strife is a result of misunderstandings and so can be resolved through give-and-take and rational discourse. But once more September 11 has returned America to the classical view of war as a tragic, but sometimes necessary, option for humans when unchallenged evil threatens civilization.

In 1986 a panel of the United Nations declared that war was an aberration and not in any way natural or innate to humans. Yet the Greek philosopher Heraclitus twenty-five centuries earlier had dubbed it "the father, the king of us all." After the fall of the twin towers, Americans were more likely to believe a dead Greek than the most sophisticated lawyers and social scientists of the modern Western world.

In a single morning Americans also rediscovered the Hellenic idea that it is not wars per se that are always terrible, but the people—Hitler, Tojo, Stalin, Saddam Hussein, and bin Laden—and their repugnant ideas who start them. In this present conflict, the -isms and -ologies of radical Islamic fundamentalism that have infected millions can be shown to be bankrupt only by their complete repudiation, which tragically must come out of military defeat, subsequent humiliation, and real personal costs for all who embrace them. Only that way can both adherents and the innocent alike learn the wages of allowing their country to be hijacked by agents of intolerance. Ask the Japanese about the terrible sequelae to Okinawa.

The enemy in battle is never a person per se, but the fanaticism that has taken hold of him. Battle likewise is sometimes the only exorcist strong enough to rid the zombie host of such deadly demons. The brilliant memoir of E. B. Sledge about his ghastly experiences in the inferno of Okinawa is often cited as an antiwar tract. It is. But we remember that his recollection is also more than that—as the last lines of the book reveal: "As the troops used to say, 'If the country is good enough to live in, it's good enough to fight for.' With privilege goes responsibility."

Even we in the supposedly enlightened West may also relearn from fighting rich and educated terrorists that conflicts can often arise not out of real, but rather perceived grievances—or, as the Greeks taught us, from old-fashioned but now passé ideas like hatred, envy, fear, and self-interest. The agitators for secession were not the millions of poor and nonslaveowning Southern whites who lived hand-to-mouth, but the few plantationists whose antebellum cotton sales had made them among the wealthiest men in the history of civilization. Japan had as many people and as little land in 1941 as it does now, but a very different perception then of its own grievance, national right, and imperial destiny. People and their leaders can go to war not because their bellies ache with hunger, but out of the belief that they may otherwise lose—or even not augment—the sizable fortune, influence, or real power they hold.

The terrorists of al-Qaeda, like the Japanese militarists, attacked America not simply because they were poor, exploited, abused, or maladjusted, but perhaps as much out of loathing, trepidation, and resentment of the West. That fact in and of itself seemed somewhat a refutation of perhaps the entire twentieth-century confidence in the assertions of social science that man's nature is not absolute, unchanging, and timeless, but simply a construct of his contemporary environment and (often pathological) upbringing. After September 11 we were reminded that our own prosperous and peaceful era, not history's long centuries, was the true aberration in its denial of an unchanging human character driven by timeless passions and appetites.

Battles that seem to allow horrible things to transpire as ordinary events—as we saw from Shiloh and Delium—can also transform more subtly the lives of thousands of both the renowned and ordinary, well apart from the grand cosmology of politics, war, and culture. Rudolph Giuliani before September 11 was a lame-duck mayor of New York City, a sort of has-been limping out of office, pilloried by the press, and caught in personal scandal and gossip—his unique potential for leadership still unchanged, but the requisite arena for its manifestation long ago gone by. After the attacks he immediately emerged from Ground Zero to steady the city in the twilight of his tenure—reenergizing himself as the embodiment of New York grit and calm under fire, and so acclaimed as *Time* magazine's Man of the Year and America's *civis princeps*. Given his character, a Plutarch would suggest, his time was not over as we thought, but waiting all along for the eye of the storm.

George W. Bush, who lacked his predecessor's encyclopedic knowledge of names, places, and dates, was—after the election fiasco in Florida—considered a near-illegitimate president, tongue-tied and in over his head, his impoverished vocabulary purported proof of his intellectual levity. But the terrorists' war proved that he, like the Greek iambic poet Archilochus's hedgehog, "knew one thing, but a big one": how to galvanize his people and lead them to battle against an evil enemy in the hour of his country's great peril. That "big one" should never have had the opportunity to appear, but then conflicts also are illogical things and should also perhaps not occur. Few before 9/11 would have remembered that the original prime directive of the founders' presidency was to protect the citizenry from foreign attack rather than to ensure healthy GNP, the Dow above 11,000, and an approval rating of over 60 percent.

We learned in the early part of the Afghanistan war that a slain Johnny Spann was an unheralded middle-class American with a fine record at the CIA, a captured John Walker a "mixed-up" child of affluence cavorting among the Taliban. The one died doing his duty for his country, the other fought for its enemies confused and searching for personal fulfillment. Both were caught in battle on videotape, their respective fates instantly suggesting that there were two very different Americans at cross-purposes even six thousand miles away. Not all reputations, then, were won and lost among the elite. Amid the grieving and less well known after September 11, there are right now thousands of undiscovered brave and anonymous souls who will vow to remember their fallen in all that they do and say for the duration of their lives. If the past is any guide to the future, Americans will see their spirit soon enough at shops, on television, and in bookstores for decades hence—and with it the knowledge that the voices of the battlefield dead can still speak among us in the here and now.

Whatever battles like Okinawa did to thousands of servicemen, it surely taught them that there are many in the world who do not like the United States and seek to use their wealth and power to kill as many Americans as they can; thus it was no surprise that throughout the national debate over the proper response to September 11, crusty veterans were neither shrill in their bloodlust nor apologetic pacifists, but rather reminded younger generations that they had seen it all before and unfortunately knew precisely what to do and how it must end.

Other than the distant bombing and hundred-hour ground war in the Gulf during a few days in 1991, and isolated actions in Grenada, Panama, Somalia, Bosnia, and Kosovo, we have been mostly at peace from real organized killing for thirty years and so have forgotten in a brief generation that since the birth of civilization entire worlds have changed, both abruptly and insidiously, in minutes—once thousands fall to the fire and explosions unleashed by others. Americans are startled at pronouncements that "nothing is the same after 9/11," dumbfounded that their own comfortable and relatively predictable worlds are now changed—and will continue to be differ-ent—for years to come. But if history demonstrates that Lexington and Con-cord, Fort Sumter, and Pearl Harbor all turned America into a different nation in a matter of minutes, why should we now be any less immune from the far greater bloodletting on September 11? If our understanding of Greek tragedy, art, philosophy, politics, and war were changed by a relatively ob-scure battle at Delium, why would not the destruction of the World Trade Center and the bombing of the Pentagon not similarly alter American cul-ture? The Athenian fifth century was ushered in by the defeat of Xerxes—but only after the destruction of the first Parthenon, the desolation of Athens itself, the Persian effort to destroy or absorb Hellenic civilization, and the miraculous Greek counterresponse at Salamis.

Millions of the anonymous have had their lives altered in ways we can-not grasp for centuries, as a single battle—with all its youth, confined space, and dreadful killing—insidiously warps the memory of the friends and fam-ilies of the fallen, twists the thoughts and aspirations of the veterans of the ordeal, and abruptly ends the accomplishments of the dead. In that sense the ripples of battle are also immune from and care little for what people write and read, in or outside the dominant West. They simply wash up on us all as we speak and in ways that cannot fully be known until centuries after we are gone.

Acknowledgments

Secondary literature is discussed in the following brief bibliographical essay, with page numbers cited for direct quotations in the text. I would like to thank veterans of F Company, 2nd Battalion, 29th Regiment, 6th Marine Division, for their letters, phone calls, photographs, and notes concerning Victor Hanson—especially Richard Whitaker, Robert Sherer, William Twigger, Louis Ittmann, Michael Senko, Edward Hewlik, and others. Some fifty-seven years after Victor Hanson perished on Okinawa, I finally know *how* he died, have his pictures from the war, and his ring, all thanks to the generosity of these brave veterans.

Classics students at California State University–Fresno, Kristi Hill and Sabina Robinson, helped with selection and acquisition of the photographs, as well as typing and proofreading duties. Rebecca and Raymond Ibrahim and Ray Sanchez aided with bibliographical tasks. Katherine Becker, a doctoral student in military history at Ohio State University, made available a great number of sources not otherwise available here at CSU Fresno and read the manuscript. My colleague in Classics, Professor Bruce Thornton, offered invaluable insight about the organization of the book and critiqued the text at its penultimate stage. Professor M. C. Drake once again drew the maps and the rendition of the warrior grave of Saugenes.

My wife Cara read the entire manuscript and helped in efforts to locate members of F Company from the 29th Marines—and took up many of my obligations on our farm that I often was obliged to neglect these past three years. My literary representatives of a decade, Glen Hartley and Lynn Chu, gave invaluable advice throughout preparation of the manuscript as both agents and friends. I thank once again my editor of a decade, Adam Bellow, at Doubleday, for continued confidence and support.

Bibliography

1. The Wages of Suicide

Recipe for a Holocaust
There are especially fine official histories of Okinawa, written by prominent American historians. See first R. Appleman, J. M. Burns, R. A. Gugeler, and J. Stevens, *Okinawa: The Last Battle* (Rutland, Vt., and Tokyo, 1960). Its appendices contain most of the statistics on troops committed and lost at the battle; cf. 322–23 for accounts of the 29th Marines on Sugar Loaf Hill; 58 for the Japanese suicides; and 473–74 for final judgments.

See also the official history of the U.S. Marine Corps on Okinawa, by C. S. Nichols and H. I. Shaw, *Okinawa: Victory in the Pacific* (Washington, D.C., 1955), 180–83 for Company F on Sugar Loaf Hill and its environs. And cf. especially P. Carleton, *The Conquest of Okinawa: An Account of the Sixth Marine Division* (Washington, D.C., 1947); and K. Stockman, *The Sixth Marine Division on Okinawa* (Washington, D.C., 1946).

An interesting account of the Japanese defenses on Okinawa is offered by Col. Hiromichi Yahara, who was in great part responsible for the effective tactics of attrition and rugged defense rather than open counterassaults: H. Yahara, *The Battle for Okinawa* (translated by R. Pineau and M. Uehara), New York, 1995; cf. 143 for his thoughts of the suicide of Japanese soldiers, and 200 for Frank Gibney's appraisals of the civilian suicides.

For Okinawa as "The England of the Pacific," see J. H. Alexander, *The Final Campaign: Marines in the Victory on Okinawa* (Washington, D.C., 1996), 2; and cf. 33 for the suicides at the Asa River. See also B. M. Frank, *Okinawa: Capstone to Victory* (New York, 1970), 20–21 for a discussion of the nature of the Japanese defenses; and T. M. Huber, *Japan's Battle of Okinawa, April–June 1945* (Leavenworth, Kans., 1990), 38, 65 for Japanese impressions of the nearly impassable terrain on the island, and the Americans' lack of imagination in circumventing the Japanese defenses. In general, there are revealing oral histories in G. Astor, *Operation Iceberg: The Invasion and Conquest of Okinawa in World War II* (New York, 1995).

Divine Wind
On the ideology of the Japanese suicide bombers, see R. Leckie, *Okinawa: The Last Battle of World War II* (New York, 1995). For the skill of American sailors in fighting

the kamikazes, and their attitude about the use of suicide bombers, see too, A. Lott, *Brave Ship, Brave Men* (Annapolis, Md., 1986), especially 164–74.

There is a growing literature on the kamikazes, both American accounts and memoirs of Japanese veterans who survived the squadrons; oddly, American rather than Japanese histories are more apt to praise the bravery, rather than condemn the fanaticism, of the pilots. For a narrative of the special squadrons of both kamikaze and *Okha* pilots from the Japanese perspective, see H. Naito, *Thunder Gods: The Kamikaze Pilots Tell Their Story* (New York, 1989). For Tojo's code of ethics, see 20; and for dissension and fright among the suicide ranks, 96, 209.

See also E. Hoyt, *The Kamikazes* (New York, 1983); B. Millot, *Divine Thunder: The Life and Death of the Kamikazes* (New York, 1971), especially 229–31 for the letter of Teruo Yamaguchi. The origins of the kamikazes are discussed in depth by J. Field, *The Japanese at Leyte Gulf: The Sho Operation* (Princeton, 1947), and R. Inoguchi and T. Nakajima, *The Divine Wind: Japan's Kamikaze Force in World War II* (Westport, Conn., 1959). For their remarks on the unique nature of the suicide corps, see xxi; Ensign Heiichi Okabe's letter is found at 190.

R. Spurr, *A Glorious Way to Die* (New York, 1981), has a detailed account of the last voyage of the *Yamato*. Westerners, who did not embrace suicide, could write in starry-eyed tributes, "Japanese heroes gave the world a great lesson in purity. From the depth of their ancient past they brought a forgotten message of human grandeur" (Millot, *Divine Thunder*, 233). For the civilian experience, see R. Keyso, *Women of Okinawa* (Ithaca, N.Y., 2000); for the accounts of Junkyo Isa, cf. 6–7, 11–12.

The Military Lessons

For Churchill's quote and other assessments of Okinawa's importance, see I. Gow, *Okinawa 1945: Gateway to Japan* (New York, 1985), 213–15. George Feifer's *Tennozan: The Battle of Okinawa and the Atomic Bomb* (New York, 1992) has an incisive analysis of the connection between Okinawa and Hiroshima; cf. 583–84; for the remarks of Thomas Hannaher, cf. 544. See also P. Fussell, *Thank God for the Atomic Bomb and Other Essays* (New York, 1988), who points out that those who were removed from the frontline fighting—in both time and space—were most likely to oppose use of the bomb; in contrast, the relieved veterans of the Pacific fighting knew the carnage that lay ahead on the Japanese mainland.

Epilogue: The Men of Okinawa

For details about Ernie Pyle's death and his writing during the war, see J. Tobin, *Ernie Pyle's War: America's Witness to World War II* (New York, 1997); and for his earlier work, cf. D. Nichols, *Ernie's America* (New York, 1989). The American Marine experience on the island is brilliantly recorded by two excellent memoirs: E. B. Sledge, *With the Old Breed: At Peleliu and Okinawa* (Novato, Calif., 1981), cf. 253, 314–15 for his memories of the fighting; W. Manchester, *Goodbye Darkness: A Memoir of the Pacific War* (Boston, 1979), cf. 378–79. For oral histories of the struggle to take Sugar Loaf Hill, see J. H. Hallas, *Killing Ground on Okinawa: The Battle for Sugar Loaf Hill* (Westport, Conn., 1996), especially 43ff.

2. Shiloh's Ghosts

Morning

For accounts of Sherman's surprise, wounding at Shiloh, and his general bravery, consult L. Daniel, *Shiloh: The Battle That Changed the Civil War* (New York, 1997), 137–39, 158, 171, 177–78, 310–11; and J. McDonough, *Shiloh: In Hell Before Night* (Knoxville, Tenn., 1977). Sherman's remarks to his subordinate colonel the morning before the battle are in B. Simpson and J. Berlin, eds., *Sherman's Civil War: Selected Correspondence of William T. Sherman, 1860–1865* (Chapel Hill, N.C., 1999), 168; on his contemplated suicide, 174; on the horrid nature of Shiloh and his calmness before fire, 202; for his lectures about the nature of war during the Atlanta campaign, 706, 708. J. Marszalek, *Sherman: A Soldier's Passion for Order* (New York, 1993), 186–87, quotes Sherman's references to Shiloh at the 1881 reunion of the Army of the Tennessee.

For his candor when shot and unhorsed, see W. Sword, *Shiloh: Bloody April* (New York, 1974), 176; "coolest man I saw that day," 209. Sherman's talk with Grant after the battle is from his autobiography, W. T. Sherman, *Memoirs of Gen. W. T. Sherman* (New York, 1875), vol. 1, 254; and for his remarks after Shiloh, see M. A. Howe, ed., *Home Letters of General Sherman* (New York, 1909).

M. Fellman, *Citizen Sherman* (Lawrence, Kans., 1995), 113–48, discusses the psychological implications of Sherman's amazing turnaround after Shiloh, and quotes from Sherman's letters concerning suicide and shame. On Grant's plans on the night of the sixth, see U. S. Grant, *Personal Memoirs of U.S. Grant* (New York, 1885), vol. 1, 346–50. For an excellent appraisal of Sherman's overall conduct at Shiloh, see L. Lewis, *Sherman: Fighting Prophet* (New York, 1932), 219–31, where Sherman's famous quotes during the first minutes of the battle are reviewed (cf. 222–23 for his confident banter with Grant's aide-de-camp), and more recently, L. Kennett, *Sherman: A Soldier's Life* (New York, 2001).

In general, for Sherman's quotes during the battle proper, consult as well J. Merrill, *William Tecumseh Sherman* (Chicago, 1971), 195–211, 207. B. H. Liddell-Hart, *Sherman: Soldier, Realist, American* (New York, 1958), 427–31, has an astute assessment of Sherman and his impact on modern war; see also V. D. Hanson, *The Soul of Battle* (New York, 1999), 232–60, for Sherman's desire to avoid casualties and his legacy of waging a war of moral retribution.

Afternoon

An enormous hagiography of some third of a million words, *The Life of Gen. Albert Sidney Johnston, Embracing his Services in the Armies of the United States, the Republic of Texas, and the Confederate States* (New York, 1879), written by his oldest son, William Preston Johnston, is a storehouse of nearly everything written and spoken by Johnston over a forty-year period—and includes nearly every positive remark recorded about him as well. For General Johnston's words in the moments before his death, see 614–15; his aphorisms during the fighting are quoted at 563–64; 566; 584–85; 612. For the assessments of General Bragg and other Confederate generals, see 549; 553; 632–33; 635–36. Jefferson Davis's eulogies are found at 658; 730–32. Quotes taken from the Southern Historical Society, 732; the proclamation of the Texas Legislature, 696; various descriptions of Johnston's appearance, 726–28.

William Preston Johnston also wrote a description of his father's record at Shiloh, "Albert Sidney Johnston at Shiloh," in C. Buel and R. Johnson, eds., *Battles and Leaders of the Civil War*, 4 vols. (New York, 1956), vol. 1, 540–68. See 556 for his remarks moments before the firing began.

There is an excellent biography of Johnston that seeks balanced assessment through additional primary research, which nevertheless comes to a similarly positive assessment of his war record. See Charles P. Roland, *Albert Sidney Johnston: Soldier of Three Republics* (Austin, Tex., 1964), 347 for the judgment of Richard Taylor, and 336–46 for Johnston's last recorded moments and postmortem appraisals of his character and record.

There is an appendix devoted to the circumstances surrounding Johnston's death in W. Sword, *Shiloh: Bloody April* (New York, 1974), 443–46; and see 446 for Sword's conclusion that Johnston's death was central to the loss of Confederate hope.

The bibliography of the Lost Cause is enormous and begins with E. A. Pollard, *The Lost Cause: A New Southern History of the War of the Confederates* (New York, 1866), especially 241, and 729 for the importance of Shiloh and the general belief of Southern moral superiority. There are a number of excellent contemporary essays in P. Gerster and N. Cords, eds., *Myth and Southern History, Volume 1: The Old South* (Urbana, Ill., 1989), and G. W. Gallagher and A. T. Nolan, eds., *The Myth of the Lost Cause and Civil War History* (Bloomington, Ind., 2000). Cf. also more generally, C. Vann Woodward, *The Burden of Southern History* (Baton Rouge, 1960); T. Connelly and B. Bellows, *God and General Longstreet: The Lost Cause and the Southern Mind* (Baton Rouge, 1982).

Grant has a number of astute observations about Shiloh and the Lost Opportunity as well as a rather harsh assessment of Johnston; see especially his U. S. Grant, *Personal Memoirs of U.S. Grant* (New York, 1885), vol. 1, 359–65.

Evening

The final chapters of Lew Wallace's massive *An Autobiography*, 2 vols. (New York, 1906) were completed by his wife, Susan Wallace, after the general's death in 1905; the account nevertheless devotes an inordinate amount to his Civil War experiences (420 of its 1,003 pages)—Shiloh in particular: Cf. his remarks after Donelson (373–433), his lengthy description of the battle of Shiloh (459–570), and the controversy over the Shunpike route (462–73). Prominent too in his recollections are his later exchanges with Grant, during and after the battle (463, 544, 566, 807–10), and with Sherman (662–66)—and his explanations for writing *Ben-Hur*, along with the favorable reactions of Grant, Sherman, Garfield, and others to his literary accomplishments (889, 926–37, 938, 947–56).

The direct relationship between the shame of Shiloh and Wallace's fiction is outlined well by I. McKee, *"Ben-Hur" Wallace: The Life of General Lew Wallace* (Berkeley, 1947), 166–67; 189, 206, 216; 232–34; 264–65. For the amazing sales figures about the book, the popularity of the play, and the controversies over the various movie versions, cf. 164–881; and for the snub of the literati to Wallace's fiction, 227. Although Wallace's literary career is the main focus of R. and K. Morsberger's magisterial *Lew Wallace: Militant Romantic* (New York, 1980), there is a very sympathetic narrative of the general at Shiloh, 70–102, in addition to an exhaustive discussion of the four movie versions of *Ben-Hur*, the amazing success of the play, and a history of the book's sales, 447–96. For the "Garfield edition" of *Ben-Hur*, see Lew Wallace, *Ben-Hur: A Tale of the Christ* (New York, 1892). Quotes from the novel are taken from D. Mayer (editor), Lew Wallace, *Ben-Hur* (Oxford, 1998), 136, 406–7, which has an insightful introduction to the text.

General Buell's support for Wallace and attack on Grant and Sherman is found in the first volume of the 1956 edition of C. Buel and R. Johnson, eds., *Battles and Leaders of the Civil War*, 4 vols. (New York, 1956), vol. 1, 487–536, together with a much more detailed response from Grant that shows little sympathy for Wallace's late arrival (465–86). For Grant's famous footnote and later correction of long-standing criticism against Wallace, see 468. In the same volume Wallace gives an account of Grant's victory at Donelson, with his own leadership figuring (too) prominently (398–428). See U. S. Grant, *Personal Memoirs of U. S. Grant* (New York, 1885), vol. 1, 337–38, and 351–52, for both criticism of Wallace and his retraction. At least in the immediate aftermath of the battle, Sherman was especially sympathetic to Wallace's dilemma; cf. B. Simpson and J. Berlin, eds., *Sherman's Civil War: Selected Correspondence of William T. Sherman, 1860–1865* (Chapel Hill, N.C., 1999), 526–28.

In general accounts of Shiloh, Wallace's march looms large with wide-ranging critique: outright criticism for the delay and Wallace's timidity on Shiloh's second day, in L. Daniel, *Shiloh: The Battle That Changed the Civil War* (New York, 1997), 257–59, 285, 291; sympathy for Wallace and criticism of Grant in J. McDonough, *Shiloh: In Hell Before Night* (Knoxville, Tenn., 1977), 156–61; neutral without assessment of blame, W. Sword, *Shiloh: Bloody April* (New York, 1974), 345–54.

Night

Two recent and mostly favorable biographies of Nathan Bedford Forrest draw on a number of nineteenth- and early-twentieth-century hagiographies published at least a half century earlier: Cf. B. S. Wills, *A Battle from the Start: The Life of Nathan Bedford Forrest* (New York, 1992) for quotes about Forrest's decision to go home after Lee's armistice, 316; his admission of his general hatred of the North, 334; his inflammatory speech to the Brownsville crowd, 349; and advice to Judge Blackford, 362. See also J. Hurst, *Nathan Bedford Forrest: A Biography* (New York, 1993) for Lee and the Klan, 286–87; the murder of George Ashburn in Georgia, 295; Forrest's controversial interview with the *Cincinnati Commercial*, 312–13; his misleading congressional testimony, 339–44. Cf. Hurst's assessment of Forrest after Shiloh: "To him, everything always had depended on final triumph, not on the gentlemanly gamesmanship so many affected in seeking it. Like all the frontier fights he had made, this was not a game. It was a struggle for no less than survival—this time, not only individually but collectively and nationally. After Shiloh, he seemed to begin to wage war more nearly the way he had lived the rest of his life: not only single-mindedly, but confident in his own counsel and following his own rules."

The oral tradition surrounding Forrest's exploits was collected by T. Jordan and J. P. Pryor, *The Campaigns of General Nathan Bedford Forrest and of Forrest's Cavalry* (with a fine new introduction by Albert Castel) (New York, 1996); both were Confederate veterans (Jordan was also a roommate of W. T. Sherman at West Point), and there is, not surprisingly, little in either account about Fort Pillow, Forrest's Klan activity, or his purported shooting and dueling. See also the new edition of the classic by J. A. Wyeth, *That Devil Forrest: Life of General Nathan Bedford Forrest* (with a new foreword by Albert Castel; Baton Rouge, 1989), that has a good account of Forrest at Shiloh (64–65). See also J. H. Mathes, *General Forrest* (New York, 1902), and R. S. Henry, *"First with the Mostest" Forrest* (New York, 1944). There are fascinating essays about Forrest by Gen. Viscount Wolseley, who argued that Forrest was among the most astute generals of any time, as well as other Confederate veterans in R. S. Henry, ed., *As They Saw Forrest: Some Recollections and Comments of Contemporaries* (Jackson, Tenn., 1956).

For the controversy over the Fallen Timbers incident and whether Forrest really did pick up a Union soldier as a human shield, see McDonough, *Shiloh: In Hell Before Night* (Knoxville, Tenn., 1977), 209–10; W. Sword, *Shiloh: Bloody April* (New York, 1974), 300. L. J. Daniel, *Shiloh: The Battle That Changed the Civil War* (New York, 1997), 219–20, recounts Forrest's comments at Lick Creek. Sherman's disappointments about Fallen Timbers are found in B. Simpson and J. Berlin, eds., *Sherman's Civil War: Selected Correspondence of William T. Sherman, 1860–1865* (Chapel Hill, N.C., 1999), 218; and cf. 808 for his wish to have Forrest hunted down and killed.

An invaluable inside view of the Klan's early years is found in J. C. Lester and D. L. Wilson, *Ku Klux Klan: Its Origin, Growth, and Disbandment* (with introduction and notes by W. L. Fleming; New York, 1971). A popular account of the rise and evolution of the Klan is found in Wyn Craig Wade, *The Fiery Cross: The Ku Klux Klan in America* (New York, 1987). For Wade's quotations concerning the Forrest interview with the *Cincinnati Commercial*, the idea that Forrest was commanding more brave men in the Klan than during the war, and the disgust his pardon drew from Northern veterans, see 16, 40, 50–55. See also A. W. Trelease, *White Terror: The Ku Klux Klan Conspiracy and Southern Reconstruction* (Westport, Conn., 1971), and W. P. Randel, *The Ku Klux Klan: A Century of Infamy* (Philadelphia, 1965), who argues that Forrest's dissolution of the Klan two years after its inception was for show only and accordant with the terms of his own parole. In fact, the Klan continued as it had in the past, albeit in a less manifest way.

On Forrest's sometimes misleading testimony before the congressional committee formed to investigate the Klan and other efforts to thwart Reconstruction, see the congressional report, *Report of the Joint Select Committee to Inquire into the Condition of Affairs in the Late Insurrectionary States, Volume 13: Miscellaneous and Florida* (Washington, 1871), 3–41. Forrest's infamous interview with the *Cincinnati Commercial* and his later letter to the paper alleging error is quoted verbatim at 32–35. D. M. Chalmers, *Hooded Americanism: The First Century of the Ku Klux Klan, 1865–1965* (New York, 1965), also discusses the prominent role of Nathan Bedford Forrest III, the grandson, whose rise in the Klan was predicated on the general impression that his grandfather had founded the organization.

3. The Culture of Delium

The Battle

Direct quotations are from the two brief ancient narratives of the battle found at Thucydides 4.91–101 and Diodorus 12.69–70. For a detailed commentary on the Greek of Thucydides' contemporary account, see A. W. Gomme, *A Historical Com-*

mentary on Thucydides, Volume III (Oxford, 1956), 558–71; and S. Hornblower, *A Commentary on Thucydides, Volume II* (Oxford, 1996), 301–10. Cf. also G. Busolt, *Griechische Geschichte bis zur Schlacht bei Chaeroneia* (3. vols.; Gotha, 1893–1904), III.2, 1147–51.

Delium is discussed fully and with an astute strategic assessment by D. Kagan, *The Archidamian War* (Ithaca, 1987), 282–90, and afforded a lengthy treatment in the classic history of G. Grote, *A History of Greece*, vol. 6 (4th ed.; London, 1872), 379–97. There is also a very general article on the battle by V. D. Hanson, "Delium," *Quarterly Journal of Military History* 8.1 (1995): 28–35. The topographical problems are discussed by W. K. Pritchett, *Studies in Ancient Greek Topography, Part 2 (Battlefields)* (Berkeley and Los Angeles, 1969), 24–36; *Studies in Ancient Greek Topography, Part 3 (Roads)* (Berkeley and Los Angeles, 1980), 295–97; as well as in the earlier survey of J. Kromayer, *Antike Schlachtfelder*, v.4 (Berlin, 1903–31), 177–98 (written by J. Beck).

Euripides and the Rotting Dead

The quotations are my own translations from the Greek text of Euripides' *Suppliants*, and are found at the following lines: "violation of what all Greece holds to be lawful" (311); "they are violent and deprive the dead of their due burial" (308); "Sparta is savage and duplicitous in its character" (187); "The mothers wish to bury in the earth the corpses of those destroyed by the spear" (16–17); "Save the corpses, take pity on my misfortunes, and on the mothers whose children have been slain" (168–70); "A city based on an equal vote" (353); "The city is not governed by a single man, but is free. And the people themselves rule, and the offices are held by annual turns. Nor does the citizenry assign the highest honors to the rich, but the poor also have an equal share" (405–8); "A struggle evenly balanced" (706); "Making [their] way over to the struggling wing of the army" (709); "Whenever the issue of war comes before a vote of the people, no one reckons on his own death; that misfortune, he thinks, will come to others than himself. If death stood before his eyes as he cast his vote, Greece would not be self-destructing from a madness for the spear" (481–85); "There are three classes of citizens. The rich are of no use and always lusting after more gain; the poor who lack a livelihood are dangerous folk, who invest too much in envy, trying to goad the rich, as they are hoodwinked by the tongues of wicked leaders. But of these three classes those in the middle save states, since they preserve the order which the city has established" (238–45); "Freedom is simply this: Who has a good proposal and wishes to bring it before the citizenry? He who does so, enjoys repute, while he who does not merely keeps silent. What can be more just for a city than this?" (439–41); "Let the dead be covered by the earth, and let each thing return to that place from whence it came into the light of day, the spirit of a man to the upper air, his body back into the earth. For we do not possess our bodies altogether as our own: we live our lives in them and then the earth, our nourisher, must take them back" (531–36).

For the controversies of connecting Delium with Euripides' *Suppliants* and the exact parallels between the real and fictional battles, see C. Pelling, *Greek Tragedy and the Historian* (Oxford, 1997), 45–51; S. Mills, *Theseus, Tragedy, and the Athenian Empire* (Oxford, 1997), 91–97; C. Kuiper, "De Euripidis Supplicibus," *Mnemosyne* 51 (1923): 102–28; C. Collard, *Euripides: Supplices*, 2 vols. (Groningen, 1975); and

P. Giles, "Political Allusions in the Suppliants of Euripides," *Classical Review* 4 (1890): 95–98.

Thespian Tragedies

I have written at length of the Thespian holocaust with reference to the Greek sources in V. D. Hanson, "Hoplite Obliteration: The Case of the Town of Thespiae," in J. Carman and A. Harding, *Ancient Warfare: Archaeological Perspectives* (Trow-bridge, U.K., 1999), 203–18. On the remains of Thespiae, see J. Fossey, *Topography and Population of Ancient Boeotia* (Chicago, 1986), 135–40; and W. K. Pritchett, *Studies in Ancient Greek Topography, Part 5* (Berkeley, 1989), 138–65. For a history of the city, see in general P. Roesch, *Thespies et la confédération béotienne* (Paris, 1965); and C. Fiehn, "Thespeia," in A. Pauly, G. Wissowa, and W. Kroll, *Paulys Real-Encyclopäedia des classischen Altertumswissenschaft* (Berlin, 1936), 37–59. For Phili-ades' epigram of the Thespians, see J. M. Edmonds (translator), *Greek Elegy and Iambus*, Vol. 1 (Cambridge, Mass., 1961), 439. For the Spartan epigrams for the family dead, see W. R. Paton (translator), *The Greek Anthology, Books VII–VIII* (Cambridge, Mass., 1993), 239.

For the Thespians and the Persian Wars, cf. Herodotus 7.202, 222, 226; 8.75, 50; 9.25; and cf. C. Hignett, *Xerxes' Invasion of Greece* (Oxford, 1963), 146–48; 371–78; J. Lazenby, *The Defence of Greece, 490–479 B.C.* (Warminster, 1993), 144–47.

For the purported grave of the roughly three hundred Thespians slain at Delium, the casualty list of Delium with a partial accounting of its dead, and the black lime-stone sepulchral stelai of some of the prominent Boeotians killed, see W. K. Pritch-ett, *The Greek State at War*, Vol. 4 (Berkeley and Los Angeles, 1974), 132, 141–43, 192–94; N. Demand, *Thebes in the Fifth Century: Heracles Resurgent* (London, 1982), 110–18.

The Faces of Delium

On the career of Alcibiades, cf. W. M. Ellis, *Alcibiades* (London, 1989); S. Forde, *The Ambition to Rule: Alcibiades and the Politics of Imperialism in Thucydides* (Ithaca, 1989); J. Kirchner, *Prosopographia Attica* (Berlin, 1901), Vol. 1, 43–49; J. K. Davies, *Athenian Propertied Families, 600–300 B.C.* (Oxford, 1971), 18–20. For the main points of Laches' career, see Kirchner, Vol. 2, 6–7; and for Pyrilampes, Kirchner, Vol. 2, 244–45; Davies, 329–31. For Hippocrates, see Kirchner, Vol. 1, 502–3; Davies, 456. A chronology of the major events in Plato's life is found in Kirchner, Vol. 2, 204–6.

Plutarch's quote about Alcibiades, *Alcibiades* 23.5; Hippocrates' speech is at Thucydides 4.95; Pausanias' suggestion that Hippocrates died in the early moments at Delium is in *Description of Greece*, 361. For the relevant passages in Plato's *Laches*, see 181 A–B; 182 A; 189 B; for passages in Plato's *Republic* that seem to allude to Delium, see 5.468A–70D; cf. *Laws* 8.829A–C.

Socrates Slain?

There is a vast hagiographic account of Socrates' mettle at the battle found in the works of Plato (*Laches*, 181 B; *Symposium*, 221; *Apology*, 28 E) and Plutarch (*Alcib-iades*, 7; *Moralia*, 581 D). Later sources sought either to magnify his achievements or deny his presence largely on the grounds that his courage is not mentioned by Thucy-dides; see, for example, Athenaeus 5.215; Simplicius, *Commentary on Epictetus*, 65.19; Stobaeus, 3.750; Theodoretus, *Ecclesiastical History*, 12.26. A common theme in the Delium tradition was that Socrates' inner voice or *daimon* had steered him in the right direction during the retreat (Cicero, *On Divination*, 1.54). Similarly, an en-tire tradition of false knowledge grew up concerning his followers at the battle, often citing individuals as taking part in the battle who did not (Strabo, 9.403), or mistak-ing names and chronologies (Andocides, *Against Alcibiades*, 13). On Aristophanes' *Clouds* and the playwright's treatment of Socrates, see K. J. Dover, *Aristophanes' Clouds* (Oxford, 1968). For general information about the life of Socrates, his thought, and his relationship with his contemporaries, see G. Grote, *Plato and the Other Companions of Socrates* (London, 1875); A. H. Chroust, *Socrates, Man and Myth: The Two Socratic Apologies of Xenophon* (Notre Dame, 1957); and G. Vlastos, *Socrates: Ironist and Moral Philosopher* (New York, 1991).

Beauty from the Dead

Diodorus (12.70.5) discusses the Theban artistic renaissance following Delium. On Aristeides and his art that is to be connected with Delium, see N. Demand, *Thebes in the Fifth Century: Heracles Resurgent* (London, 1982), 42–43; 114–15. For publi-cation of the warrior steles from Delium, see A. Keramopoullos, "Eikones polemiston tes en Delio maches (424 B.C.)," *Archaiologikon Ephemeris* (1920): 1–36. See also R. Higgins, *Tanagra and the Figurines* (Princeton, 1986), 52–53. The inscriptions of the Boeotian dead from Tanagra and Thespiae are published in C. Clairmont, *Patrios Nomos* (Oxford, 1983), 231; and *Inscriptiones Graecae* VII 585, 1888.

The Birth of Tactics

On the status of Greek cavalry at the time of Delium, see for example, most recently, L. Worley, *Hippeis: The Cavalry of Ancient Greece* (Boulder, 1994), especially 93–96; I. G. Spence, *The Cavalry of Classical Greece: A Social and Military History with Par-ticular Reference to Athens* (Oxford, 1993), 40, 153, 155. On the Athenian surprise at the sudden appearance of the Boeotian horsemen, see F. E. Adcock, *The Greek and Macedonian Art of War* (Berkeley, 1957), 85. For the innovations in Greek warfare, the Theban pedigree, and the later development at Macedon, see V. D. Hanson, "Epaminondas, the Battle of Leuctra (371 B.C.) and the 'Revolution' in Greek Battle Tactics," *Classical Antiquity* 7 (1988): 190–207.

The depths of Greek phalanxes are discussed in W. K. Pritchett, *The Greek State at War, Part I* (Berkeley and Los Angeles, 1971), 134–43. For the *heniochoi* and *para-batai*, see J.A.O. Larsen, *Greek Federal States: Their Institutions and History* (Oxford, 1968), 106–71. On such specialized troops in general, see L. Tritle, "*Epilektoi* at Athens," *Ancient History Bulletin* 3.3/4 (1989): 54–59; and for the origins of the Sa-cred Band, cf. J. G. DeVoto, "The Theban Sacred Band," *The Ancient World* 23.2 (1992): 3–19. In V. D. Hanson, *The Soul of Battle* (New York, 1999), 420–21, there is a discussion of strategic and tactical traditions in Boeotia.

On Pagondas's family, his connection to Pindar, and his age at Delium (about sixty?), see C. M. Bowra, *Pindar* (Oxford, 1964), 98–99.

Index